THE DIGITAL PUBLIC DOMAIN

Melanie Dulong de Rosnay is a researcher at the CNRS Institute for Communication Sciences and associated researcher at CERSA (CNRS University Paris 2) where she is Creative Commons France legal lead. In 2011 she co-founded Communia international association on the digital public domain, which she currently chairs. She works on comparative public policies for open access and on transformation of regulation introduced by distributed architectures.

Juan Carlos De Martin is a Faculty Fellow at the Berkman Center for Internet & Society at Harvard University and co-director of the NEXA Center for Internet & Society at the Turin Polytechnic (Politecnico di Torino), Italy, which he co-founded in 2006. He is a Professor of Computer Engineering, with research interests focusing on digital media processing and transmission. De Martin also serves as a member of the Scientific Board of the Institute of the Italian Encyclopedia Treccani and of the Biennale Democrazia.

The Digital Public Domain: Foundations for an Open Culture

Edited by

Melanie Dulong de Rosnay
and Juan Carlos De Martin

OpenBook Publishers

Open Book Publishers CIC Ltd.,
40 Devonshire Road, Cambridge, CB1 2BL, United Kingdom
http://www.openbookpublishers.com

As with all Open Book Publishers titles, digital material and resources
associated with this volume are available from our website:
http://www.openbookpublishers.com/product/93

ISBN Hardback: 978–1-906924–46–1
ISBN Paperback: 978–1-906924–45–4
ISBN Digital (pdf): 978–1-906924–47–8
ISBN Digital ebook (epub version): 978–1-906924–75-1
ISBN Digital ebook (mobi version): 978–1-906924–76-8

Typesetting by www.bookgenie.in

The cover image by John Pryere Coleman is also licensed under the Creative
Commons Attribution 3.0 unported license. His work is available at:
www.flickr.com/photos/26628378@N03

The book was funded by the European Union under the eContentplus
framework project ECP-2006-PSI-610001

All paper used by Open Book Publishers is SFI (Sustainable Forestry Initiative),
PEFC (Programme for the Endorsement of Forest Certification Schemes) and
Forest Stewardship Council (FSC) certified.

Printed in the United Kingdom and United States by
Lightning Source for Open Book Publishers

Contents

Contributors

Hal Abelson is Professor of Electrical Engineering and Computer Science at MIT and a founding director of Creative Commons.

Ben Adida is Tech Lead on Identity and User Data at Mozilla and a technical advisor to Creative Commons.

Roland Alton-Scheidl is founder of the Public Voice Lab, a Board Member of the International Media Association co-operative and Vice President of the Creative Industries Association in Austria. He teaches at the Vorarlberg University of Applied Sciences where he has recently established courses on media and business ethics. He can be reached at roland@alton.at.

Joe Benso is a professional music manager, member of the International Media Association and founder of OneLoudr.com. He is teaching at Southern Illinois University and is based in Dornbirn and Nashville. He can be reached at joe.benso@gmail.com.

Enrico Bertacchini is a researcher at the Department of Economics "Cognetti De Martiis", University of Turin, and Fellow of the Nexa Center for Internet & Society, Turin Polytechnic (Politecnico di Torino). He can be reached at enrico.bertacchini@unito.it.

Tom Dedeurwaerdere is Professor at the Université Catholique de Louvain, Director of the BIOGOV Unit at the Centre for the Philosophy of Law (CPDR) and Research Associate of the National Foundation for Scientific Research, Belgium (FSR-FNRS). He can be reached at tom.dedeurwaerdere@uclouvain.be.

Giancarlo Frosio was serving as the Chief Editor and author of the Communia Final Report from 2010 to 2011, and is the Assistant Director of the LLM in Intellectual Property jointly organized by WIPO and the University of Turin. He can be reached at LLMADir@itcilo.org.

Lucie Guibault is Assistant Professor at the Institute for Information Law, University of Amsterdam. She can be reached at L.Guibault@uva.nl.

Mike Linksvayer has served as Vice President and CTO at Creative Commons. He can be reached at ml@gondwanaland.com.

Giuseppe Mazziotti worked as an attorney and then as counsel with Nunziante Magrone in Rome from 2007 to 2011. From 2009 to 2011 he was Assistant Professor of intellectual property law at the University of Copenhagen. He is now a Fellow at the Berkman Center for Internet and Society at Harvard Law School and can be reached at giuseppe.mazziotti@gmail.com.

Charles R. Nesson is the William F. Weld Professor of Law at Harvard Law School, and Founder and Faculty Co-Director of the Berkman Center for Internet & Society. He can be reached at nesson@gmail.com.

Unai Pascual is Senior Lecturer at the Department of Land Economy, University of Cambridge and Professor (Ikerbasque) at the Basque Centre for Climate Change (BC3) in Bilbao. He can be reached at up211@cam.ac.uk

Rufus Pollock was a Director and co-founder of the Open Knowledge Foundation and Mead Fellow in Economics at Emmanuel College, University of Cambridge (until September 2010). He is currently a Director of the Open Knowledge Foundation, a Shuttleworth Foundation Fellow and an Associate at the Centre for Intellectual Property and Information Law, University of Cambridge. He can be reached at okfn.rufus.pollock@gmail.com.

Marco Ricolfi is Professor of Intellectual Property at the Turin Law School and co-Director of the LLM in Intellectual Property (jointly organized by WIPO and the University of Turin), and of the Nexa Center for Internet & Society, Turin Polytechnic. He is also a Partner at Tosetto, Weigmann & Associati and can be reached at marco.ricolfi@studiotosetto.it.

Martin Springer is a research manager based in Berlin and was active for Semantic Copyright Standardisation at IEEE. He is also a member of the International Media Association and can be reached at ms@osAlliance.com.

Per M. Stromberg is Visiting Research Fellow at the Institute of Advanced Studies, United Nations University, Yokohama. He also works as an economist at the Policy Analysis Unit of the Swedish Environmental Protection Agency. He can be reached at Per.Stromberg@naturvardsverket.se.

Kaitlin Thaney managed the science division of Creative Commons, formerly known as "Science Commons", from 2006 to July 2010. She is now the Manager of External Partnerships at Digital Science, and can be reached at kaitlin@digital-science.com.

Karen Van Godtsenhoven was working on the DRIVER project at Ghent University Library and is now curator of the Fashion Museum (www.momu.be) in Antwerp. She can be reached at karen.vg83@gmail.com.

Jo Walsh has been on the Open Knowledge Foundation Board and is Project Manager at EDINA, University of Edinburgh.

Nathan Yergler is Senior Software Engineer at Eventbrite and was previously CTO at Creative Commons. He can be reached at nathan@yergler.net

Foreword

Charles R. Nesson

The public domain is the sovereign space of all citizens of the world. Like the air we breathe, it is free for all people to use, without restriction, no rights reserved. Our public ownership of this domain of knowledge should be understood as a fundamental human right to access our shared knowledge, the use of which is not the result of a grant by any specific government.

In this book, the members of Communia not only articulats this positive conception of our public domain, but also seek to make the European public domain *actionable*. The book defines the public domain of the European nations and studies the environment in which it operates. Most importantly, it recommends a set of actions to build and make use of that domain as an environment of shared intellectual property and multifaceted cultural heritage.

This book could not come at a more important time. In a little over a decade, technological developments have shifted information production and distribution methods throughout the world. The way we interact with information has changed radically. Names like Wikipedia, Google, YouTube and, increasingly, Europeana speak for themselves. Our public domain is a wellspring of common wealth that provides ways to share that were inconceivable just a short time ago. The potential for growth that a free and accessible public domain presents to a networked Europe, rich in cultural heritage and with such a highly educated populace, is incredible. Yet the immediate implications can be hard to grasp, and policy interventions, quite often driven by special interests, painfully myopic.

Communia bucks this trend. Each recommendation in this book addresses a genuine long-term concern. Their principle objective is to ensure a strong, free and accessible public domain. Any intervention concerning intellectual property laws will have an impact on innovation, education and economic growth for decades into the future. Communia's proposals offer benefits for innovation, creation and societal enrichment that are not only immediate, they also grow with the passage of time. These proposals are designed to further propel the creative revolution that has been rising in the networked economy, providing the people of Europe with competitive advantage among developed nations.

Seen from the perspective of users of the public domain, the greatest legal constraint on dissemination of public knowledge is from the threat of copyright litigation. This report recommends the action of developing a digital registry for intellectual works. This is, in my view, the single most important Communia recommendation, and I would like to expand upon it.

A legal system of intellectual property in cyberspace without a digital registry makes no more sense than would a legal system of property without a registry of deeds. From a user's viewpoint the cyber world offers access to three kinds of works: public domains works, which are legally free to use but it is up to the user to make the legal determination that the work is in the public domain; copyrighted works including information sufficient to allow the user to find the copyright holder and negotiate legal permission to use; and copyrighted works, orphaned by the absence of tracking information and therefore legally unusable. Determining the status of most works is a task beyond the vast majority of people, and can even be challenging to lawyers. For many individuals and institutions, even a 99% certainty that a work is in the public domain is not comforting, if there is still a 1% chance that use of the work could subject them to financially crippling litigation.

This ambiguity regarding the copyright status of countless works, compounded by the threat of crushing litigation if one makes a misjudgment, blights our shared common domain and cries out for a better system. To the extent that we want to have an open and accessible public domain, which is to say, to the extent that we want our public domain to be *usable*, a reliable digital registry is a necessity.

Communia proposes that each country — helped by Europeana and the great universities of Europe — sets up a registry by legally curating works in their nation's public domain. Each registry should be backed by legal strength to defend its declarations. Each registry should be linked with other national registries and accessible to all countries. When aggregated, the registries will form a global consortium in support of our public domain in cyberspace, and hence a coherent force to hold litigation at bay.

Cyberspace is structured by law and engineering. Communia seeks to build its national parks. The recommendations of this report are timely, wise and important. They should be carefully studied and then adopted.

Introduction

Melanie Dulong de Rosnay
Juan Carlos De Martin

In a context of extension of copyright duration and scope, the public domain is at risk, and with it, the vibrant expression of our culture and democracies. A group of academic and think-tank researchers, librarians, government representatives, museum curators, copyright and human rights activists, information technology entrepreneurs and non-profits worked between 2007 and 2011 to understand the notion of the public domain. Often lacking a positive definition, this concept has been poorly represented in the public debate. The political scene, since the expansion of the Internet in the last couple of decades, has been giving a larger space to concepts of piracy, cybercriminality, technical protection, lawsuits and internet filtering, forgetting that lawful and peaceful creative activities can only take place if an unregulated space remains available around copyright protection.

A reason for the public domain to be forgotten is that copyright—initially developed in the eighteenth century as a temporary and limited monopoly granting exclusive rights to authors in order to provide them an incentive to create and disseminate their work within society—has been increasing and undermining the potential of members of the public, who can also be creators and inventors, to produce cultural wealth and economic value for the society as a whole when reusing works.

The project around this book intended to revert the definition and put back the public domain at its original position: "the public domain is the rule, copyright protection is the exception". The foreword of this book by Charles Nesson recalls the simple yet powerful idea that the public domain belongs to the public and that no private interest should undermine it.

The citations in this introduction have been extracted from *The Public Domain Manifesto*, which is reproduced in full later in this volume. The Manifesto was produced within the context of Communia, the European Thematic Network, which was funded by the European Commission.[1] The Communia project had several developments that were not initially planned in the grant agreement. At its beginning, neither the coordinators nor the members could have imagined the number and the nature of the activities, many of which went well beyond the scope of organizing conferences and publishing papers. As the project progressed, partners decided to work on a voluntary basis between conferences to perform public outreach.

The most emblematic output of the Communia project is *The Public Domain Manifesto*, which was translated in over twenty languages. In particular, it takes a broad definition of the public domain:

> The public domain, as we understand it, is the wealth of information that is free from the barriers to access or reuse usually associated with copyright protection, either because it is free from any copyright protection or because the right holders have decided to remove these barriers. It is the basis of our self-understanding as expressed by our shared knowledge and culture. It is the raw material from which new knowledge is derived and new cultural works are created. The public domain acts as a protective mechanism that ensures that this raw material is available at its cost of reproduction — close to zero — and that all members of society can build upon it.

The Manifesto defines the public domain as including not only works for which copyright restrictions have expired, but also the space where copyright does not apply because the law foresees some exceptions and limitations. It also includes resources which are part of the commons, either because they were not subjected to copyright (such as facts, ideas, information and data) or because their authors decided to freely share them by publishing them under free and open licenses, such as Creative Commons licenses.

Another outcome of the project is that legal scholars changed their mind during the course of the almost four years of common work to define the nature of the public domain and how it could and should be protected. Librarians self-organized activities for the annual Public Domain Day which celebrates the books which have joined the public domain because copyright restrictions have ended (more or less seventy years after the

---

1   Communia's project website is available at http://www.communia-project.eu; *The Public Domain Manifesto* is also available at http://www.publicdomainmanifesto.org.

death of their authors).[2] The copyright term is difficult to calculate due to complex and unharmonized legislation varying among jurisdictions. Therefore, researchers and developers of the network gathered to produce Public Domain Calculators, partnering with major actors of the field, namely the Open Knowledge Foundation and Europeana, the European Digital Library Portal.[3] These simple web-based applications are designed to allow the public to evaluate whether a work is in the public domain. After almost four years of activity, many members willing to pursue the activities of the network decided to form an international association based in Brussels in order to continue to educate about, advocate for, offer expertise and lead research on the public domain in the digital age.[4] As a network, Communia has published hundreds of news posts and publication items on its website. Another academic book was also initiated during the course of the project, as most of its editors and authors were members of the consortium.[5]

This book does not intend to constitute the proceedings of a European project. On the contrary, it aims to present how a vision has been built internationally along the course of four years of meetings and collaboration among interdisciplinary experts. Starting with *The Public Domain Manifesto*, Communia defends a European vision of the public domain and presents concrete policy proposals to protect the public interest. Most of the subsequent chapters had a first version which was published on the project website. Some have been updated, and others have been kept in their original version, mostly from 2007 or 2008, as a testimony of the project as a process which reached the conclusion presented as the starting point of the book. Chapters were selected to support and justify the Manifesto and its policy recommendations. They demonstrate how the project developed and outline the most valuable lessons that were learned along the way. The book attempts to capture the most structured part of the output of Communia in the hope that it will represent the foundations for a new awareness in Europe and elsewhere of the role of the public domain for cultural, civic and economic development in the twenty-first century.

---

2   See the Public Domain Day website: http://www.publicdomainday.org.
3   Background at http://wiki.okfn.org/Public_Domain_Calculators; application at http:// www.publicdomainworks.net/api; see also http://outofcopyright.eu.
4   See http://www.communia-association.org/home.
5   *Intelligent Multimedia: Sharing Creative Works in a Digital World*, ed. by Danièle Bourcier, Pompeu Casanovas, Melanie Dulong de Rosnay and Catharina Maracke (Florence: European Press, 2010), available at http://creativecommons.fr/wordpress/wp-content/ uploads/2011/05/CCiBook_printedversion_IntelligentMultimedia1.pdf.

The first chapter by Giancarlo Frosio investigates the state of the digital public domain in Europe, and recommends policy strategies for enhancing a healthy public domain and making digital content in Europe more accessible and usable. The second chapter also contains academic articles building the legal framework of the public domain. With his Copyright 2.0 proposal, Marco Ricolfi makes concrete proposals for changes in copyright legislation to fit the digital environment in the context of the i2010 strategy. Lucie Guibault presents an evaluation of the Directive 2001/29/EC on the harmonization of certain aspects of copyright and related rights in the digital information society in the light of the recommendation on digitization and accessibility of material preserved by libraries, archives and museums. Giuseppe Mazziotti seeks to explore how the implementation of open access licences onto recordings and other forms of digital performance of creative works which have entered the public domain, complements the notion of digital commons.

The third section gathers developments and case studies. The first two papers of this section analyse the research commons in biological sciences. Enrico Bertacchini surveys the main economic issues concerning the emergence of contractually-constructed research commons, with a particular attention to the field of biological/genetic resources and biotechnologies. Tom Dedeurwaerdere, Per M. Stromberg and Unai Pascual study the social motivations and incentives in *ex situ* conservation of microbial genetic resources.

The three next chapters describe the founding principles of key institutions and projects engaged in promoting the digital public domain within research and society. Rufus Pollock and Jo Walsh present some of the concepts underlying the work led by the Open Knowledge Foundation, while Kaitlin Thaney introduces how Science Commons helps building the "Research Web". Karen Van Godtsenhoven presents the European DRIVER project (Digital Repository Infrastructure Vision for European Research), a portal for open access scientific communication. The last two chapters present technical developments implementing the digital public domain. Hal Abelson, Ben Adida, Mike Linksvayer and Nathan Yergler developed Creative Commons Rights Expression Language (CC REL), the standard recommended by Creative Commons to the W3C for machine-readable expression of copyright licensing terms and related information. Roland Alton Scheidl, Joe Benso and Martin Springer describe good practices for online registration services of creative works.

The Public Domain Manifesto

Le livre, comme livre, appartient à l'auteur, mais comme pensée, il appartient — le mot n'est pas trop vaste — au genre humain. Toutes les intelligences y ont droit. Si l'un des deux droits, le droit de l'écrivain et le droit de l'esprit humain, devait être sacrifié, ce serait, certes, le droit de l'écrivain, car l'intérêt public est notre préoccupation unique, et tous, je le déclare, doivent passer avant nous.[1]

Our markets, our democracy, our science, our traditions of free speech, and our art all depend more heavily on a public domain of freely available material than they do on the informational material that is covered by property rights. The public domain is not some gummy residue left behind when all the good stuff has been covered by property law. The public domain is the place we quarry the building blocks of our culture. It is, in fact, the majority of our culture.[2]

The public domain, as we understand it, is the wealth of information that is free from the barriers to access or reuse usually associated with copyright protection, either because it is free from any copyright protection or because the right holders have decided to remove these barriers. It is the basis of our self-understanding as expressed by our shared knowledge and culture. It is the raw material from which new knowledge is derived and new cultural works are created. The public domain acts as a protective mechanism that ensures that this raw material is available at its cost of reproduction — close to zero — and that all members of society can build upon it. Having a healthy and thriving public domain is essential to the social and economic well-being of our societies.

---

1   "The book, in and as a book, belongs to the author, but as a thought, it belongs — and I am not overstating — to all humanity. All sentient beings have a right to that thought. If one of these two rights (the author's right to the book and the people's right to the thoughts) has to be sacrificed, this should be, for sure, the rights of the author. This is because the public good is our primary concern, and I declare this [as an author], the people's rights come before ours." Victor Hugo, *Discours d'ouverture du Congrès littéraire international* (Paris: Lévy, 1878). Translation by Derek Kerton.

2   James Boyle, *The Public Domain: Enclosing the Commons of the Mind* (New Haven: Yale University Press, 2008), pp. 40–41.

It plays a capital role in the fields of education, science, cultural heritage and public sector information. A healthy and thriving public domain is one of the prerequisites for ensuring that the principles of Article 27 (1) of the Universal Declaration of Human Rights ("Everyone has the right freely to participate in the cultural life of the community, to enjoy the arts and to share in scientific advancement and its benefits") can be enjoyed by everyone around the world.

The digital networked information society has brought the issue of the public domain to the foreground of copyright discussions. In order to preserve and strengthen the public domain we need a robust and up-to-date understanding of the nature and role of this essential resource. This Public Domain Manifesto defines the public domain and outlines the necessary principles and guidelines for a healthy public domain at the beginning of the twenty-first century. The public domain is considered here in its relation to copyright law, to the exclusion of other intellectual property rights (like patents and trademarks), and where copyright law is to be understood in its broadest sense to include economic and moral rights under copyright and related rights (inclusive of neighboring rights and database rights). In the remainder of this document copyright is therefore used as a catch-all term for these rights. Moreover, the term "works" includes all subject-matter protected by copyright so defined, thus including databases, performances and recordings. Likewise, the term "authors" includes photographers, producers, broadcasters, painters and performers.

The public domain in the twenty-first century

The public domain as aspired to in this Manifesto is defined as cultural material that can be used without restriction, absent copyright protection. In addition to works that are formally in the public domain, there are also lots of valuable works that individuals have voluntarily shared under generous terms creating a privately constructed commons that functions in many ways like the public domain. Moreover, individuals can also make use of many protected works through exceptions and limitations to copyright, fair use and fair dealing. All of these sources that allow for increased access to our culture and heritage are important and all need to be actively maintained in order for society to reap the full benefit of our shared knowledge and culture.

The public domain

The structural public domain lies at the core of the notion of the public domain and is comprised of our shared knowledge, culture and resources that can be used without copyright restrictions by virtue of current law. Specifically, the structural public domain is made up of two different classes of material:

1. **Works of authorship where the copyright protection has expired.** Copyright is a temporary right granted to authors. Once this temporary protection has come to its end, all legal restrictions cease to exist, subject in some countries to the author's perpetual moral rights.

2. **The essential commons of information that is not covered by copyright.** Works that are not protected by copyright because they fail the test of originality, or are excluded from protection (such as data, facts, ideas, procedures, processes, systems, methods of operation, concepts, principles, or discoveries, regardless of the form in which they are described, explained, illustrated, or embodied in a work, as well as laws and judicial and administrative decisions). This essential commons is too important for the functioning of our societies to be burdened with legal restrictions of any nature even for a limited period.

The structural public domain is an historically grown balance to the rights of authors protected by copyright and it is essential to the cultural memory and knowledge base of our societies. In the second half of the twentieth century all two elements identified here have been strained by the extension of the term of copyright protection and the introduction of more copyright-like regimes of legal protection.

Voluntary commons and user prerogatives

In addition to this structural core of the public domain, there are other essential sources that enable individuals to freely interact with copyright protected works. These represent the "breathing space" of our current culture and knowledge, ensuring that copyright protection does not interfere with specific requirements of society and the voluntary choices of authors. While these sources increase access to protected works, some of them make this access conditional on certain forms of use or restrict access to certain classes of users:

1. **Works that are voluntarily shared by their rights holders.** Creators can remove use restrictions from their works by either freely licensing them, or by using other legal tools to allow others to use their works without restrictions, or by dedicating them to the public domain.[3]

---

3   For free licencing definitions see the definition of free software http://www.gnu.org/philosophy/free-sw.html, the definition of free cultural works http://freedomdefined.org/, and the open knowledge definition http://opendefinition.org/1.0/ for reference.

2. **The user prerogatives created by exceptions and limitations to copyright, fair use and fair dealing.** These prerogatives are an integral part of the public domain. They ensure that there is sufficient access to our shared culture and knowledge, enabling the functioning of essential social institutions and enabling social participation of individuals with special needs.

Taken together, the public domain, the voluntary sharing of works and exceptions and limitations to copyright, fair use and fair dealing go a long way to ensure that everyone has access to our shared culture and knowledge in order to facilitate innovation and cultural participation for the benefit of the entire society. It is therefore important that the public domain in both its incarnations is actively maintained so that it can continue to fulfill this key role in this period of rapid technological and social change.

General Principles

In a period of rapid technological and social change the public domain fulfills an essential role in cultural participation and digital innovation, and therefore needs to be actively maintained. Active maintenance of the public domain needs to take into account a number of general principles. The following principles are essential to preserve a meaningful understanding of the public domain and to ensure that the public domain continues to function in the technological environment of the networked information society. With regard to the structural public domain these are as follows:

1. **The public domain is the rule, copyright protection is the exception.** Since copyright protection is granted only with respect to original forms of expression, the vast majority of data, information and ideas produced worldwide at any given time belongs to the public domain. In addition to information that is not eligible for protection, the public domain is enlarged every year by works whose term of protection expires. The combined application of the requirements for protection and the limited duration of the copyright protection contribute to the wealth of the public domain so as to ensure access to our shared culture and knowledge.

2. **Copyright protection should last only as long as necessary to achieve a reasonable compromise between protecting and rewarding the author for his intellectual labour and safeguarding the public interest in the dissemination of culture and knowledge.** From neither the perspective of the author nor the general public do any valid arguments exist (whether historical, economic, social or otherwise) in support of an exceedingly long term of copyright protection. While the author should be able to reap the fruits of his intellectual labour, the general public should not be

deprived for an overly long period of time of the benefits of freely using those works.

3. **What is in the public domain must remain in the public domain.** Exclusive control over public domain works must not be reestablished by claiming exclusive rights in technical reproductions of the works, or using technical protection measures to limit access to technical reproductions of such works.

4. **The lawful user of a digital copy of a public domain work should be free to (re-)use, copy and modify such work.** The public domain status of a work does not necessarily mean that it must be made accessible to the public. The owners of physical works that are in the public domain are free to restrict access to such works. However once access to a work has been granted then there ought not be legal restrictions on the re-use, modification or reproduction of these works.

5. **Contracts or technical protection measures that restrict access to and re-use of public domain works must not be enforced.** The public domain status of a work guarantees the right to re-use, modify and reproduce. This also includes user prerogatives arising from exceptions and limitations, fair use and fair dealing, ensuring that these cannot be limited by contractual or technological means.

In addition, the following principles are at the core of the voluntary commons and user prerogatives described above:

1. **The voluntary relinquishment of copyright and sharing of protected works are legitimate exercises of copyright exclusivity.** Many authors entitled to copyright protection for their works do not wish to exercise these rights to their full extent or wish to relinquish these rights altogether. Such actions, provided that they are voluntary, are a legitimate exercise of copyright exclusivity and must not be hindered by law, by statute or by other mechanisms including moral rights.

2. **Exceptions and limitations to copyright, fair use and fair dealing need to be actively maintained to ensure the effectiveness of the fundamental balance of copyright and the public interest.** These mechanisms create user prerogatives that constitute the breathing space within the current copyright system. Given the rapid pace of change in both technology and society it is important that they remain capable of ensuring the functioning of essential social institutions and the social participation of individuals with special needs. Therefore, exceptions and limitations to copyright, fair use and fair dealing should be construed as evolutionary in nature and constantly adapted to account for the public interest.

In addition to these general principles, a number of issues relevant to the public domain must be addressed immediately. The following recommendations are aimed at protecting the public domain and ensuring that it can continue to function in a meaningful way. While these recommendations are applicable across the spectrum of copyright, they are of particular relevance to education, cultural heritage and scientific research.

General Recommendations

1. **The term of copyright protection should be reduced.** The excessive length of copyright protection combined with an absence of formalities is highly detrimental to the accessibility of our shared knowledge and culture. Moreover, it increases the occurrence of orphan works, works that are neither under the control of their authors nor part of the public domain, and in either case cannot be used. Thus, for new works the duration of copyright protection should be reduced to a more reasonable term.

2. **Any change to the scope of copyright protection (including any new definition of protectable subject-matter or expansion of exclusive rights) needs to take into account the effects on the public domain.** Any change of the scope of copyright protection must not be applied retroactively to works already subject to protection. Copyright is a time-limited exception to the public domain status of our shared culture and knowledge. In the twentieth century its scope has been significantly extended, to accommodate the interests of a small class of rights holders at the expense of the general public. As a result, most of our shared culture and knowledge is locked away behind copyright and technical restrictions. We must ensure that this situation will not be worsened at a minimum, and be affirmatively improved in the future.

3. **When material is deemed to fall in the structural public domain in its country of origin, the material should be recognized as part of the structural public domain in all other countries of the world.** Where material in one country is not eligible for copyright protection because it falls under a specific copyright exclusion, either because it does not meet the criterion of originality or because the duration of its protection has lapsed, it should not be possible for anyone (including the author) to invoke copyright protection on the same material in another country so as to withdraw this material from the structural public domain.

4. **Any false or misleading attempt to misappropriate public domain material must be legally punished.** In order to preserve the integrity of the public domain and protect users of public domain material from inaccurate and deceitful representations, any false or misleading attempts to claim exclusivity over public domain material must be declared unlawful.

5. **No other intellectual property right must be used to reconstitute exclusivity over public domain material.** The public domain is integral to the internal balance of the copyright system. This internal balance must not be manipulated by attempts to reconstitute or obtain exclusive control via regulations that are external to copyright.

6. **There must be a practical and effective path to make available "orphan works" and published works that are no longer commercially available (such as out-of-print works) for re-use by society.** The extension of the scope and duration of copyright and the prohibition of formalities for foreign works have created a huge body of orphan works that are neither under the control of their authors nor part of the public domain. Given that such works under current law do not benefit their authors or society, these works need to be made available for productive re-use by society as a whole.

7. **Cultural heritage institutions should take upon themselves a special role in the effective labeling and preserving of public domain works.** Not-for-profit cultural heritage organizations have been entrusted with preservation of our shared knowledge and culture for centuries. As part of this role they need to ensure that works in the public domain are available to all of society, by labeling them, preserving them and making them freely available.

8. **There must be no legal obstacles that prevent the voluntary sharing of works or the dedication of works to the public domain.** Both are legitimate exercises of exclusive rights granted by copyright and both are critical to ensuring access to essential cultural goods and knowledge and to respecting authors' wishes.

9. **Personal non-commercial uses of protected works must generally be made possible, for which alternative modes of remuneration for the author must be explored.** While it is essential for the self-development of each individual that he or she be able to make personal non-commercial uses of works, it is just as essential that the position of the author be taken into consideration when establishing new limitations and exceptions on copyright or revising old ones.

I. Introducing the Digital Public Domain

1. Communia and the European Public Domain Project: A Politics of the Public Domain

Giancarlo Frosio

What am I then? Everything that I have seen, heard, and observed I have collected and exploited. My works have been nourished by countless different individuals, by innocent and wise ones, people of intelligence and dunces. Childhood, maturity, and old age all have brought me their thoughts, their perspectives on life. I have often reaped what others have sowed. My work is the work of a collective being that bears the name of Goethe.[1]

The following chapter is an amended version of the Final Report of the Communia Network on the Digital Public Domain. The Report was undertaken (i) to review the activities of Communia; (ii) to investigate the state of the digital public domain in Europe; and (iii) to recommend policy strategies for enhancing a healthy public domain and making digital content in Europe more accessible and usable. As a result, together with the review of the definition, value and role of the public domain, the chapter will examine the challenges and bottlenecks impinging on the public domain. In addition, it will discuss the opportunities that digitization and the Internet revolution have been offering to the public domain as well as access to

---

1   Johann Wolfgang von Goethe, cited in Martha Woodmansee and Peter Jaszi, "The Law of Text: Copyright in the Academy", *College English*, 57 (1995), 769-87.

knowledge. Finally, general guidelines for a politics of the public domain will be drafted together with the sketching of a positive view of Europe with a stronger public domain. Each of the subjects discussed in this chapter are further developed and detailed in Annex II of the Communia Final Report.

1. What is the public domain?

Defining the boundaries and inner meaning of the public domain is conducive to the aim of strengthening its protection and its promotion. There are many public domains that change in shape according to the hopes and the agenda they embody.[2] The diversity of the Communia network has provided an opportunity to internalise this protean nature of the public domain. The outcome has been a comprehensive vision that projects the understanding of the European public domain in a global international dimension. This vision conveys the perception that the public domain is never a definition but instead a statement of purpose, and a project of enhanced democracy, globalised shared culture and reciprocal understanding. Communia has attempted to propel a process of definitional re-construction of the public domain in positive and affirmative terms. It envisions the public domain as having a very substantial element of attraction to aggregate social forces devoted to promoting public access to culture and knowledge.

The traditional definition regarded the public domain as a "wasteland of undeserving detritus" and did not "worry about 'threats' to this domain any more than [it] would worry about scavengers who go to garbage dumps to look for abandoned property".[3] This definitional approach has been discarded in the last thirty years. In 1981, David Lange published his seminal work, *Recognizing the Public Domain*, and departed from the traditional line of investigation. Lange suggested that "recognition of new intellectual property interests should be offset today by equally deliberate recognition of individual rights in the public domain".[4] In January 2008, Séverine Dusollier reinstated that idea at the first Communia Workshop by speaking of a "positively defined public domain":

> In legal regimes of intellectual property, the public domain is generally defined in a negative manner, as the resources in which no IP right is vested. This no-rights perspective entails that the actual regime of the public

---

2   See James Boyle, "The Second Enclosure Movement and the Construction of the Public Domain", *Law and Contemporary Problems*, 66 (2003), 33-74 (p. 62).

3   Pamela Samuelson, "Mapping the Digital Public Domain: Threats and Opportunities", *Law and Contemporary Problems*, 66 (2003), 147-61.

4   David Lange, "Recognizing the Public Domain", *Law and Contemporary Problems*, 24 (1981), 147-81.

domain does not prevent its ongoing encroachment, but might conversely facilitate it. In order to effectively preserve the public domain, an adequate legal regime should be devised so as to make the commons immune from any legal or factual appropriation, hence setting up a positive definition and regime of the public domain.[5]

The affirmative public domain was a powerfully attractive idea that propelled the "public domain project".[6] Many authors in Europe and elsewhere attempted to define, map and explain the role of the public domain as an alternative to the commodification of information that threatened creativity. This ongoing public domain project offers many definitions that attempt to construe the public domain positively. A positive, affirmative definition of the public domain is a political statement, the endorsement of a cause.

As *The Public Domain Manifesto* puts it, the public domain is the "cultural material that can be used without restriction", and which includes a structural core and a functional portion. The structural core encompasses the "works of authorship where the copyright protection has expired" and the "essential commons of information that is not covered by copyright". The functional portion of the public domain consists of the "works that are voluntarily shared by their rights holders" and "the user prerogatives created by exceptions and limitations to copyright, fair use and fair dealing".[7]

However, notwithstanding many complementing definitional approaches, consistency is to be found in the common idea that the public domain is the material that composes our cultural heritage. The public domain envisioned by Communia becomes the "place we quarry the building blocks of our culture", as put by James Boyle, the co-director of the Duke Center for the Study of the Public Domain, and a member of the Communia network.[8] At the same time, the public domain is the building itself. It is, in the end, the majority, if not the entirety, of our

---

5 Séverine Dusollier, "Towards a Legal Infrastructure for the Public Domain", paper delivered at the first Communia workshop, Turin, Italy (18 January 2008). Please note that any of the materials cited in this Report and Annexes related to proceedings of Communia meetings can be found at http://www.communia-project.eu.

6 Michael D. Birnhack, "More or Better? Shaping the Public Domain", in *The Future of the Public Domain: Identifying the Commons in Information Law*, ed. by P. Bernt Hugenholtz and Lucie Guibault (Kluwer Law International, 2006), 59-86 (p. 60).

7 See *The Public Domain Manifesto* at the beginning of this volume; also available at http://publicdomainmanifesto.org.

8 James Boyle, *The Public Domain: Enclosing the Commons of the Mind* (New Haven: Yale University Press, 2008), p. 40.

culture. Therefore, the public domain must be free for all to use, and copyright expansionism is a welfare loss against which society at large must be guarded.

The modern discourse on the public domain owes much to the legal analysis of the governance of the commons, that is, natural resources used by many individuals in common. Commons and the public domain are in fact two different things: the public domain is free from property rights and control whilst a commons may be restrictive. However, this kind of control is different than under traditional property regimes because no permission or authorisation is required to enjoy the resource. These resources are protected by a liability rule rather than a property rule.[9] Free Software, Open Source Software and Creative Commons are examples of intellectual commons.[10]

Although the public domain and commons are diverse concepts, since the origin of the public domain discourse, the environmental metaphor has been largely used to refer to the cultural public domain.[11] Therefore, the traditional environmental conception of the commons was ported to the cultural domain and applied to intellectual property policy issues. Under this conceptual scheme, the individual, legal, and market-based control of the property regime is juxtaposed to the collective and informal controls of the well-run commons.[12] Environmental and intellectual property scholars started to look at knowledge as a commons—a shared resource, as defined by the Nobel laureate Elinor Ostrom.[13] The environmental metaphor has propelled what can be termed as cultural environmentalism.[14]

---

9   See Lawrence Lessig, "The Architecture of Innovation", *Duke Law Journal*, 51 (2002), 1783-1801 (p. 1788); but see James Boyle, "The Second Enclosure Movement and the Construction of the Public Domain", pp. 33, 69 n., 145.

10 See Yochai Benkler, *The Wealth of Networks: How Social Production Transforms Markets and Freedom* (New Haven: Yale University Press, 2006), pp. 63–68. Benkler describes free software as "the quintessential instance of commons-based peer production".

11 See Mark Rose, "Copyright and its Metaphors", *UCLA Law Review*, 50 (2002), 1-15; William St Clair, "Metaphors of Intellectual Property", in *Privilege and Property: Essays on the History of Copyright*, ed. by Ronan Deazley, Martin Kretschmer and Lionel Bently (Cambridge: Open Book Publishers, 2010), 369-95 (pp. 391–92).

12 See James Boyle, "Foreword: The Opposite of Property?", *Law and Contemporary Problems*, 66 (2003), 1-32 (p. 8).

13 See Charlotte Hess and Elinor Ostrom, "Introduction: An Overview of the Knowledge Commons", in *Understanding Knowledge as a Commons: From Theory to Practice*, ed. by Charlotte Hess and Elinor Ostrom (Cambridge, MA: MIT Press, 2007), pp. 3–26.

14 See James Boyle, "Cultural Environmentalism and Beyond", *Law and Contemporary Problems*, 70 (2007), 5-21; and James Boyle, *Shamans, Software, and Spleens: Law and the Construction of the Information Society* (Cambridge, MA: Harvard University Press, 1996).

In the last decade, we have witnessed the emergence of a new understanding of the public domain in terms of affirmative protection and the sustainable development of a common pool of resources, especially in the digitally networked environment. This enhanced understanding of the value of the public domain has been undergoing a multi-faceted evolution with academic, civic, institutional and more practical ramifications. Today, the Institute for Information Law at Amsterdam University, the Berkman Center for Internet and Society at Harvard, the Cambridge Centre for Intellectual Property and Information Law, the Nexa Center for Internet and Society at the Politecnico di Torino, the Haifa Center of Law and Technology, the Duke Center for the Study of the Public Domain, the Stanford Center for Internet and Society, and a variety of other academic centres devote a substantial amount of their time to investigate the proper balance between intellectual property and the public domain, as detailed by the Communia *Survey of Existing Public Domain Competence Centers* delivered to the European Commission on 30 September 2009.[15] Several advocacy groups are committed to the preservation of the public domain and the promotion of a shared commons of knowledge including, among many others: the Open Knowledge Foundation, Open Rights Group, LaQuadratureduNet, Knowledge Ecology International, the Access to Knowledge (A2K) movement, Public Knowledge, and the Electronic Frontier Foundation. Civil advocacy of the public domain and access to knowledge has also been followed by several institutional variants, such as the "Development Agenda" at the World Intellectual Property Organization (WIPO), setting specific policy recommendations to protect and strengthen the public domain.[16] The WIPO efforts for the promotion of the public domain were presented at the fifth and seventh Communia workshops.[17] In addition,

---

15 See also Communia, *Survey of Existing Public Domain Competence Centers*, Deliverable No. D6.01 (Draft, 30 September 2009) (survey by Federico Morando and Juan Carlos De Martin for the European Commission—on file with the author). The survey reviews the present situation of European competence and excellence centres for the study of the public domain and related issues from different disciplinary perspectives.

16 See Development Agenda for WIPO, http://www.wipo.int/ip-development/en/agenda; see also Séverine Dusollier, "Scoping Study On Copyright And Related Rights and the Public Domain", prepared for the Word Intellectual Property Organization (30 April 2010), p. 69, available at http://www.wipo.int/edocs/mdocs/mdocs/en/cdip_4/cdip_4_3_rev_study_inf_1.pdf.

17 See Richard Owens, "WIPO and Access to Content: The Development Agenda and the Public Domain", paper delivered at the fifth Communia workshop, London (27 March 2009); see also Richard Owens, "WIPO Project on Intellectual Property and the Public Domain", paper delivered at the seventh Communia workshop, Luxembourg

developments in commons theory have been coupled by efforts to turn theory into practice. For example, Creative Commons and the free and open-source software movement have created a commons through private agreement and technological implementation.[18] Again, private firms in the biotechnological and software fields, have decided to forgo property rights to reduce transaction costs.[19] The issue of voluntary sharing, private ordering and contractually constructed commons was widely investigated at the first and second Communia conferences.

The emergence and growth of an environmental movement for the public domain and, in particular, the digital public domain, is morphing the public domain into the commons. The public domain is our cultural commons: it is like our air, water and forests. We must look at it as a shared resource that cannot be commodified. As much as water, knowledge cannot be constructed mainly as a profitable commodity, as recently argued by Stefano Rodotà, one of the members of the Communia Advisory Committee.[20] As for the natural environment, the public domain and the cultural commons that it embodies need to enjoy a sustainable development. There is also a need, as for the natural environment, to promote a "balanced and sustainable development" of our cultural environment as a fundamental right that is rooted in the Charter of Fundamental Rights of the European Union.[21] As we will detail later in this report, overreaching property theory and overly protective copyright law disrupt the delicate tension between access and protection. Unsustainable cultural development, enclosure and commodification of our cultural commons will produce cultural catastrophes. As unsustainable environmental development has polluted our air, contaminated our water, mutilated our forests, and disfigured our natural landscape, unsustainable

---

(1 February 2010).

18 See Lawrence Lessig, *The Future of Ideas: The Fate of The Commons in a Connected World* (New York: Vintage, 2002); see also Michael J. Madison, Brett M. Frischmann and Katherine J. Strandburg, "Constructing Commons in the Cultural Environment", *Cornell Law Review*, 95 (2010), 657-609 (p. 659); Molly Shaffer Van Houweling, "Cultural Environmentalism and the Constructed Commons", *Law and Contemporary Problems*, 70 (2007), 23-50 (pp. 25-26, 40-48); Jerome H. Reichman and Paul F. Uhlir, "A Contractually Reconstructed Research Commons for Scientific Data in a Highly Protectionist Intellectual Property", *Law and Contemporary Problems*, 66 (2003), 315-462.

19 See Robert P. Merges, "A New Dynamism in the Public Domain", *University of Chicago Law Review*, 71 (2004), 183-203 (pp. 186-91).

20 See Stefano Rodotà, "Se il mondo perde il senso del bene comune", *La Repubblica*, 10 August 2010.

21 See Charter of Fundamental Rights of the European Union, 18 December 2000, 2000 O.J. (C364), pp. 1, 8, 37.

cultural development will outrage and corrupt our cultural heritage and information landscape. A cultural development neglectful of the public domain, if not redressed, will negatively affect society at large in consequence of the loss of economic and social value that may be extracted from the public domain, especially from the digital public domain.

2. The value of the public domain for Europe

The public domain is a valuable global asset; a forward-looking approach would allow the extraction of considerable economic and, especially, social value from it. In particular, Communia asserts that open and public domain approaches can produce economic and social value, as spelled out at the first Communia conference, which was devoted to the assessment of the economic and social impact of digital public domain in Europe, and the second Communia conference. Unfortunately, so far this value has been left unattended. In addition, the intellectual property rhetoric has hidden the public costs of extreme propertisation of the public domain. Rufus Pollock has noted that the current paradigm "binds us to a narrow and erroneous viewpoint in which innovation is central but access is peripheral".[22]

This imbalance should be redressed. This is far more relevant now because this disproportion between innovation and access prevents us from taking full advantage of the possibilities offered by the digital age. Digitization and internet distribution have multiplied the potentialities and opportunities offered by the use of public domain material. On one hand, digitization offers the opportunity to extract economic value out of the public domain by benefiting the public with free or inexpensive cultural resources. On the other hand, digitization may produce immense social value by opening society up to immediate and unlimited access to culture and knowledge. In addition, the economic and social value of the public domain is enhanced by the mass production capacities of the digital environment. A new peer-based culture of sharing is changing our cultural landscape through the revolutionary technological ability of multiplying references instantaneously and endlessly. Openness and access fuel this new culture of shared production of knowledge. Commodification and enclosure of the public domain threaten its growth and survival.

22　Rufus Pollock, "The Value of the Public Domain" (UK Institute for Public Policy Research, 2006), p. 4.

The value of the public domain is a complex variable made up of many components. It is a source of value in both economic and social terms. In addition, value can be extracted from the structural and the functional aspects of the public domain. The contribution of the public domain can be assessed in positive or negative terms by estimating the economic and social loss of enclosure and commodification. The positive value of the public domain can be the effect of direct use, indirect use or reuse of public domain works, the application of public domain business models, its market efficiency or, again, its democratic function. In any event, social and economic value is always very much tangled up in the assessment of the riches of the public domain.

As per the value of a work entering into the public domain or public domain effect, the revenue value is to be distinguished from the social value, as the economic utility generated for society.[23] If, after entering into the public domain, a work is sold for €5 instead of the €10 charged previously, the social value of the work entering into the public domain will be €5. In addition, the social value of a work entering into the public domain will also include the deadweight loss of restricting access to a good that is spared to society. Finally, the assessment of the value of a work entering into the public domain must also take into account the value of reuse. Reducing the public domain or retarding the entrance of a work into the public domain shall deprive the community of the correspondent social value of developing derivative works or invention from the original cultural artefact. The value of reuse is a dynamic value that boosts society both economically and culturally.

Practice is often more explanatory than theory. A few examples may help to pinpoint the value of the "public domain effect", the entrance of a work into the public domain, and other social and economic values that can be extracted from the public domain. In 2010, the works of Sigmund Freud entered the public domain in Italy. This event propelled the publication of 36 works by Freud in the first nine months of 2010 by ten publishers. This is an astonishing figure if compared with the previous years: from 1999 to 2009, only 16 works by Freud were published in Italy.[24]

Secondly, 2007 saw the end of the copyright protection of the works of Louis Vierne, a renowned French organist and composer. Upon expiration of Vierne's copyright, new editions of Vierne's works finally corrected

---

23   See ibid., p. 5.
24   See International Book Shop, www.ibs.it.

many mistakes and inaccuracies included in the original scores. Vierne was born nearly blind, and such mistakes were obviously due to his wobbly handwriting. Up to the expiration of Vierne's copyright, none of the publishers tried to correct the mistakes, because the copyright laws prevented them from editing the original works in any way.[25]

Similarly, the film *It's a Wonderful Life,* directed by Frank Capra, fell into the public domain in 1974 after the copyright holder failed to renew it. The film had been largely ignored since its original release. However, in 1975, a television station discovered that the movie was freely available and ran it during the Christmas period because its climax comes on Christmas Eve. Within a few years, *It's a Wonderful Life* was being shown on television stations across the United States every Christmas. The success was terrific. Watching the film at Christmastime became a cultural tradition in the US.[26]

Together with the value that may be immediately extracted from the entrance of a work into the public domain, a public domain approach to knowledge management may be a source of value on many different levels. Although a quantitative measurement is impossible, some quantitative conclusions on the value of the public domain can be inferred by examining a few examples of public domain approaches to knowledge production.[27] In general, these examples show the role and the value of the digital public domain in allowing new business models to emerge.

In the case of file sharing, for example, few studies have found significant benefits of free access. The studies have found that the impact of peer-to-peer file sharing on sales does not seem that relevant.[28] Furthermore, data on the supply of new works seem to support the argument that the advent of file sharing did not discourage creators and creativity at large.[29] In fact, the impact of file sharing

---

25 See Massimo Nosetti, "Il maestro dell'organo fuori dal copyright", in *Il Giornale della Musica*, November 2008, p. 38.

26 See Paul A. David and Jared Rubin, "How Many Scanned Books on the Web?" (SIEPER Policy Briefs, December 2008), pp. 6–7.

27 See Pollock (2006), p. 8.

28 See, for example, Felix Oberholzer-Gee and Koleman Strumpf, "File-Sharing and Copyright", *Innovation Policy and the Economy*, 10 (2010), 19-55 (pp. 19, 34–38); Felix Oberholzer-Gee and Koleman Strumpf, "The Effect of File Sharing on Record Sales: An Empirical Analysis", *Journal of Politcal Economy*, 115 (2004), 1-42; Fabrice LeGuel and Fabrice Rochelandet, "P2P Music-Sharing Networks: Why the Legal Fight Against Copiers May Be Inefficient?" (Social Science Research Network Working Paper Series, 2005), which uses a unique dataset collected from more than 2,500 French households; but, for example, Stan J. Liebowitz, "How Reliable is the Oberholzer-Gee and Strumpf Paper on File-Sharing?" (University of Texas at Dallas, Working Paper, August 2007); Stan J. Liebowitz, "File Sharing: Creative Destruction or Just Plain Destruction?", *Journal of Law and Economics*, 49 (2006), 1-28.

29 See Oberholzer-Gee and Strumpf (2010), pp. 46–49.

on creators may be positive due to the increase of the demand for complements to protected works, such as concerts, special editions or merchandising.

The value of other examples of public domain models, as singled out by Pollock's study, *The Value of the Public Domain*, can be more immediately appreciated.[30] Open source software is a quintessential example of the value of an open approach, or functional public domain approach, as *The Public Domain Manifesto* puts it, to the production of information goods. The Internet and the World Wide Web are further examples of the great wealth that can be built upon public domain material. These technologies were non-proprietary and openness was the key to their revolutionary success. Again, online search engines, such as Google, produce relevant social benefit through their service and generate very large revenue by copying "open" information on the web.

Finally, several studies have highlighted that a public domain approach to weather, geographical data, and public sector information (PSI) in general, may yield a substantial long-run value for Europe, running into the tens of billions or hundreds of billions of euros.[31] The benefit of access to and reuse of public sector information has been widely investigated during the Communia proceedings by Paul Uhlir, member of the Communia Advisory Committee, among others.[32] In particular, the fifth Communia workshop, co-organised by the Open Knowledge Foundation and the London School of Economics, focused on accessing, using and reusing public sector content and data.

Additionally, the value of privileged and fair use of copyrighted material is also to be taken into account when assessing the overall value of the public domain. Privileged and fair uses of copyrighted material are an integral part of the functional public domain. As a recent study has shown, companies benefiting from fair use and copyright exceptions exceeded GDP, employment, productivity and export growth of the overall

---

30 See Pollock (2006), pp. 11–13.
31 Ibid., p. 14; Pira International, "Commercial Exploitation of Europe's Public Sector Information" (30 October 2000) (report prepared for the European Commission, Information Society Directorate General); Richard E. W. Pettifer, "Towards a Stronger European Market in Applied Meteorology", *Meteorological Applications*, 15/2 (2008), 305-12; see also Peter Weiss, "Borders in Cyberspace: Conflicting Government Information Policies and their Economic Impact", summary report (February 2002), available at http://www.nws.noaa.gov/sp/Borders_report.pdf.
32 See Paul Uhlir, "Measuring the Economic and Social Benefits and Costs of Public Sector Information Online: A Review of the Literature and Future", paper delivered at the first Communia conference, Louvain-la-Neuve, Belgium (30 June 2010).

economy.[33] Fair use-enhanced industries include manufactures of consumer devices allowing for individual copying of protected content, educational institutions, software developers, and internet search and web-hosting providers. The study also reveals that fair use industries have grown dramatically within the past twenty years, since the advent of the Internet and the digital information revolution. These data may help to argue that in the digital environment, open and public domain business models may spur growth at a faster pace than proprietary traditional business models. Promoting fair use and the functional public domain, thus related fair use industry, may also have a considerable added value for Europe.

When contrasted with the US case-by-case fair use model, the European list of predefined limitations and exceptions may be a vantage point for fair use industries in Europe. Fair use decisions are inherently complex and unpredictable in the US.[34] As a consequence of the inherent unpredictability of fair use in the US, transaction costs will be higher and commercial endeavours will be chronically open to legal challenge. Europe should maximise the advantages that our legal framework offer to industries based on fair use. The enhanced legal certainty and lower transaction costs of the European legal framework will make that sector flourish in Europe and will boost the international investments. However, to that end, Europe needs to advance harmonisation of exceptions and limitations across national jurisdictions, and introduce an open fair dealing provision to close any loopholes that predefined exceptions and limitations may have, as sought by the Communia policy recommendation #3.

Further, the public domain plays a relevant role in terms of market efficiency. From an economic standpoint, a market with a shrinking public domain would be especially inefficient. Nobel laureate Joseph Stiglitz stressed this point by noting that:

> [i]t is imperative to understand the ways in which the production and distribution of knowledge differs from that of goods like steel and cars. [...] The fact that knowledge is, in central ways, a public good and that there are important externalities means that exclusive or excessive reliance on the market may not result in economic efficiency.[35]

---

33 See Thomas Rogers, Andrew Szamosszegi and Peter Jaszi, "Fair Use in the U.S. Economy: Economic Contribution of Industries Relying on Fair Use" (September 2007). Study prepared for the Computer & Communications Industry Association (ccianet.org).

34 See Dellar v. Samuel Goldwyn, Inc., 104 F.2d 661, 662 (2d Cir. 1939) (per curiam), which describes the fair use doctrine as "the most troublesome doctrine in the whole of copyright".

35 Joseph E. Stiglitz, "Public Policy for a Knowledge Economy", address to the Department

Restricting access to information would increase the inefficiency of the market because perfect information makes the perfect market.[36] A market that commodifies information excessively will be less efficient in allocating resources in our society since key information to facilitate that allocation will be more difficult to find. In addition, by raising the costs of information, we will undermine creativity since the building blocks of future creations will be inaccessible to a portion of our society.[37]

Finally, as we will better detail later, the public domain is an engine of democratisation because it ensures proper access to information for EU citizens regardless of the market power of the players. The value of the public domain as a building block of our capacity for free expression has been immensely enhanced by the ubiquity of the interconnected society and the power of propagation of digitization. Technological advancement makes the public domain the perfect democratic forum.

For the purpose of the Communia project, digitization and the Internet revolution are an extraordinary opportunity to multiply the value of the public domain and exploit humanities' riches as never before. Several authors have described the Internet revolution as a monumental shift that we are undergoing. David Bollier, speaker at the third Communia conference, notes:

> I believe we are moving into a new kind of cultural if not economic reality. We are moving away from a world organized around centralized control, strict intellectual property rights and hierarchies of credentialed experts, to a radically different order. The new order is predicated upon open access, decentralized participation, and cheap and easy sharing.[38]

Digital networks fuel new forms of user-based creative sharing and collaboration. This mass collaboration may stifle social and economic enrichment to a far greater extent than in the past. Yochai Benkler described the high generative capacity of online commons as the "wealth of networks".[39] The wealth of networks lies

---

for Trade and Industry and Center for Economic Policy Research (1999), p. 25, available at http://akgul.bilkent.edu.tr/BT-BE/knowledge-economy.pdf.

36   See Sanford J. Grossman and Joseph E. Stiglitz, "On the Impossibility of Informationally Efficient Markets", *American Economic Review*, 70/3 (1980), 393–408.

37   Boyle (2008), pp. 39–41.

38   David Bollier, "The Commons as New Sector of Value Creation: It's Time to Recognize and Protect the Distinctive Wealth Generated by Online Commons", remarks at the Economies of the Commons: Strategies for Sustainable Access and Creative Reuse of Images and Sounds Online Conference, Amsterdam (12 April 2008).

39   See Benkler (2007).

in social and networked peer production that is highly generative, because it is modular, granular and inexpensive to integrate the results.[40] At the first Communia workshop, Rishab Aiyer Ghosh explored the need to protect and foster open standard in the research community worldwide, to best embrace the collaborative networked projects. Ghosh noted that "our technology future will be based on collaborative, open projects of such large scale that global policies and regulations will become more flexible to meet the needs of every stakeholder involved".[41]

A great deal of attention has been paid by Communia to sharing and networked peer collaboration in education and research, especially at the second and eighth Communia conferences. In particular, at the second Communia conference, Jerome H. Reichman, a member of the Communia Advisory Committee, discussed the introduction of a contractually reconstructed commons via the *ex ante* acceptance of liability rules to promote the exchange of materials in a globally distributed and digitally integrated research commons.[42] At the same conference, Uhlir proposed a model of open knowledge environments (OKEs) for digitally networked scientific communication. OKEs would "bring the scholarly communication function back into the universities" through "the development of interactive portals focused on knowledge production and on collaborative research and educational opportunities in specific thematic areas".[43]

However, the revolution is far more massive and distributed than collaboration in education and research. Technological change has brought about cultural change, because the audience has become an active participant in its own culture. Open networks and networked peer collaboration have transformed markets by enabling amateurs to innovate. Individual experimentation, sub-cultures, and a community of social trust have created Linux, Wikipedia, Facebook, YouTube, and major political websites. Flexibility, decentralisation, cooperative creation, and customisation out-performed corporate bureaucracies unwilling to experiment because it was thought to be too risky and costly. Moreover, new models of decentralised and cooperative creation out-perform themselves, as it

---

40 Ibid., p. 101; see also Jerome H. Reichman, "Of Green Tulips and Legal Kudzu: Repackaging Rights in Subpatentable Innovation", *Vanderbilt Law Review*, 53 (2000), 1743-98.

41 Rishab Aiyer Ghosh, "Technology, Law, Policy and the Public Domain", paper delivered at the first Communia workshop, Turin (18 January 2008).

42 See Jerome H. Reichman, "Formalizing the Informal Microbial Commons: Using Liability Rules to Promote the Exchange of Materials", paper delivered at the second Communia conference, Turin (30 June 2009).

43 See Paul F. Uhlir, "Revolution and Evolution in Scientific Communication: Moving from Restricted Dissemination of Publicly-Funded Knowledge to Open Knowledge Environments", paper delivered at the second Communia conference, Turin (28 June 2009).

is the case for open alternatives to Facebook like the Diaspora project.[44] Faced with Facebook's centralised nature and desire to control online identities by trampling on privacy norms, the online community has been responding with the emergence of projects and experiments to redress the deficiencies of the Facebook model. The specificity of the Diaspora project resides also in crowd-sourced funding that was largely raised out of the dissatisfaction for the centralised social networking models.[45]

The Musopen project provides an additional example of the potential of public domain works when exploited within an open and peer-based project. Musopen is a charity that aims to produce and distribute recordings and sheet music of public domain music. The project allows users to suggest pieces that they would like to have recorded and to pledge funds to pay for the recording. Recently, the project crowd-funded US$70,000 through a KickStarter campaign.

The interactive nature of the Web 2.0 has propelled user-generated creativity and defined a peculiar form of digital culture that has been termed as "free culture".[46] "Remix" and "mash up" are now keywords of the cultural process taking place in the digital environment.[47] Remix culture has emphasised the potential for reuse of public domain material. Open networks, user-generated creativity, and remix culture have made the public domain highly generative. The public domain, once regarded as a "virtual wasteland of undeserving detritus,"[48] has become "a fertile paradise... a commons".[49]

The revolution brought by the Web 2.0 has called for a Copyright 2.0. This call is urged, as Marco Ricolfi put it at the first Communia conference, by the fact that:

> ...the social and technological basis of creation has been radically transformed. The time has come for us to finally become aware that, in our post-post-industrial age, the long route which used to lead the work from its creator to the public by passing through different categories of businesses is gradually being replaced by a short route, which puts in direct contact creators and the public.[50]

---

44   See Diaspora: https://joindiaspora.com.

45   See Kickstarter, "Decentralize the Web with Diaspora", available at http://www.kickstarter.com/projects/196017994/diaspora-the-personally-controlled-do-it-all-distr.

46   See Lawrence Lessig, *Free Culture: The Nature and Future of Creativity* (London: Penguin, 2005).

47   See Lawrence Lessig, *Remix: Making Art and Commerce Thrive in the Hybrid Economy* (New York: Penguin, 2008).

48   Samuelson (2003), p. 147.

49   Bollier (2008).

50   Marco Ricolfi, "Copyright Policies for Digital Libraries in the Context of the i2010 Strategy", paper presented at the first Communia conference, Louvain-la-Neuve (1 July 2008).

Copyright 2.0 stands for a relaxed and more flexible set of rules that may adapt to the new mechanics of creative production in the digital age. In particular, Copyright 2.0 should serve and pave the way for the "short route" that enhances an unrestrained discourse between authors and the public.

Together with the cultural revolution of networked peer production, the nature of digital information and digitization may also greatly enrich the public domain. Digital information is inexpensive and easy to collect, store, and make available via digital networks. The nature of digital information has propelled the creation of databases of legislative, jurisprudential and governmentally produced material; digital libraries, such as Europeana,[51] Project Gutenberg, Google Books, the Online Books Page,[52] the Hathi Trust Digital Library;[53] digital repositories; scientific libraries of reusable code; databases of scientific and technical information; vast non-profit digital archives, such as the Internet Archive; electronic journals; and MP3 files of music posted by bands wanting to attract a new audience.

Again, digital tools such as high-performance computers and digitized archives are transforming research in science and scholarship in history, literature and the arts.[54] The human genome project is an example of how computational analysis of digitized data has changed scientific research. The emerging field of digital humanities encompasses a wide range of activities, including online preservation, digital mapping, data mining and the use of geographic information systems. Digital humanities can reveal unexplored patterns and trends by analysing unprecedented amounts of data.[55]

The digital environment has the potential to make knowledge a truly global public good. As Charles Nesson reminded us at the third Communia conference, the "challenge is how to use this environment to create knowledge".[56] Human inventiveness has provided us with a ground-breaking solution to underdevelopment, isolation, and cultural and social divide. The open question

---

51 See Europeana: http://www.europeana.eu/portal.
52 See The Online Books Page: http://onlinebooks.library.upenn.edu.
53 See The Hathi Trust Digital Library: http://www.hathitrust.org/about.
54 See Patricia Cohen, "Digital Keys for Unlocking the Humanities' Riches", *The New York Times*, 16 November 2010.
55 See Google Books' Ngram Viewer, http://books.google.com/ngrams/ (discussing the gigantic database made by Google from nearly 5.2 million digitized books available to the public for free downloads and online searches); see also Patricia Cohen, "In 500 Billion Words, New Window on Culture", *The New York Times*, 16 December 2010.
56 Charles Nesson with Juan Carlos De Martin, "Communia and Universities", welcome address at the third Communia conference, Turin (28 June 2010), available at http://www.communia-project.eu/node/459

is whether we, as a society, are up to the task of re-inventing, and challenging our notions of democracy, education, economy and social interaction.

Communia maintains that Europe should not be afraid of changing and flourishing. It believes that policy strategies implementing openness in information management are the key to any change that may fully exploit technological advancement. Any actions towards the enclosure of the public domain should be reversed. Outmoded intellectual property models should be re-invented. Again, Ricolfi, reminds us that the time to take up this challenge has come, regardless of how daunting the task may be.[57] This solicited change is sought to address the many challenges and tensions that the present intellectual property system is presenting to the public domain. The discussion of the most relevant of those challenges and tensions will be the focus of the next portion of this essay.

3. Public domain challenges and bottlenecks

There is an undeniable tension between the public domain and the copyright system. This tension is represented by an equation where the enclosure of the public domain is proportional to the expansion of the copyright protection.[58] This tension is unavoidable and originates from the dual functionality of knowledge as a commodity and as a driving social force. At the second Communia conference, Bernt Hugenholz referred to this tension as the "paradox of intellectual property", because intellectual property is a "system that promotes, or at least, aspires to promote knowledge, dissemination, cultural dissemination by restricting it", by creating temporary monopolies in expressed ideas or in applied invention.[59]

In Europe, the paradox is heightened by the intensity of moral rights. The strength of moral rights, especially the moral right of integrity, conversely weakens the public domain. In Europe, moral rights are inalienable and potentially perpetual. Any copyright expirations, public domain dedications or the licensing of a creative work under open access and reuse models will only enrich the structural and functional public domain under the assumption and to the extent that moral rights are not infringed. The

---

57   Ricolfi (2008), p. 15.
58   See Jerome H. Reichman and Jonathan A. Franklin, "Privately Legislated Intellectual Property Rights: Reconciling Freedom of Contract with Public Good Uses of Information", *University of Pennsylvania Law Review*, 147 (1999), 875-970.
59   See P. Bernt Hugenholtz, "Owning Science: Intellectual Property Rights as Impediments to Knowledge Sharing", paper delivered at the second Communia conference, Turin (29 June 2001).

capacity of the heirs and descendants of an author to claim infringement in perpetuity threatens the public domain with legal uncertainty. Adaptations and re-interpretations of works, abridged versions of works, colourisations of movies, or the application of other future unforeseeable technological tools, which may somehow temper with or modify the perception of the original work, may all trigger the reaction of the author's estate in perpetuity.

However, digitization and internet distribution have exacerbated these traditional tensions between copyright protection and the public domain. The misperception of the "Internet threat" has led to a reaction that endangers the public domain.[60] Concurrently, the opportunities that digitization and Internet distribution offer to our society make enclosure and commodification of our information environment even more troublesome. As Paul A. David, keynote speaker at the first Communia conference, noted:

> [t]oday, the greater capacity for the dissemination of knowledge, for cultural creativity and for scientific research carried out by means of the enhanced facilities of computer-mediated telecommunication networks, has greatly raised the marginal social losses that are attributable to the restrictions that those adjustments in the copyright law have placed upon the domain of information search and exploitation.[61]

With large agreement, scholars and the civil society have warned that "we are in the midst of an enclosure movement in our information environment".[62] Boyle has talked about a second enclosure movement that it is now enclosing the "commons of the mind".[63] As for the natural commons, fields, grazing lands, forests, and streams that were enclosed in the sixteenth century in Europe by landowners and the state, relentlessly expanding intellectual property rights are enclosing the intellectual commons and the public domain. In a very similar fashion, Peter Drahos and John Braithwaite have spoken of an "information feudalism".[64] Enclosure is promoted by a mix of technology and legislation. According

---

60 Boyle (2008), pp. 54–82.
61 Paul A. David and Jared Rubin, "Restricting Access to Books on the Internet: Some Unanticipated Effects of U.S. Copyright Legislation", *Review of Economic Research on Copyright Issues*, 5 (2008), 23-53 (p. 50).
62 Yochai Benkler, "Free as the Air to Common Use: First Amendment Constraints on the Enclosure of the Public Domain", *New York University Law Review*, 74 (1999), 354-446.
63 See Boyle (2003 and 2008); see also Keith Maskus and Jerome H. Reichman, "The Globalization of Private Knowledge Goods and The Privatization of Global Public Goods", *Journal of International Economic Law*, 7 (2004), 279-320; David Bollier, *Silent Theft: The Private Plunder of Our Common Wealth* (New York: Routledge, 2002).
64 See Peter Drahos with John Braithwaite, *Information Feudalism: Who Owns the Knowledge Economy?* (London: Earthscan, 2002).

to Hugenholtz and Lucie Guibault, the public domain is under pressure from the "commodification of information".

> [T]he public domain is under pressure as a result of the ongoing march towards an information economy. Items of information, which in the "old" economy had little or no economic value, such as factual data, personal data, genetic information and pure ideas, have acquired independent economic value in the current information age, and consequently become the object of property rights making the information a tradable commodity. This so-called "commodification of information", although usually discussed in the context of intellectual property law, is occurring in a wide range of legal domains, including the law of contract, privacy law, broadcasting and telecommunications law.[65]

Commodification of information is propelled by the ability of new technologies to capture resources previously unowned and unprotected, as in a new digital land grab.[66]

However, this digital land grab is the continuation of a well-settled analogue trend whose limits and fallacies have already been shown and rebutted. In the past, law and economics scholars have launched a crusade to expose the evil of the commons,[67] the evil of not propertising.[68] A much-quoted article written by Garret Hardin in 1968 termed the evil of not propertizing as the tragedy of the commons.[69] Hardin identified the tragedy of the commons in the environmental dysfunctions of overuse and underinvestment found in the absence of a private property regime. He made it clear that any commons open to all, ungoverned by custom or law, will eventually collapse. The fear of the tragedy of the commons propelled the idea that more property rights will necessarily lead to the production of more information together with the enhancement of its

---

65 P. Bernt Hugenholtz and Lucie Guibault, "The Future of the Public Domain: An Introduction", in *The Future of the Public Domain: Identifying the Commons in Information Law*, ed. by Lucie Guibault and P. Bernt Hugenholtz (Kluwer Law International, 2006), 1-6.

66 See Hess and Ostrom (2007), p. 12.

67 See H. Scott Gordon, "The Economic Theory of a Common-Property Resource: The Fishery", *Journal of Political Economy*, 62 (1954), 124-42; and Anthony D. Scott, "The Fishery: The Objectives of Sole Ownership", *Journal of Politcal Economy*, 63 (1955), 116-24, which introduces an economic analysis of fisheries that demonstrates that unlimited harvesting of high-demand fish by multiple individuals is both economically and environmentally unsustainable); see also Chander Anupam and Sunder Madhavi, "The Romance of the Public Domain", *California Law Review*, 92 (2004), 1331-74 (pp. 1332–33).

68 See generally Lee A. Fennell, "Commons, Anticommons, Semicommons", in *Research Handbook on the Economics of Property Law*, ed. by Kenneth Ayotte and Henry E. Smith (Cheltenham: Edward Elgar, 2010), 35-56.

69 See Garrett Hardin, "The Tragedy of the Commons", *Science*, 162 (1968), 1243-48.

diversity.[70] In this perspective, the prevailing assumption is that anything of value within the public domain should be commodified.[71] The recent tremendous expansion of intellectual property rights has been justified by this and similar statements.

To put it bluntly, this statement and the like are wrong. No economic theory of intellectual property and commons management supports the prediction stated.[72] Ostrom powerfully advocated the cause of the commons against the mantra of propertisation. Her work showed the inaccuracies of Hardin's ideas and brought attention to the limitations of the tragedy of the commons.[73] Empirical studies by Ostrom and others have shown that common resources can be effectively managed by groups of people under suitable conditions, such as appropriate rules, good conflict-resolution mechanisms, and well-defined group boundaries.[74] Under suitable conditions and proper governance, the tragedy of the commons becomes "the comedy of the commons".[75]

Culture is quintessential comedic commons, because it is enriched

---

70 Paul Goldstein, *Copyright's Highway: From Gutenberg to the Celestial Jukebox* (Stanford: Stanford University Press, 1994), p. 236; see also Wagner R. Polk, "Information Wants to Be Free: Intellectual Property and the Mythologies of Control", *Columbia Law Review*, 103 (2003), 995-1034 (arguing that "increasing the appropriability of information goods is likely to increase, rather than diminish, the quantity of 'open' information").

71 See William Landes and Richard A. Posner, *The Economic Structure of Intellectual Property Law* (Cambridge, MA: Harvard University Press, 2003); William Landes and Richard A. Posner, "Indefinitely Renewable Copyright", *University of Chicago Law Review*, 70 (2003), 471-518 (pp. 475, 483).

72 See Yochai Benkler, "A Political Economy of the Public Domain: Markets in Information Goods Versus the Marketplace of Ideas", in *Expanding the Boundaries of Intellectual Property: Innovation Policy for the Knowledge Society*, ed. by Rochelle Dreyfuss, Diane L. Zimmerman and Harry First (Oxford: Oxford University Press, 2001), pp. 267–94 (pp. 270–72).

73 See generally Elinor Ostrom, *Governing the Commons: The Evolution of Institutions for Collective Action* (Cambridge: Cambridge University Press, 1990); Elinor Ostrom, Roy Gardner and James Walker, *Rules, Games, and Common-Pool Resources* (Ann Arbor: University of Michigan Press, 1994); and Elinor Ostrom, *The Drama of the Commons* (Washington, DC: National Academies Press, 2002).

74 See Hess and Ostrom, p. 11; *Rights to Nature: Ecological, Economic, Cultural, and Political Principles of Institutions for the Environment*, ed. by Susan S. Hanna, Carl Folke, and Karl-Gören Mäler (Washington, DC: Island Press, 1996); *Making the Commons Work: Theory, Practice and Policy*, ed. by Daniel W. Bromley, David Feeny et al. (San Francisco: ICS Press, 1992); *Commons Without Tragedy: The Social Ecology of Land Tenure and Democracy*, ed. by Robert V. Andelson (London: Center for Incentive Taxation, 1991); David Feeny, Fikret Berkes, Bonnie J. McCay, and James M. Acheson, "The Tragedy of the Commons: Twenty-Two Years Later", *Human Ecology*, 18 (1990), 1-19.

75 See Carol M. Rose, "The Comedy of the Commons: Custom, Commerce, and Inherently Public Property", *University of Chicago Law Review*, 53 (1986), 711-81.

through reference as more people consume it.[76] The carrying capacity of cultural commons is endless. Cultural commons are non-rivalrous. One person's use does not interfere with another's. Unlike eating an apple, my listening of a song does not subtract from another's use of it. Therefore, cultural commons unveil the inaccuracy of the tragedy of the commons more than any other commons. Propertisation and enclosure in the cultural domain may be a wasteful option by cutting down social and economic positive externalities, particularly in peer-based production environments.

Reviewing the peculiar nature of cultural commons, the academic literature has turned upside down the paradigm of underuse of common resources by developing the idea of the "tragedy of the anti-commons".[77] The tragedy of the anti-commons lies in the underuse of scarce scientific resources because of excessive intellectual property rights and all of the transaction costs accompanying those rights. David exposed the perverse resource allocation in an anti-commons scenario at the first Communia conference.[78]

By increasing the asset value of copyright interests, copyright term extension is one basic tool of commodification of information and creativity. Copyright term extension may be singled out as the clearest evidence of the progressive expansion of property rights against the public domain. Any temporal extension of copyright deprives and impoverishes the structural public domain. The policy choice has so far privileged private interest over public, and copyright protection over the public domain.

The timeline of temporal extension of copyright protection shows a steady elongation in all international jurisdictions. From the original protection encompassing a couple of decades, copyright protection has expanded to last for over a century and a half. As an example, today the oldest work still in copyright in the United Kingdom dates back to 1859.[79] The Statute of Anne, the first copyright law enacted in England in 1709, provided only for 14 years of protection, which was renewable for a term

---

76   Lawrence Lessig, "Re-crafting a Public Domain", *Yale Journal of Law and the Humanities*, 18 (2006), 56-83 (p. 64).

77   Michael A. Heller, "The Tragedy of the Anticommons: Property in the Transition from Marx to Markets", *Harvard Law Review*, 111 (1998), 621-88.

78   See Paul A. David, "New Moves in 'Legal Jujitsu' to Combat the Anti-commons: Mitigating IPR Constraints on Innovation by a 'Bottom-up' Approach to Systemic Institutional Reform", paper presented at the first Communia conference, Louvain-la-Neuve (30 June 2008).

79   See Anna Vuopala, "Assessment of the Orphan Works Issue and Cost for Rights Clearance" (May 2010), p. 10. Report prepared for the European Commission, DG Information Society and Media, Unit E4, Access to Information.

of an additional 14 years if the author was still alive at the expiration of the first term.[80] This expansionistic course does not appear to be interrupted or reversed and the line between temporary and perpetual protection is blurred. The words of Lord Kames, discussing the booksellers' request for a perpetual common law right on the printing of books a couple of centuries ago, act as a powerful warning from the past: "[i]n a word, I have no difficulty to maintain that a perpetual monopoly of books would prove more destructive to learning, and even to authors, than a second irruption of Goths and Vandals".[81]

Recently, an extension of the term of protection for performers and sound recordings has been adopted by the European Parliament.[82] Communia is opposing any such re-adoption and asking the Member States not to implement the directive. Extending the terms of protection for related rights endangers a valuable public domain, as argued by Stef van Gompel at the second Communia workshop.[83] Communia Policy Recommendation #2 asked for the withdrawal of the proposal of the directive later adopted. In particular, Communia is challenging the appropriateness of any retroactive extension of the copyright term. It opposes any blanket extension of copyright and neighbouring rights, as detailed in Communia Policy Recommendation #1 and #2. Once the incentive to create is assured, any extension of the property right beyond that point should at least require affirmative proof that the market is incapable of responding efficiently to consumer demand.

The most palpable example of the destructive effect of copyright extension on our cultural environment is the case of orphan works. Orphan works are those whose rights-holders cannot be identified or located and, thus, whose rights cannot be cleared. Publishers, film-makers, museums, libraries, universities and private citizens worldwide face daily insurmountable hurdles in managing risk and liability when a copyright owner cannot be identified or located. Too often, the sole option left is a silent unconditional surrender to the intricacies of copyright law. Many historically significant and sensitive records

---

80 See Statute of Anne, 1709, 8 Ann., c. 19 (Eng.)

81 Hinton v. Donaldson, Mor 8307 (1773) (Lord Kames).

82 See European Parliament and Council Directive 2011/77/EU Amending Directive 2006/116/EC on the Term of Protection of Copyright and Related Rights, 2011 O.J. (L 265) 1 (27 September 2011).

83 Stef van Gompel, "Extending the Terms of Protection for Related Rights Endangers a Valuable Public Domain", paper presented at the second Communia workshop, Vilnius (31 March 2008).

will never reach the public. Society at large is being precluded from fostering enhanced understanding.

The cultural outrage over orphan works is a by-product of copyright expansion, the retroactive effect of some copyright legislation, and the intricacies of copyright law. A study from the Institute for Information Law at Amsterdam University (IViR) attributed the increased interest in the issue of orphan works to the following factors: (1) the expansion of the traditional domain of copyright and related rights; (2) the challenge of clearing the rights of all the works included in derivative works; (3) the transferability of copyright and related rights; and (4) the territorial nature of copyright and related rights.[84] In Europe the problem is further complicated by the difficulty of determining whether the duration of protection has expired. As mentioned earlier, the complexities related to copyright term extensions, such as war extensions, blur the contours of the public domain, thereby making more uncertain and costly any attempt to clear copyrights.

The clearing process can take from several months to several years. In many instances, the cost of clearing rights may amount to several times the digitization costs. The unfulfilled potentials of digitization projects worsen the cultural outrage over orphan works in terms of loss of opportunities and value that may be extracted from the public domain. The challenges of digitizing works today were widely investigated at the sixth Communia workshop in Barcelona. The European institutions are also aware of the potential loss of social and economic value if the orphan works problem remains unsolved. As the European Commission noted, "there is a risk that a significant portion of orphan works cannot be incorporated into mass-scale digitization and heritage preservation efforts such as Europeana or similar projects".[85] Communia Policy Recommendation #9 urges a solution to the orphan works problem.

As additional tools of commodification, term extension of copyright has been aided by copyright subject matter expansion, multiplication of strong commercial rights, and erosion of fair dealing prerogatives, exceptions and limitations. Firstly, the expansion of copyright has caused the contraction of the structural public domain. The protected subject matter has been systematically expanded from books to maps and photographs, to sound

---

84   See P. Bernt Hugenholtz et al., "The Recasting of Copyright & Related Rights for the Knowledge Economy" (November 2006), report to the European Commission, DG Internal Market, pp. 164–66.

85   Commission Communication on Copyright In The Knowledge Economy, COM (2009) 532 final (19 October 2009), pp. 5–6.

recordings and movies, to software and databases. In some instances, new quasi-copyrights have been created, as in the case of the introduction of *sui generis* database rights in the EU, a quintessential example of the process of commodification of information.[86] Additionally, subject-matter expansion has been coupled with the attribution of strong commercial distribution rights, especially the right to control imports and rental rights, and the strengthening of the right to make derivative works.

Together with the contraction of the structural public domain, the functional public domain has been similarly eroded by the narrowing of the scope of fair dealing or fair use, exceptions and limitations to copyright, and public interest rights. The erosion of public interest rights reached its peak in recent times as a side effect of the transposition of the authorship rights from the analogue to the digital medium. In particular, the enactment of anti-circumvention provisions as a response to the "Internet threat" played a decisive role in the process of contraction of fair dealing rights.

There is, finally, an additional dimension of the process of copyright expansion. Traditionally, the public domain was the default rule of our system of creativity, and copyright was the exception. The abolition of formalities changed it all. As a consequence of the international abolition of formalities enclosed in Article 5(2) of the Berne Convention, copyright was declared the default, and public domain was the exception.[87] By default, intellectual works are created under copyright protection, and public domain dedication must be properly spelled out. Communia opposes any such overreaching expansion of copyright protection and strongly upholds the view embodied in the first general principle of *The Public Domain Manifesto* that "[t]he Public Domain is the rule, copyright protection is the exception." Communia upholds the position that the abolition of formalities no longer serves the purpose that it was served in the analogue world.[88] In the field of international law, the mandatory adoption of a "no

---

86   Mark Davison, "Database Protection: The Commodification of Information", in *The Future of the Public Domain: Identifying the Commons in Information Law*, ed. by Lucie Guibault and P. Bernt Hugenholtz (Kluwer Law International, 2006), pp. 167–89.

87   See Berne Convention for the Protection of Literary and Artistic Works, Art. 5(2), 9 September 1886, as last revised at Paris on 24 July 1971 and amended on 28 September 1978, 1161 U.N.T.S. 30.

88   See also Stef van Gompel, "Formalities in the Digital Era: An Obstacle or Opportunity?", in *Global Copyright: Three Hundred Years Since the Statute of Anne, from 1709 to Cyberspace*, ed. by Lionel Bently, Uma Suthersanen and Paul Torremans (Cheltenham: Edward Elgar, 2010), pp. 395–424. Van Gompel argues that, in the pre-digital era, the objections against copyright formalities were real and, in the light of the changes caused by the advent of digital technologies, there is now sufficient reason to reconsider subjecting copyright to

formalities" approach had a precise target: it was an anti-discrimination norm, introduced to avoid any kind of hidden disadvantages for foreign authors. The digitized and interconnected world allows for instantaneous sharing of information and minimises the space and time hurdles that persuaded the international community to abolish formalities. Today, the non-discriminatory goal of Article 5(2) of the Berne Convention may be reached using alternative tools: for instance, a simple and free online copyright register could be easily implemented and made accessible from every country in the world. A carefully crafted registration system may enhance access and the reuse of creative works by attenuating some of the structural tensions between access and property rights encapsulated in our copyright system. Communia has embodied this position in Recommendation #8.

The crucial driver of the modern drift toward commodification of the public domain is a mix of technology and legislation. Technology was able to appropriate and fence informational value that was previously unowned and unprotected. That value was appropriated by means of the adoption of technological protection measures (TPMs) to control the access and use of creative works in the digital environment, including uses that previously could not be restrained. The seal on a policy of control was set by the introduction of the so-called "anti-circumvention provisions" aimed to forbid the circumvention of copyright protection systems. In addition, the law banned any technology potentially designed to circumvent technological anti-copy protection measures.

Anti-circumvention provisions have negative effects both on the structural and the functional public domain. Communia Policy Recommendation #7 pleads for an immediate intervention to protect the public domain against the adverse effect of TPMs. Additionally, Communia would like European institutions to carefully reconsider the adoption of any stronger protection of TPMs included in the last proposed text of the Anti-Counterfeiting Trade Agreement (ACTA), as also recently requested by several European academics.[89] The foremost concern with this legal and technological bundle is that TPMs and anti-circumvention provisions can make copyright perpetual.[90] The legally protected encryption, in fact, would continue after the expiration

---

formalities.

89   See "Opinion of European Academics on Anti-Counterfeiting Trade Agreement", p. 6, available at http://www.iri.uni-hannover.de/tl_files/pdf/ACTA_opinion_200111_2.pdf.

90   See Boyle (2008), p. 104; Samuelson (2003), p. 161.

of the copyright term. Because circumventing tools are illegal, users will be incapable of accessing public domain material fenced behind TPMs. In addition, TPMs will affect the public domain by restricting or completely preventing fair dealings, privileged and fair uses.[91] TPMs cannot make any determination of purpose that is necessary to assess whether a use is privileged or not. In the absence of that determination, copyright will be technologically enforced regardless of the fairness of the use, the operation of a copyright exception or limitation, or a private use. As per Directive 2001/29/EC, as with many other pieces of international legislation, circumventing a digital right management technology that restricts acts permitted by the law is a civil wrong, and perhaps a crime.[92] Exceptions and limitations, and in particular the limitations included in Article 6(4) of the Directive 2001/29/EC, will be of no avail to exclude infringement of the anti-circumvention provisions.[93]

In recent years, contract law has also been deployed to commodify and appropriate information supposedly in the public domain.[94] Contracts may be employed to restrict or prohibit uses of works that would otherwise be permitted

---

91   See Lucie Guibault et al., "Study on the Implementation and Effect in Member States' Laws of Directive 2001/29/EC on the Harmonisation of Certain Aspects of Copyright and Related Rights in the Information Society" (February 2007), report prepared for the European Commission, DG Internal Market, ETD/2005/IM/D1/91, pp. 102–33 (discussing the relation between limitation and TPMs); see also Mireille Van Eechoud, P. Bernt Hugenholtz, Lucie Guibault, Stef Van Gompel and Natali Helberger, *Harmonizing European Copyright Law: The Challenges Of Better Lawmaking* (Kluwer Law International, 2009), pp. 131–79.

92   See Common Position No. 48/2000 of 28 September 2000 adopted by the Council, with a view to adopting a Directive of the European Parliament and of the Council on the harmonisation of certain aspects of copyright and related rights in the information society, 2000 O.J. (C 344) 01, 19 (1 December 2000), available at http://eur-lex.europa.eu/LexUriServ/LexUriServ.do?uri=OJ:C:2000:344:0001:0022:EN:PDF; see also Kamiel J. Koelman, "The Public Domain Commodified: Technological Measures and Productive Information Use", in *The Future of the Public Domain: Identifying the Commons in Information Law*, ed. by Lucie Guibault and P. Bernt Hugenholtz (Kluwer Law International, 2006), pp. 108–09.

93   Guibault et al., Study on Directive 2001/29/EC, p. 106; see also Nora Braun, "The Interface Between The Protection of Technological Measures and the Exercise of Exceptions to Copyright and Related Rights: Comparing the Situation in the United States and the European Community", *European Intellectual Property Review*, 25 (2003), 496-503 (p. 499).

94   See Lucie Guibault, "Wrapping Information in Contract: How Does it Affect the Public Domain?", in *The Future of the Public Domain: Identifying the Commons in Information Law*, ed. by Lucie Guibault and P. Bernt Hugenholtz (Kluwer Law International, 2006), pp. 87–104; Lucie Guibault, *Copyright Limitations and Contracts: An Analysis of the Contractual Overridability of Limitations on Copyright* (Kluwer Law International, 2002); Lydia Pallas Loren, "Slaying the Leather-Winged Demons in the Night: Reforming Copyright Owner Contracting with Clickwrap Misuse", *Ohio Northern University Law Review*, 30 (2004), 495-535; Samuelson (2003), pp. 155–58, 163; P. Bernt Hugenholtz, "Copyright, Contract and Code: What Will Remain of the Public Domain?", *Brooklyn Journal of International Law*, 26 (2000), 77-90; Niva Elkin-Koren, "Copyright Policy and the Limits of Freedom of Contract", *Berkeley Technology Law Journal*, 12 (1997), 93-113.

under copyright law. The digital information marketplace has seen the emergence of standard form contracts restricting the capacity to use information not or no longer qualifying for intellectual property protection or whose use is privileged. The most powerful example is that of click-wrap agreements stating that some uses of scanned public domain material are restricted or prohibited. A glimpse of such a practice has been implemented by Google as part of its project to partner with international libraries to digitize public domain materials. If you download any public domain books from the Google Books website, quite awkwardly the Usage Guidelines included at the front of each scan read as follows: "We also ask that you: + Make non-commercial use of the files. We designed Google Book Search for use by individuals, and we request that you use these files for personal, non-commercial purposes". In the preamble to the Usage Guidelines, Google justifies these restrictions by stating that the digitization work carried out by Google "is expensive, so in order to keep providing this resource, we have taken steps to prevent abuse by commercial parties". Communia Policy Recommendations #5 and #6 set up principles to protect affirmatively the public domain against the misappropriation of public domain works with special emphasis on their digital reproduction.

However, the synergy between mass-market licenses and technological protection measures poses the major threat to the availability of digital information in the public domain. As Guibault has noted at the first Communia conference:

> The digital network's interactive nature has created the perfect preconditions for the development of a contractual culture. Through the application of technical access and copy control mechanisms, rights owners are capable of effectively subjecting the use of any work made available in the digital environment to a set of particular conditions of use.[95]

This was never the case in the analogue environment. The purchase of a book, the enjoyment of a painting or a musical piece never entailed the obligation of entering into a contract in the past. Hence, the emergence of this contractual culture, coupled with strict technological enforcement, has been endangering the public domain with a new set of threats.

Technological protection measures empower the application and enforcement of mass-market licenses on the Internet that may restrict

---

95   Lucie Guibault, "Evaluating Directive 2001/29/EC in the Light of the Digital Public Domain", paper presented at the first Communia conference, Louvain-la-Neuve (1 July 2008); an updated version of Guibault's paper can be found in this volume (Chapter 3).

the lawful use of unprotected information by the users. Technological protection measures act as a substitute for the traditional exceptions and limitations provided by copyright law. Therefore, Guibault concluded that "the widespread use of technological protection measures in conjunction with contractual restrictions on the exercise of the privileges recognised by copyright law does affect the free flow of information".[96] The control over the dissemination of ideas and facts or other unprotected and non-protectable information will unduly hinder democratic discourse and freedom of expression by restricting productive uses of unprotected information.

Any encroachment upon the public domain is an encroachment upon our capacity for free and diverse expression. Freedom of expression and the public domain are overlapping concepts that share the same goal. Public domain and free speech both have a democratic function in that they propel personal and political discourse. The public domain is pivotal to our ability to express ourselves freely regardless of the market power of the speakers. Any decrease in the public domain will produce the most relevant repercussions on people with less ability to finance creation and dissemination of their speech.[97] Thus, any contraction of the public domain will push Europe away from the goal of bringing "the millions of dispossessed and disadvantaged Europeans in from the margins of society and cultural policy in from the margins of governance", to quote a European report drafted as a specific complement to the World Commission on Culture and Development's 1996 report on global cultural policy.[98]

As an interrelated issue, copyright expansion and public domain enclosure affect our freedom of expression by impinging on cultural diversity. Historically, cultural diversity has been a fundamental value in the EU. Very recently, in looking at the implementation of a digital agenda for Europe, the European Commissioner, Nellie Kroes, powerfully reclaimed the value of cultural diversity by saying that "we want '*une Europe des cultures*'".[99] In addition, since ratification in 2007, all of the

---

96 Ibid.

97 Benkler, "Free as the Air to Common Use" (1999), p. 393; see also Christopher S. Yoo, "Copyright and Democracy: A Cautionary Note", *Vanderbilt Law Review*, 53 (2000), 1933-63 (pp. 1935–52); Neil W. Netanel, "Market Hierarchy And Copyright in Our System of Free Expression", *Vanderbilt Law Review*, 53 (2000), 1879-1932; Neil W. Netanel, "Copyright and Democratic Civil Society", *Yale Law Journal*, 106 (1996), 283-387.

98 The European Task Force on Culture and Development, "In From the Margins: A Contribution to the Debate on Culture and Development in Europe" (1997), report prepared for the Council of Europe, p. 276.

99 Neelie Kroes, "A Digital World of Opportunities", speech delivered at the Forum

relevant European policy decisions should be compelled to conform to the UNESCO Convention on the Protection and Promotion of the Diversity of Cultural Expressions' obligations. In this regard, a recent study on the state of the implementation of the Convention in Europe noted that, while some copyright is necessary, too much copyright is detrimental to diversity of cultural expression. Diversity of cultural expression is particularly threatened by intellectual property rights "in markets that are dominated by big corporations exercising collective power as oligopolies".[100] Cultural conglomerates deepen their market dominance through horizontal and vertical integration.[101] The high degree of control over the entire distribution process in a number of different areas of cultural output makes it possible to run any alternative, non-infringing creative material out of the market.[102] As a consequence, global media and entertainment oligopolies will impose an homogenising effect on local culture. Fiona Macmillan argues that cultural filtering, homogenisation and the loss of the public domain have exacerbated the "dysfunctional relationship between copyright and cultural diversity".[103]

In particular, public domain enclosure and copyright expansion are very pernicious for the diversity and decentralisation of modern forms of peer information production:

---

d'Avignon: Les Rencontres Internationales de la Culture, de l'Économie et des Medias, Avignon, France, SPEECH/10/619 (5 November 2010).

100 Germann Avocats et al, "Implementing the UNESCO Convention of 2005 in the European Union" (May 2010), study prepared for the European Parliament Directorate General for Internal Policies, Policy Department B: Structural and Cohesion Policies, Culture and Education, available at http://www.diversitystudy.eu/ms/ep_study_long_version_20_nov_2010_final.pdf.

101 See Fiona Macmillan, "Public Interest and The Public Domain in an Era Of Corporate Dominance", in *Intellectual Property Rights: Innovation, Governance and The Institutional Environment*, ed. by Brigitte Andersen (Cheltenham: Edward Elgar, 2006), pp. 46-69 (pp. 49–52); and Fiona Macmillan, "Commodification and Cultural Ownership", in *Copyright And Free Speech: Comparative And International* Analyses, ed. by Jonathan Griffiths and Uma Suthersanen (Oxford: Oxford University Press, 2003), pp. 35-65 (pp. 44–48).

102 See Guy Pessach, "Copyright Law as a Silencing Restriction on Noninfringing Materials: Unveiling the Scope of Copyright's Diversity Externalities", *Southern California Law Review*, 76 (2003), 1067-1104 (p. 1068).

103 Fiona Macmillan, "The Dysfunctional Relationship Between Copyright and Cultural Diversity", *Quaderns Del CAC*, 27 (2007), 101–10; see also Fiona Macmillan, "Copyright, the World Trade Organization, and Cultural Self-Determination", in *New Directions in Copyright Law*, vol. 6, ed. by Fiona Macmillan (Cheltenham: Edward Elgar, 2007), pp. 307–34 (pp. 313–19); and Fiona Macmillan, "The Cruel ©: Copyright and Film", *European Intellectual Property Review*, 24 (2002), 483–92 (pp. 488–89).

In a digital environment where distribution costs are very small, the primary costs of engaging in amateur production are opportunity costs of time not spent on a profitable project and information input costs. Increased property rights create entry barriers, in the form of information input costs, that replicate for amateur producers the high costs of distribution in the print and paper environment. Enclosure therefore has the effect of silencing non-professional information producers.[104]

Amateur production has been the driving force of the Internet informational revolution. Blogs, listservs, forums, and user-based communities re-calibrated the meaning of diversity and freedom of expression toward a higher standard. Non-professional information production empowered the civic society with the ability to produce truly independent and diverse speech. Any policy intervention should not underestimate the decreased production by organisations using strategies that do not benefit from copyright expansion.[105] Increased copyright protection and public domain enclosure, in fact, may "lead, over time, to concentration of a greater portion of the information production function in society in the hands of large commercial organizations that vertically integrate new production with owned-information inventory management".[106]

Ironically, copyright law may end up serving the old enemy against which it was originally unleashed. Widely recognised as a tool to counter censorship so common in the old patronage system, copyright law may turn out to restrict free and diverse speech by its steady expansion and converse public domain enclosure and commodification. Moreover, and more regretfully, an unwise expansionistic copyright policy may empower again that old enemy of any democratic society at the very moment when technological progress may lead us close to its very annihilation.

It is worth mentioning that Communia has also been investigating the problem of the tension between cultural heritage protection laws (CHPLs) and the public domain. In some EU Member States, cultural heritage legislation may impose an additional layer of restrictions over works that are otherwise copyright free. In particular, in some instances, CHPLs may set up a permission system to reproduce cultural resources and monuments. The Communia Working Group 3 gathered in Istanbul in December 2010 to explore the issue and produce a set of recommendations. The policy

---

104 Benkler (1999), p. 410.
105 See Benkler (2001), pp. 272–85 (reviewing in detail the effects of intellectual property approaches to organizing information production); see also Benkler (1999), pp. 400–08.
106 Benkler (1999), p. 410.

options discussed by the group ranged from the abolition of CHPLs, the harmonisation of CHPLs across the EU, and the gradual transition towards less and more rational restrictions. In particular, the most important conclusion of the meeting was that CHPLs could be used in order to mark and protect the public domain, if the permission system possibly in place is accompanied by an obligation to mark the work as a public domain work.[107] Together with the more substantial and specific factors troubling the public domain so far described, there are other more generic aspects of the legislative process that should be redressed to better protect and promote the European public domain. Lack of representation of the interest of users and the public, lack of transparency of the legislative process, obscurity of copyright legal provisions, and lack of legal harmonisation are all factors that aggravate the tension between public domain and copyright protection.

Enclosure and commodification of the public domain are also the result of an unbalanced legislative process. Lobbying from cultural conglomerates played an important role in amplifying the process of copyright expansion beyond strict public interest.[108] The public at large has always had very limited access to the bargaining table when copyright policies had to be enacted. This is due to the dominant mechanics of lobbying that largely excluded the users from any decision on the future of creativity management. In accordance with Mançur Olson's work, copyright policy is driven by a small group of concentrated players to the detriment of the more dispersed interest of smaller players and the public at large.[109] The final outcome has been the implementation of a copyright system that is strongly protectionist and pro-distributors with an overbroad expansion of private property rights followed by a correspondent restriction of public prerogatives and enclosure of the public domain.

Legal uncertainty is an additional hurdle to the public enjoyment of a healthy and rich public domain. By blurring the contours of the structural and functional public domain, legal uncertainty will augment the

---

107 See Federico Morando and Prodromos Tsiavos, *Cultural Heritage Rights in the Age of Digital Copyright* (forthcoming).

108 For an account of copyright industry political influence in the US and worldwide, see Jessica Litman, *Digital Copyright* (Amherst: Prometheus, 2001), pp. 22–69; see also Neil W. Netanel, "Why Has Copyright Expanded?: Analysis and Critique", in *New Directions in Copyright Law*, vol. 6, ed. by Fiona Macmillan (Cheltenham: Edward Elgar, 2008), pp. 3–34 (pp. 3–11).

109 See Mançur Olson, *The Logic of Collective Action: Public Goods and the Theory of Groups* (Cambridge, MA: Harvard University Press, 1971).

unpredictability of the European public domain. As a consequence, users' prerogatives will be variable and ambiguous, transaction costs will rise, and the efficiency of the European Internal Market will be lowered, therefore undermining *A Digital Agenda for Europe*'s goal of a "vibrant digital single market".[110] The fundamental drivers of legal uncertainty are obscure laws and a lack of harmonisation.

Authors including Jessica Litman have argued that copyright laws are too obscure and complex for the users.[111] Copyright law is drafted for the market players, and its obscurity causes a high level of uncertainty among users regarding what they can or cannot do with creative content. Because of the complexity of copyright provisions, users are discouraged from enforcing privileged or fair uses of copyrighted content in court. The obscurity of copyright law has perpetuated and propelled its misuse and abuse by copyright conglomerates. The problem is exacerbated by the fact that users are involved far more than before in the creative process. Digitization, the Internet and user-generated culture have made everybody a potential author as well as a potential infringer.

The public domain suffers also from legal uncertainty that is the effect of lack of harmonisation among European national jurisdictions. Firstly, Europe's diverse legal frameworks heighten the indeterminacy of that portion of the European structural public domain that may be termed the ontological public domain. The ontological public domain is defined by the application of the idea-expression dichotomy, the subject matters protected, the criteria for protection, either the requirement of originality or substantial investment, and the exhaustion doctrine. In Europe, subject matters of protection have been harmonised only with respect to new or controversial subject matters, such as software, databases and photographs.[112] The concept of originality is still largely unharmonised throughout Europe and fundamental differences between continental and common law systems still remain.

The diversity of the European legal framework also adds peculiar complexity to the issue of copyright duration. Despite the fact that

---

110   European Commission, *A Digital Agenda for Europe*, Communication from the Commission to the European Parliament, the Council, the European Economic and Social Committee and the Committee of the Regions, COM (2010) 245, Brussels (19 June 2010), available at http://ec.europa. eu/information_society/digital-agenda/documents/digital-agenda-communication-en.pdf, p. 7

111   See Litman (2001) and Jessica Litman, "Real Copyright Reform", *Iowa Law Review*, 96 (2010), 1-55.

112   See Hugenholtz, et al. (2006), pp. 31–41.

efforts have been made toward harmonisation, the intricacies of length of protection and copyright extension (such as war extensions) in national jurisdictions aggravate the tension between copyright protection and the public domain. Communia Policy Recommendation #4 calls for further harmonisation of rules of copyright duration. Further, lack of harmonisation of exceptions and limitations in Europe plays a nefarious role for the public domain, as spelled out by Guibault at the first Communia conference.[113] Notwithstanding the Information Society Directive aimed at harmonising exceptions and limitations, legal uncertainty still persists. All but one of the limitations in the regime set up by the Information Society Directive was optional, and the regime provides the Member States with ample discretion to decide if and how they implement the limitations.[114]

This variety of different rules applicable to a single situation across the European Community has an adverse effect on the functional public domain thus undermining the users' prerogatives. Communia Policy Recommendation #3 asks for further harmonisation and revision of exceptions and limitations across Europe, together with the introduction of an open fair dealing exception to close any loopholes that predefined exceptions and limitations may have. Europe has the opportunity to acquire a leading international role in the fair use industry, by taking full advantage from the European system of predefined exceptions and limitations, if contrasted with the more unpredictable United States case-by-case fair use model.

Finally, the promotion of the public domain calls for an effort towards harmonisation of the definition of the moral right of integrity and duration of moral rights after the death of the author. Communia trusts that moral rights should not extend longer than economic rights. This arrangement would be compliant with the minimum standard set by Article 6bis (2) of the Berne Convention, which states that the moral rights of the author "shall, after his death, be maintained, at least until the expiry of the economic rights".

---

113   See Guibault (2008), pp. 5–7.
114   See Council Directive 2001/29/EC on the harmonisation of certain aspects of copyright and related rights in the information society, Art. 5, 2001 O.J. (L 167) 10, 17 (22 May 2001).

4. The public domain and the European Commission strategy

So far much of the value residing in the public domain has been left unattended. Much of the emphasis has been placed on private commodification of information rather than exploitation of the public domain for the public good. Unfortunately, no international player has yet focused upon the value of openness and public domain business models by reversing the present trend of extreme propertisation. As detailed throughout the report, the emerging online culture of sharing and remixing has enhanced the value of the public domain. User-generated content, online collaborative endeavours and peer-production, such as open source software, are founded on the value of reuse and inherently diminished by increased propertisation. The same applies to blogging, tweeting and modern forms of online information that have radically changed our democratic landscape. So far, no jurisdiction has really tackled the question of creativity in the digital age by shifting the paradigm of steady commodification of information, overlooking the fact that digitization and the Internet have changed everything. In contrast, digitization and the Internet have become a misperceived justification of extreme propertisation. Europe can become an international leader in extracting value from the public domain with a few key solutions that do not substantially harm the current state copyright and do not entail overbroad efforts.

The large benefits that Europe could reap from preserving and promoting the public domain will substantially come at no additional costs. The assets of the public domain are ready to be profitably used. The public domain is a cultural mine enriched over the centuries. Today, the riches of the public domain can be enjoyed with the click of a computer mouse. The power of propagation through the Internet and the endless productivity of digitization have made exploitation easier and the public domain exponentially more valuable.

Additionally, mechanisms and tools to make the public domain and the value attached to it a priority for further intervention are already in place at the EU level. Since the i2010 strategy, European institutions have greatly valued digitization and preservation of the European public domain, open access to information, and the protection of users' prerogatives in the digital environment. The same priorities have been upheld by the most recent efforts of the EU. In this regard, as one of the seven flagship initiatives of the Europe 2020 strategy, the *Digital Agenda* is setting up several key principles and guidelines to redress many of the tensions challenging the full exploitation of the value of the digital public domain. Many of the key actions proposed by the *Digital Agenda* strengthen the conclusions and the call for policy actions put forward by Communia. In particular:

i.   Digitization of the European cultural heritage and digital libraries are key aspects of the recently implemented *Digital Agenda* of the EU. The *Digital Agenda* notes that fragmentation and complexity in the current licensing system also hinder the digitization of a large part of Europe's recent cultural heritage. Therefore,

    a.   rights clearance must be improved;

    b.   Europeana—the EU public digital library—should be strengthened and increased public funding is needed to finance large-scale digitization, alongside initiatives with private partners;

    c.   funding to digitization projects is to be conditioned to general accessibility of Europe's digitized common cultural heritage online;

ii.   The *Digital Agenda* calls for a simplification of copyright clearance, management and cross-licensing. In particular, the European Commission should create a legal framework to facilitate the digitization and dissemination of cultural works in Europe by proposing a directive on orphan works;

iii. The review of the Directive on the Re-Use of Public Sector Information to oblige public bodies to open up data resources for cross-border application and services has been prioritised by the *Digital Agenda*;

iv.   Promoting cultural diversity and creative content in the digital environment, as an obligation under the 2005 UNESCO Convention, is an additional relevant goal of the *Digital Agenda*;

v.   The *Digital Agenda* is also very much concerned with harmonisation and simplification of laws by calling for the creation of a "vibrant single digital market" and promoting the necessity of building digital confidence as per the EU citizens' digital rights that are scattered across various laws and are not always easy to grasp.

The mentioned European strategies have been translated in a vast array of projects and endeavours to protect and propel the public domain in Europe and to investigate its capacity to produce value for society at large. Communia is one of the outcomes of this strategic vision, especially conceived to investigate the challenges and the opportunities brought by digitization.

5. Communia and the European Public Domain project

Communia is aggregating a strong coalition that is promoting the public domain and a sustainable cultural development in Europe. Communia has been strengthening a European network of organisations that have been developing a new perspective on the importance of the public domain for Europe and the international arena at large. Communia aims to solve the typical collective action problem raised by copyright policy by promoting the dispersed interests of smaller players and the public at large.[115]

Several Communia members have embodied the Communia perspective and values in *The Public Domain Manifesto*. Conscious of the challenges and opportunities for the public domain in the technological environment of the networked society, *The Public Domain Manifesto* endorses fundamental principles and recommendations to actively maintain the structural core of the public domain, the voluntary commons and user prerogatives. With regard to the structural public domain, the manifesto states the following principles:

> 1. The public domain is the rule, copyright protection is the exception. [...]
> 2. Copyright protection should last only as long as necessary to achieve a reasonable compromise between protecting and rewarding the author for his intellectual labour and safeguarding the public interest in the dissemination of culture and knowledge . [...] 3. What is in the public domain must remain in the public domain. [...] 4. The lawful user of a digital copy of a public domain work should be free to (re-)use, copy and modify such work. [...]
> 5. Contracts or technical protection measures that restrict access to and re-use of public domain works must not be enforced. [...]

Together with the structural core of the public domain, *The Public Domain Manifesto* promotes the voluntary commons and user prerogatives by endorsing the following principles:

> 1. The voluntary relinquishment of copyright and sharing of protected works are legitimate exercises of copyright exclusivity. [...] 2. Exceptions and limitations to copyright, fair use and fair dealing need to be actively maintained to ensure the effectiveness of the fundamental balance of copyright and the public interest.

Further, *The Public Domain Manifesto* puts forward the following general recommendations to protect, nourish and promote the public domain:

---

115   See Olson (1971).

1. The term of copyright protection should be reduced. [...] 2. Any change to the scope of copyright protection (including any new definition of protectable subject-matter or expansion of exclusive rights) needs to take into account the effects on the public domain. [...] 3. When material is deemed to fall in the structural public domain in its country of origin, the material should be recognised as part of the structural public domain in all other countries of the world. [...] 4. Any false or misleading attempt to misappropriate public domain material must be legally punished. [...] 5. No other intellectual property right must be used to reconstitute exclusivity over public domain material. [...] 6. There must be a practical and effective path to make available "orphan works" and published works that are no longer commercially available (such as out-of-print works) for re-use by society. [...] 7. Cultural heritage institutions should take upon themselves a special role in the effective labeling and preserving of public domain works. [..] 8. There must be no legal obstacles that prevent the voluntary sharing of works or the dedication of works to the public domain. [...] 9. Personal non-commercial uses of protected works must generally be made possible, for which alternative modes of remuneration for the author must be explored.

In addition, the European-wide relevance of the public domain has been strengthened by other policy statements endorsing the same core principles of *The Public Domain Manifesto*. The Europeana Foundation has published the *Public Domain Charter* to stress the value of public domain content in the knowledge economy.[116] The many relations between *The Public Domain Manifesto* and the Europeana Charter were discussed at the seventh Communia workshop in Luxembourg.[117] The Free Culture Forum released the *Charter for Innovation, Creativity and Access to Knowledge* to plead for the expansion of the public domain, the accessibility of public domain works, the contraction of the copyright term, and the free availability of publicly funded research.[118] Again, Open Knowledge Foundation launched the

---

116 See The Europeana Public Domain Charter, http://version1.europeana.eu/web/europeana-project/publications.

117 See Jill Cousins, "The Public Domain, the Manifesto, his Charter and her Dilemma", paper delivered at the seventh Communia workshop, Luxembourg (1 February 2010).

118 See "Charter for Innovation, Creativity and Access to Knowledge: Citizens' and Artist's Rights in the Digital Age", Barcelona Free Culture Forum, http://fcforum.net/. It states in its preamble that "[f]ree culture opens up the possibility of new models for citizen engagement in the provision of public goods and services. These are based on a 'commons' approach. 'Governing of the commons' refers to negotiated rules and boundaries for managing the collective production and stewardship of and access to, shared resources. Governing of the commons honours participation, inclusion, transparency, equal access, and long-term sustainability. We recognise the commons as a distinctive and desirable form of governing. It is not necessarily linked to the state or other conventional political institutions and demonstrates that civil society today is a potent force. [...]. In

Panton Principles for Open Data in Science in February 2010, to endorse the concept that "data related to published science should be explicitly placed in the public domain".[119]

Triggered by a forward-looking approach of the European institutions, Europe is putting together a very diversified and multi-sector network of projects for the promotion of the public domain and open access. The European public domain project is emerging in a strong multi-tiered fashion. Together with Communia, as part of the i2010 policy strategy, the EU launched the Europeana digital library network to digitize Europe's cultural and scientific heritage.[120] The LAPSI project was started to build a network covering policy discussions and strategic action on all legal issues related to access and the reuse of public sector information in the digital environment.[121] Further, to assess the value and to define the scope and the nature of the public domain, the European Commission has promoted the Economic and Social Impact of the Public Domain in the Information Society project.[122] The project, together with its methodology, was presented at the first Communia conference in 2008.[123]

Again, many other projects focus on extracting value from our scientific and cultural riches in the digital environment. The European DRIVER project, presented at the first Communia conference and the first Communia workshop,[124] builds a repository infrastructure, combined with a search portal, for all of the openly available European scientific communications.[125] The project ARROW (Accessible Registries of Rights

---

this context, the public interest is best served by supporting and ensuring continued creation of intellectual works of significant societal value, and to ensure all citizens have unfettered access to such works for a wide variety of uses..."; see also Evolution Summit 2010, http://d-evolution.fcforum.net/en (endorsing very similar principles).

119   See Panton Principles: Principles for Open Data in Science, http://pantonprinciples.org.

120   See Europeana: Think Culture, http://www.europeana.eu/portal.

121   See LAPSI: Legal Aspects of Public Sector Information, http://www.lapsi-project.eu.

122   See Public Domain in Europe, Rightscom, http://www.rightscom.com/Default. aspx?tabid=20397.

123   See Mark Isherwood, "European Commission Project: Economic and Social Impact of the Public Domain. Introduction to Methodology", paper presented at the first Communia conference, Louvain-la-Neuve (30 June 2008).

124   See Sophia Jones and Alek Tarkowski, "Digital Repository Infrastructure Vision for European Research: DRIVER project", paper delivered at the first Communia workshop, Turin (18 January 2008); Karen Van Godtsenhoven, "The DRIVER Project: On the Road to a European Commons for Scientific Communication", paper delivered at the first Communia conference, Louvain-la-Neuve (30 June 2008). An updated version of Van Godtsenhoven's paper can be found in this volume (Chapter 9).

125   See DRIVER, Digital Repository Infrastructure Vision for European Research, http://www.driver-repository.eu; see also Van Godtsenhoven, "The DRIVER Project".

Information and Orphan Works), encompassing national libraries, publishers, writers' organisations and collective management organisations, aspires to find ways to identify rights-holders and rights, clear the status of a work, or possibly acknowledge the public domain status of a work.[126] Finally, the Digital Research Infrastructure for the Arts and Humanities (DARIAH) aims to enhance and support digitally-enabled research across the humanities and the arts.[127]

With the support of the Open Knowledge Foundation, the UK government announced the launch of www.data.gov.uk, a collection of more than 2,500 UK government databases, which is now freely available to the public for consultation and reuse. The Open Knowledge Foundation launched the Public Domain Calculators project as part of the Public Domain Works project, an open registry of artistic works that are in the public domain.[128] The Public Domain Calculators project, presented at the third Communia workshop, creates an algorithm to determine whether a certain work is in the public domain based on certain details, such as date of publication, date of death of author, etc.[129] The activities and goals of the Open Knowledge Foundation, a very active Communia member, were presented at the first Communia workshop.[130]

Many other civic society endeavours have been working toward the goal of promoting open access and safeguarding the public domain throughout Europe. Among them, La Quadrature du Net, an advocacy group that promotes the rights and freedoms of citizens on the Internet, is very active within and outside of the Communia network.[131] The European Association for Public Domain was recently initiated as a project to promote and defend the public domain. Again, Knowledge Exchange is a co-operative effort run by European libraries and research foundations that supports the goal of making a layer of scholarly and scientific content openly available on

126 See ARROW: Accessible Registries of Rights Information and Orphan Works, http://www.arrow-net.eu.
127 See DARIAH: Digital Research Infrastructure for the Arts and Humanities, http://www.dariah.eu.
128 See Public Domain Works, http://www.publicdomainworks.net.
129 See Jonathan Gray, "Public Domain Calculators", presentation delivered at the third Communia workshop, Amsterdam (20 October 2008); see also Public Domain Calculators, http://wiki.okfn.org/PublicDomain Calculators.
130 See Jonathan Gray, Rufus Pollock and Jo Walsh, "Open Knowledge: Promises and Challenges", paper delivered at the first Communia workshop, Turin (18 January 2008). An updated version of this paper can be found in this volume (Chapter 7).
131 See La Quadrature du Net, http://www.laquadrature.net.

the Internet.[132] Finally, it is worth noting that commercial enterprises joined the Communia network in an attempt to investigate and promote open and public domain business models.

This distributed European public domain project is an encouraging starting point. Nonetheless, much still must be done to promote sustainability in the development of our cultural environment. The commodification of information, the enclosure of the public domain, and the converse expansion of intellectual property rights tell a story of unsustainable imbalance in shaping the informational policy of the digital society. Communia is, therefore, calling for targeted policy actions to redress the informational policy of the digital society and to maximise the economic and social value that may be extracted from the public domain, especially from the digital public domain.

6. What can Europe do for the public domain?

One of the main goals of the Communia Network is to provide policy recommendations to strengthen the public domain in Europe. The Communia recommendations are principally addressed to the Commission. However, the recommendation portion of the Report has been envisioned as an agenda and stimulus to any other entity—Member States, national libraries, the publishing industry, expert groups, etc.—that may promote or influence public domain related decisions. In addition, an inner integration between public domain projects at the European level and the international level is a goal recommended by Communia. This may be easily done by strengthening a more qualified presence of the EU during discussion and negotiations of public domain issues within the WIPO Development Agenda framework.

The Communia policy recommendations seek to re-define the hierarchy of priorities embedded in the traditional politics of intellectual productions and creativity. Any public policy of creativity should promote the idea that "information is not only or mainly a commodity; it is also a critically important resource and input to learning, culture, competition, innovation and democratic discourse".[133] The agenda of the information society cannot be dictated by commercial interests above and beyond any of the

---

132   See Knowledge Exchange, http://www.knowledge-exchange.info.
133   Samuelson (2003), p. 171.

fundamental values that shape our community. This approach would be a myopic understatement of the relevance of information in the "information society". Therefore, "intellectual property must find a home in a broader-based information policy, and be a servant, not a master, of the information society".[134] In other words, the new policy for creativity envisioned by Communia shall revolve around the founding principle that the public domain is not "an unintended by product, or "graveyard" of copyrighted works but its very goal".[135] If Europe is eager to take up a leading role in the digital environment as stated in the i2010 strategy and the *Digital Agenda*, it is time to depart from the idea that the only paradigm available is a politics of intellectual property. Instead, it is pivotal to develop a global strategy and a new politics of the public domain. To quote again from *The Public Domain Manifesto*: private incentive to create shall naturally follow like exceptions from the rule.

The Communia proposal for a new politics for the public domain shall encompass the review of the following strategic subject matters:

- Term of protection
- Copyright harmonisation
- Exceptions and limitations
- Misappropriation of public domain material
- Technological protection measures
- Registry system
- Orphan works
- Memory institutions and digitization projects
- Open access to research
- Public sector information
- Alternative remuneration systems and cultural flat rate

A politics for the public domain should (1) redress the many tensions with copyright protection by re-discussing the term of protection, re-empowering exceptions and limitations, harmonising relevant rules and adapting them to technological change; (2) positively protect the public domain against misappropriation and technological protection measures; (3) propel digitization projects and conservation of the European cultural heritage by solving the orphan works problem and implementing a registry system; (4)

---

134   Ibid., pp. 171–72.
135   Birnhack (2006), p. 60.

open access to research and public sector information; (5) and promote new business models to enhance creativity, including alternative remuneration systems and a cultural flat rate.

A politics of the public domain is needed to protect our intellectual domain as much as a strategy for national security is required to protect our physical home. Lange has argued that we are all citizens of the public domain.[136] The public domain is our country and our home. Enclosure and propertisation of the public domain correspond to depriving citizens of their country and homes. Any policy oriented to the enhancement of creativity should be respectful of our citizenship of the public domain and should nourish, protect, and promote it.

A stronger public domain will make Europe stronger and richer. It will help the region earn a central and crucial place in fostering new creativity. The ability to promote new creativity will allow Europe to appropriate unexplored social and economic value that lies in the digital realm and raise income levels across the continent.

The European advantage in promoting the public domain can be seen from multiple angles. Firstly, much value is still to be extracted from public sector information, if compared to other jurisdictions. Europe is a late entry in the market for public sector information. According to estimates, 7% of the United States GDP is coming from public sector information, whereas only 0.5% of European Union GDP is coming from that source. Several studies have highlighted that a public domain approach to weather, geographical data, and public sector information in general, may yield a substantial long-term value for Europe, running into the tens of billions or hundreds of billions of euros. Open access to public sector information will entail a considerable added value for the European market.

A stronger public domain will also help Europe to achieve its goal of creating a European digital public library. The Europeana platform is up and running. This is the only international project of its kind. Other jurisdictions are in the process of abdicating their public role in developing digital libraries and digitization projects to private parties. This is not the European vision. Europe values public interest and full public access above all. However, in order not to lag behind private projects, such as Google Books, and suffer from negative network effects, Europe should strive to build a digital public library that can fully unlock the riches of digitization

---

136 David Lange, "Reimagining the Public Domain", *Law and Contemporary Problems*, 66 (2003), 463-83 (p. 475).

to European society at large. To that end, a European digital public library must be capable of including orphan works as well as access to information, sampling, and purchase of copyrighted in-print and out-of-print material.

Open access to scientific and academic publications and new business models, such as alternative remuneration systems and cultural flat rates that favour access and the reuse and remix of information, will be the tools of European cultural growth and enhanced creativity. As discussed at Communia meetings, networks of open knowledge environments may spread across European academic and public interest institutions. Open access will propel collaborative research and educational opportunities through interactive portals and functions such as wikis, forums, blogs, journals, post publication reviews, repositories and distributed computing.

In a modern, networked Europe, open and free public sector information, together with public domain material, will be the building blocks of our cumulative knowledge and innovation. Exceptions for scientific and academic purposes, open access to academic publications and easy remix promoted by alternative business models, will empower fast and efficient processing and reuse of other protected material while lowering transaction costs. A pan-European digital library will assure access to and widen the distribution of knowledge with the enhanced tools of computational analysis to foster new research opportunities, such as the digital humanities and genomics. Additionally, a digital public library will push forth the rediscovery of currently unused or inaccessible works, open up the riches of knowledge in formats that are accessible to persons with disabilities and empower a superior democratic process by favouring access regardless of users' market power. It will be a perfectly efficient integrated environment for boosting knowledge, research, and follow-up innovation. The goal of the *Digital Agenda*—"to deliver sustainable economic and social benefits from a digital single market based on fast and ultra fast internet and interoperable applications"—perfectly supports this vision.[137] Communia policy recommendations are meant to be one initial, but substantial, step towards making this vision come true.

Additionally, if we look at the traditional market for creativity, we can see that there is a considerable added value for Europe to invest in a lead role in the market for open and public domain business models. Businesses based on legacy intellectual property models have been the strength

---

137 *A Digital Agenda*, p. 3.

of the US economy (Hollywood, Microsoft, Apple, pharmaceutical and biotechnological companies, etc.). Most of the economic value created by those models has been harvested in places other than Europe. Moreover, the dominance of imported cultural paradigms and industries has increasingly propelled pernicious forms of cultural colonisation. The negative externalities are immense, especially in terms of impoverishment and the blurring of our cultural diversity. At the same time, an open, decentralised, networked model for creativity would boost cultural diversity at unprecedented levels. The rich linguistic and cultural diversity of Europe, coupled with a net deficiency of European intellectual property industries, makes the EU the ideal candidate to extract value from an open digital agenda and for successful deployment of cooperative, network-driven enterprises. Further, as previously noted, the European Internal Market may become a haven for fair use industries, thanks to the legal certainty of its predefined list of exceptions to copyright, as opposed to the unpredictable case-by-case fair use system of the US.

If Europe takes control of creativity in the digital environment, Europe will take full control of its future. However, the sole way for Europe to acquire this edge is to promote the immense cultural diversity that lies in the European public domain, as enhanced by the ubiquity and power of propagation of digitization. In order to do so, Europe needs to be innovative, creative and unafraid to challenge outdated and inefficient business models. It should fully empower the values of public participation, collaboration and innovation. When radical innovation become the new paradigm, the innovator will leapfrog ahead of former leaders who are incapable of changing fast enough, having been trapped by the strength and privileges of the traditional gatekeepers. Radical innovation is coming along regardless of the fact that the *Ancien Régime*, as Kroes has termed it, may attempt to retard its advent.[138] As Joseph Schumpeter would have put it, to best leapfrog all of its competitors, the European Union should take the opportunity to go full sail out of the Digital Dark Age into the Digital Enlightenment, blown by the wind of creative change.[139]

---

138 See Neelie Kroes, "A Digital World of Opportunities" (2010).
139 See Joseph Schumpeter, *Capitalism, Socialism and Democracy* (New York: Harper, 1976) [1942], p. 83.

II. Legal Framework

2. Consume and Share: Making Copyright Fit for the *Digital Agenda*

Marco Ricolfi

As it often happens, the title of my chapter has an ambiguous ring to it. Are we trying to figure out which set of specific changes in copyright legislation would help to achieve the targets set by the specific policy document released by the EU Commission last year? Are we supposed to deal with a broad new vision of the role of copyright intended to foster the generation and dissemination of creativity in the new digital environment?[1] And are we talking about EU Directives or the Berne Convention—about the short term or medium term? Well, perhaps the two dimensions, different as they are, may go hand in hand. It stands to reason that a few ideas about the future—what could and indeed should happen in the next five or ten years or so—may also help us in transacting the business of today and tomorrow. So let me start from the broader picture and come back to questions of more immediate concern in the final remarks.[2]

---

1 See European Commission, *A Digital Agenda for Europe*, Communication from the Commission to the European Parliament, the Council, the European Economic and Social Committee and the Committee of the Regions, COM (2010) 245, Brussels (19 June 2010), available at http://ec.europa.eu/information_society/digital-agenda/documents/digital-agenda-communication-en.pdf.
2 In sketching out the broader picture, I draw on the final section of my paper "Copyright Policies for Digital Libraries in the Context of the i2010 Strategy", presented at the first Communia conference, Louvain-la-Neuve, Belgium (1 July 2008).

1. Creators and their public: from the long route to the short route

The case is often made that copyright, as we have known it for three centuries (which after all is a brief parenthesis in the *longue durée* of the millennial history of information technology), may no longer be an appropriate tool for the needs of creators and society in a digital environment. What is the basis for this—arguably bold; but also quite widespread—argument?[3] The reply is quite straightforward: in the last two decades or so, the social and technological basis of creation has been radically transformed. The time has come for us to be aware that, in our post-post-industrial age, the long route—which used to lead the work from its creator to the public by passing through different categories of businesses—is gradually being replaced by a short route, which puts creators and the public in direct contact. This development may be sketched as follows.[4]

In the analogue word, direct access to the market by creators was confined to a limited number of special cases.[5] Otherwise, it could be taken for granted that the intermediation of business was necessary to bring works from creators to markets. In particular, books and records needed to be printed. For this purpose some kind of "factory" was required to

---

3   See Lawrence Lessig, *Remix: Making Art And Commerce Thrive In The Hybrid Economy* (New York: Penguin, 2008); Volker Grassmuck, "The World is Going Flat(-Rate): A Study Showing Copyright Exception for Legalizing File-Sharing Feasible as a Cease-Fire in the 'War on Copyright' Emerges", *Intellectual Property Watch*, 11 May 2009, available at http://www.ip-watch.org/weblog/2009/05/11/the-world-is-going-flat-rate; Philippe Aigrain, *Internet and Création: Comment Reconnaître les Échanges sur Internet en Finançant la Création* (Cergy-Pontoise: In Libro Veritas, 2008); Yochai Benkler, "Sharing Nicely: On Shareable Goods and the Emergence of Sharing as a Modality of Economic Production", *Yale Law Journal*, 114 (2004), 273–358. A very open minded approach is also advocated by the speech made by WIPO's Director General, Francis Gurry, "The Future of Copyright", Sydney (25 February 2011), available at http://www.wipo.int/about-wipo/en/dgo/speeches/dg_blueskyconf_11.html. A theoretical framework to the re-orientation of the assessment of the rules concerning information products is arguably provided by the literature devoted to common pools resources and more specifically to its extension to knowledge and information commons; see in this connection Charlotte Hess and Elinor Ostrom, "Introduction: An Overview of the Knowledge Commons", in *Understanding Knowledge as a Commons: From Theory to Practice*, ed. by Charlotte Hess and Elinor Ostrom (Cambridge, MA: MIT Press, 2007), pp. 3–26.

4   For additional references see Marco Ricolfi, "Individual and Collective Management of Copyright in a Digital Environment" in *Copyright Law: A Handbook of Contemporary Research*, ed. by Paul Torremans (Cheltenham: Edward Elgar, 2008), pp. 283-314 (pp. 285, 308–14).

5   Such as the bohemian painter personally seeking out patrons in order to sell his paintings or the wandering gipsy carrying around his violin.

manufacture what in effect were fixed, stable, material or — as the expression now goes — "hard" copies of the work. In turn these hard copies needed to be stored, transported and distributed, before reaching the shelves on which the public would finally find them.

It was difficult for creators to engage in all these steps; and this is why, as a rule, they preferred to resort to businesses to set up the characteristic trilateral relationship between creator, business and the public, which is typical of primary exploitation of copyrighted works.[6] The kind of business that appeared to be indispensable for this purpose had features which the last two centuries made familiar. To begin with, it had to make substantial outlays to figure out whether there was a market for the work, and it had to invest and take large risks for the mass production of material copies of works and for their distribution. This was all done on a scale that increased in step with the extension of the markets. Publishers, film studios and record labels are appropriate cases in point. Radio and television came in to take care of so-called "secondary" utilization of work. This was a long route to institute contact between the creator and the public; and business was a very valuable, indeed indispensable intermediary to achieve such a goal.

In the digital environment all this dramatically changes. On the production side, perfect digital copies make "factories" of physical, material copies of works redundant, at least in principle.[7] What is particularly remarkable is that this same development is now reaching the movie industry. Until recently this sector of the entertainment business appeared to be the last bulwark in which capital-intensive business could be considered indispensable. But this is becoming less and less true as each day passes. Jean Cocteau predicted that the tools required for the creation of a movie would at some point in time become

---

6   See in this connection in W. R. Cornish, *Intellectual Property: Patents, Copyright, Trade Marks and Allied Rights* (London: Sweet & Maxwell, 1996), p. 401.

7   It may be argued that this is true only for additional copies, the ones which can be costlessly multiplied after what we could call the initial embodiment, the prototype or the "master" has been first created; and to this it may be added that, for the latter, the required investment still is huge. This objection has indeed been raised a number of times, for example by Paolo Auteri, "Il paradigma tradizionale del diritto d'autore e la nuove tecnologie" in *Proprietà digitale: diritti d'autore, nuove tecnologie e Digital Rights Management*, ed. by M. L. Montagnani and M. Borghi (Milan: Egea, 2006); but the case becomes less and less defensible as the time passes. The role of software and of digital technology in the creation and initial fixation of music is increasing all the time; and their cost is decreasing in parallel.

as cheap as paper and pencil; and digital technology may prove his vision right.[8]

On the distribution side, a similar if less visible process is taking place. Digital goods that are distributed through the Internet are light rather than heavy, and use up a limited amount of storage space. But even more so because the technological endowment held by the public at the receiving end has in the meantime deeply changed. Even In the past, the consumer had to make an investment in technology, by purchasing a radio or a television set, a record player or a tape recorder. Since the beginning of the digital age, the scale of a minimum unit of the technological endowment at the receiving end — for example, the memory of a PC — has started to be largely in excess of the average needs of the consumer;[9] and as a rule each unit is interoperable with all the others. A similar analysis can be reiterated in connection with file-sharing. Whatever legal assessment we may pass of this practice, its ultimate technological ramifications cannot be in doubt.[10] Here we have enormous excess capacity residing with the public at the receiving end; and this excess capacity can be mobilized to create distributive networks of extraordinary scale, scope and effectiveness.

In this novel context, it would seem that the setting up of a relationship between creator and business no longer has the same compelling rationale it once had. Digital copies are (nearly) perfect; and can be duplicated at no cost at the receiving end. Therefore, in a number of situations both the "factory" and the physical distribution chain are no longer indispensable.[11] Creators can increasingly access markets without engaging in the trilateral relationship that used to be characteristic of dealings in copyright. Indeed, these technological determinants enable creators to make works directly available to the public. It is even more remarkable that an increasingly large number of members of the public are in turn grabbing the opportunity offered by the technology available

---

8 See, for example, Open Source Cinema: http://www.opensourcecinema.org.

9 As noted by Benkler (2004), p. 277.

10 As indeed aptly described by the decision of the US Supreme Court of 27 June 2005, Metro-Goldwin-Mayer Studios Inc. et al. v. Grockster, Ltd. et al., 125 S. Ct. 2764 (2005). On the potential for distribution offered by open spectrum access see Lawrence Lessig, *The Future of Ideas: The Fate of The Commons in a Connected World* (New York: Vintage, 2002), pp. 78, 218, 240.

11 Both developments had been anticipated a number of years ago: see Eugene Volokh, "Cheap Speech and What It Will Do", *Yale Law Journal*, 104 (1995), 1805–50; and Ithielde Sola Pool, *Technologies of Freedom* (Cambridge, MA: Belknap, 1983), pp. 249–51.

at the receiving end and transforming themselves into producers and distributors of works.

To make a long story short: both the production and distribution functions migrate from business to the public and there they can rely on excess resources available at each consumption unit. These, if individually of small scale, may be multiplied by very large numbers to provide almost infinite manufacturing and distribution capacity in a way that dwarfs past industry investments and makes them, to a large extent, redundant.[12] The stage scenario is changing. Social sharing enters; business recedes. As a result, the long route from creators to the public may at some point become much shorter; and this is happening more and more all the time. Today creators set up their own websites and make books and music directly accessible to the public.[13] Currently, user-generated content and social networks are growing exponentially:[14] creators and their public are finally merging into each other.

2. The three requirements for a legislative agenda for the digital environment

What are the implications of this upheaval for the legislative agenda? Of course, we do not know much about the future. So much is changing all the time, and so quickly, that it is impossible to make predictions about the future. Nevertheless we can anticipate with some confidence that production and distribution of works will continue to originate from two different segments. The first is based on business and markets; the other on the production and distribution mode, which is based on decentralized

---

12 It may be questioned whether cloud computing (on which see Jonathan Zittrain, "Lost in the Cloud", *The New York Times*, 20 July 2009; and the Expert Group Report, *The Future of Cloud Computing: Opportunities for European Cloud Computing Beyond 2010*, available at http://cordis.europa.eu/fp7/ict/ssai/docs/cloud-report-final.pdf) reinforces or calls into question the direction of this process: software-as-a-service, infrastructure-as-a-service and platform-as-a-service slim down the amount of technology which both businesses and the public require in order to generate and access content; and possibly announce the emergence of a new generation of powerful intermediaries.

13 On the early beginnings of the phenomenon, when Stephen King set up a website to allow readers to download his latest short story, "Riding the Bullet", at US $2.50 per download, see Jason Epstein, "The Rattle of Pebbles", *The New York Review of Books*, 27 April 2000, pp. 57–58.

14 See *Networked Publics*, ed. by Kazys Varnelis (Cambridge, MA: MIT Press, 2008). For an early appraisal see John Horrigan, "Home Broadband Adoption 2006", 28 May 2006, available at http://www.pewinternet.org/Reports/2006/Home-Broadband-Adoption-2006.aspx.

non-market decisions, often referred to as "social sharing". This latter group taking the "short route" — currently encompassing the open content made available by Wikipedia and other wikis, websites offering free music and pictures, blogs, and the massive volumes of other user-generated content — will exponentially grow, dwarfing the market segment based on the "long route". These two components of creativity will not be mutually exclusive but will interact.

This is why any agenda for law-making for the digital environment should meet at least three requirements. First, it should incorporate rules that are appropriate not only for the long route but also for the short route.[15] Second, it should allow for the "peaceful coexistence" of the two sets of rules, making them interoperable, in such a way that the continued existence and specific contribution of the two sectors is maximized. Third, obstacles inherited by the past that unduly inhibit the emergence of the short route should be gradually phased out in ways that should minimize the disruption of the workings of the old route.

3. Copyright 2.0: interests and rules

Against this background, let us think for a moment about the set of rules which would appear to be appropriate to meet the demands of creators operating along the short route.

3.1 The interests

In the market-based model it was essential for creators and even more so for businesses to control and restrict access to works, as the monopoly granted by expansive exclusive rights enabled them to charge whatever price the market would bear. However, this would not appear to be the goal of creators currently operating along the short route. The great majority of them, be it 9 out of 10 or 95 out of 100, do not make a living out of "sales" of "copies" of their works; they earn their livelihood in another

---

15 A similar idea would appear to be shared by proponents of "dual", "hybrid" or "bipolar" systems of protection which have been cropping up in the recent past. See Christoph Geiger, "Promoting Creativity Through Copyright Limitations: Reflections on the Concept of Exclusivity in Copyright Law", *Vanderbilt Journal of Entertainment and Technology Law*, 12 (2011), 515–48; and Alexander Peukert, "A Bipolar Copyright System for the Digital Networks Environment", *Hastings Communications and Entertainment Law Journal*, 28 (2005), 1–80. For a theoretical frame of reference, see Hess and Ostrom (2007).

activity or business and devote a portion—often a very large portion—of their spare time to creating. These activities may give them a bit of extra income, professional credit and recognition which may have positive spill-over effects in their main line or just fun (or a combination of the three). Even when the creators operating along the short route are professionally engaged in the creation of works, which is usually not the case, their business model is often based on income flows different from simply the sale of copies. There is a shift whereby even singers and songwriters increasingly rely on performances, tours, endorsements, merchandising and the like rather than sales of albums and tracks.[16]

This is the business model that the Grateful Dead pioneered, possibly taking a clue from open source software and IBM, and is currently expanding to an increasing number of businesses. Economist Paul Krugman made the case that the demise of reliance on an income based on "hard" copies was being generalized and, making his case, quipped that in the long run we will all be the Grateful Dead.[17] What is important for creators engaged along the short route is that their work can be disseminated as widely as possible, on two conditions: first, that the work is correctly attributed to them, and second, that the creators may, if they so choose, reserve the right to prevent third parties from making a commercial profit out of their work unless this is agreed to by the creator herself.

3.2 The rules

If this is so, then what may currently be needed is a new kind of copyright, which we may, if you wish, label Copyright 2.0. I submit that the new system would have four basic features. Old copyright, or Copyright 1.0, would still be available; but it would have to be claimed for by the creator at the onset, for example by inserting the old copyright notice, ©, as the US did in the past, before accessing the Berne Convention.[18] If no notice was

---

16 Including revenue from product placement embedded in virally disseminated videos (as magisterially shown by Lady Gaga).

17 Paul Krugman, "Bits, Band and Books", *The New York Times*, 6 June 2008. This trend seems confirmed by the current behaviour of "traditional" businesses, which are indeed seeking to obtain a share of these novel income streams: see John Gapper, "The Music Labels Can Take a Punch", *The Financial Times*, 3 July 2008, noting that labels have started "to get a slice of the action from the artists' other earnings, including live performances and merchandising". Accordingly, "Universal is taking a share of touring and merchandise revenue in 90 per cent of contracts it signs with new artists".

18 The question of "re-formalizing" copyright has come back into discussion in recent times.

given, Copyright 2.0 would apply; and this would give creators just one right, the right to attribution. The notice could also be added after creation, but then it would only have the effect of giving exclusivity against specified non-authorized uses (in particular: subsequent commercial uses). The Copyright 1.0 protection given by the original notice could be withdrawn, and perhaps it should be deemed withdrawn after a specified period of time (for example, the 14 years of the original copyright protection), unless an extension period (of another 14 years) is specifically requested.

I confess that, a couple of years after first airing this proposal, I am now not sure that the four features I just described are exactly appropriate for the needs of our present society. The point I am making is that thinking along these lines at least allows us to conceptualize how the different sets of rules correspond to the specific needs of the people who create works along the long and short route. We assumed that Copyright 1.0 should survive; and we may anticipate that this is likely to be resorted to by creators (and businesses) choosing to operate along the long route. Indeed, the ultimate goal is not to displace old copyright, which seems to be alive and well in many situations, but to add to the menu a second possibility, Copyright 2.0, which should be better tailored to the characters of production and distribution of works prevailing in the current digital environment.

This line of reasoning might also help us in asking the next question. Which set of rules would then operate in each given situation? Well, in some way I already replied to this question: creators should opt-in for Copyright 1.0 at the time of the original release of their work; otherwise the new and more flexible Copyright 2.0 would operate as a default set of provisions. I characterize this approach as "Lessig by default" or, in a less personalized way, "Creative Commons by default". The idea behind the approach is that the very successful uptake of Creative Commons licenses and other copyleft

---

See Stef van Gompel, "Formalities in the Digital Era: An Obstacle or Opportunity?", in *Global Copyright: Three Hundred Years Since the Statute of Anne, from 1709 to Cyberspace*, ed. by Lionel Bently, Uma Suthersanen and Paul Torremans (Cheltenham: Edward Elgar, 2010), pp. 395–424; and Christopher Sprigman, "Reform(aliz)ing Copyright", *Stanford Law Review*, 57 (2004), 485–568. The idea of a copyright notice is being upgraded into the notion of global copyright registries. Today registration may become a precondition for protection, as state-of-the art technology enables the creation of global digital repositories. This gives security to the digital files that embody the works and to the identity of the person or entity claiming copyright. It also makes the corresponding filings user-friendly and inexpensive. If one were to consider that making registration into a global registry, rather than notice, a precondition for protection is too harsh a requirement, then registration might at least be required as a precondition of *extension* of protection.

licenses by creators operating along the short route shows that out there, in the digital prairies and wilderness, there is a very large number indeed of creators who prefer to reserve only some rights rather than all rights;[19] and that the time has come for legal systems to recognize this by creating a regime in which downstream freedom is the rule and a system under which creators may have the option to reserve some rights or, if they like, all the old Copyright 1.0 rights.

4. The new international framework and the role of the European Union

Of course, to go this way, one would have to change hundreds of laws and a few international conventions (including Berne and TRIPs).[20] I do not know that this is an impossibility. I am among those who, at the beginning of the digital age, insisted that it was too early to legislate. However, I believe that the time has now come, and that the EU should take the lead in this regard, for a variety of reasons. First, because it has the legitimacy and the prestige to do it. The same states which are currently EU member states coincide to a large extent with the ones that originally conceived and put in place the Berne Convention;[21] today they still have the cultural and international prestige required to take the initiative to adapt Berne to the digital environment. Taking up Copyright 2.0 is in the long-term interest not only of our society and of our culture but also of our economy. To argue the case in a detailed and comprehensive way, one would need multiple interdisciplinary volumes rather than this short essay. Let me therefore confine myself to two short—and admittedly a bit too assertive—points.

In the last three decades, much of IP policy in the developed world has turned around the idea that ratcheting up protection of IPRs is a good idea because it protects by strong property rights assets that typically belong to US and EU right-holders. The other idea is to expand enforcement standards abroad, with a view to boosting revenue generated by exports of IP-protected goods or by inflows of royalties dutifully paid by foreign users. This approach has been put at the basis of the Uruguay Round

---

19 In November 2009 the Creative Commons Monitor project calculated that more than 207 million webpages had been licensed under some Creative Commons Public License.

20 For a discussion, see Sprigman (2004).

21 See Sam Ricketson, "The Birth of the Berne Union", *Columbia-VLA Journal of Law and the Arts*, 11 (1986), 9-32.

negotiations, which finally led to the adoption of the WTO and of its IP component, TRIPs.[22] It was also quickly taken up by the EU and particularly so in connection with copyright-based products, as if our legacy of artistic creation could be a long lasting source of income flowing into Europe from the rest of the world until the long term of protection expires.

There are several grounds to believe that this strategy is both illusory and doomed. Here, leaving aside that it is easier to let the biblical camel pass through the needle's eye than to persuade our developing neighbours that strong enforcement of our rights is in their interest, I will only mention the fact that the domestic economies of our business partners have finally reached such a size that their demands that we give them access to our technology and IP as a precondition to our obtaining access to their markets are increasingly successful.[23]

While IP-based exclusivity protection would (unsurprisingly) appear not to assist our economies as much as our trade negotiators had hoped, I suggest that we would do better to place our bets on the third paradigm of innovation which seems to be emerging: distributed innovation through digital network driven cooperation. In the beginning innovation was the preserve of individuals; at a later stage the engine was to be found in organisations, be they the firms or research entities. Both modes required appropriation of the results of innovation by means of property rights over IP, to provide the incentives to creation. This has changed radically in the last few decades: while classical property rights-based IP protection has increasingly proved unequal to the new challenges of innovation,[24] at the same time network driven innovation is seen to thrive in contexts in

---

22 On the origins of the American idea, swiftly taken up by European trade diplomacy, that the lack of global IP protection and enforcement amounts to a "trade barrier" see Paul A. David, "Intellectual Property Institutions and the Panda's Thumb: Patents, Copyrights, and Trade Secrets in Economic Theory and History" in *Global Dimensions of Intellectual Property Rights in Science and Technology*, ed. by Mitchell B. Wallerstein, Mary Ellen Mogee and Roberta A. Schoen (Washington, DC: National Academy Press, 1993), pp. 19–62; and *Global Business Regulation*, ed. by John Braithwaite and Peter Drahos (Cambridge: Cambridge University Press, 2000), p. 61.

23 Anecdotal evidence from nuclear plants and high speed trains.

24 As anticipated by Jerome H. Reichman, "Legal Hybrids between the Patent and Copyright Paradigms", *Columbia Law Review*, 94 (1994), 2432–558. For a confirmation of the shortcomings of the classical approach in the new technological environment, see Michael A. Heller, "The Tragedy of the Anticommons: Property in the Transition from Marx to Markets", *Harvard Law Review*, 111 (1998), 622–88; and Michael A. Heller and Rebecca S. Eisenberg, "Can Patents Deter Innovation? The Anticommons in Biomedical Research", *Science*, 280 (1998), 698–701. For a review of the relevant literature, see Marco Ricolfi, "Is There an Antitrust Antidote Against IP Overprotection within TRIPs?", *Marquette Intellectual Property Law Review*, 10 (2006), 305–67.

which exclusivity has been relinquished and is to a large extent replaced by cooperative behaviour among the players, based on a combination of contractual arrangements and liability rules.[25]

I submit that our societies may obtain a genuine competitive advantage in fostering innovation based on this third paradigm rather than in insisting on global acceptance of strong IP rights which have in part outlived their function; and that we should consider how to make the best of the new chances offered to us. Reforming old international IP conventions, which are to a large extent based on the assumption of exclusivity, including Berne and TRIPs, should be part of this larger job.[26]

5. The 2010–2020 *Digital Agenda for Europe*

Of course, reforming international conventions takes time. In the past the EU has shown that it is able to take up the challenge of an economic crisis to explore new opportunities for innovation and growth. What are then the intermediate priorities? Which opportunities may we seize *now* in this regard, while the process leading to Copyright 2.0 and Berne 2.0 is—hopefully—kick-started?

A Digital Agenda for Europe indicates a number of current priorities that perfectly fit the broader approach I just advocated. First, orphan works should be brought into the fold of the EU digital libraries initiative by means of extended collective licenses.[27] Under this mechanism, any right holder may at any time reveal herself and opt out of the regime. Opting out of an extended collective license scheme amounts to opting in to full copyright protection. In this perspective, the orphan works regime would be a good first experiment in the direction of requiring opt-in Copyright 1.0.

Second, collective rights management organisations (CRMOs) are aptly

---

25 For examples of the working of this third paradigm see Arti K. Rai, Jerome H. Reichman, Paul F. Uhlir and Colin R. Crossman, "Pathways Across the Valley of Death: Novel Intellectual Property Strategies for Accelerated Drug Discovery", *Yale Journal of Health Policy, Law, and Ethics*, 8 (2008), 1–36 (in connection with drug discovery) and Jerome H. Reichman and Paul F. Uhlir, "A Contractually Reconstructed Research Commons for Scientific Data in a Highly Protectionist Intellectual Property Environment", *Law and Contemporary Problems*, 66 (2003), 315–462.

26 But see the refreshing remarks showing that exclusivity is not even today mandated either by Berne and by TRIPs in Geiger (2011), p. 544.

27 See *A Digital Agenda for Europe*, pp. 6–7, 29–30. The literature on ECL is significantly growing: see Tarja Koskinen-Olsson, "Collective Management in the Nordic Countries", in *Collective Management of Copyright and Related Rights*, ed. by Daniel Gervais (Kluwer Law International, 2006), pp. 257–81; and the literature quoted in Grassmuck (2009).

characterized as a fine example of contracting into liability.[28] Individual
property rights are pooled into a collecting society, which converts the full
property right over the individual work into a pro-rata share of the claim to
global compensation agreed in advance with users. What is required in the
digital age is that would-be users are not required to go around, hat in hand,
to all the twenty-seven EU CRMOs to get from each of them clearance for the
service; and that cross-border pan European licensing takes off. The *Digital
Agenda* is rightly looking into this as well.[29]

Third, public sector information is an essential input for the emergence
of the third paradigm of innovation I just sketched out. Maps, geo-data,
environmental data-sets, laws, regulations, case law and the like may be
brought together across jurisdictions through digital networks and contribute
to the emergence of new aggregated information products and services at a
pan-European level. The current text of Directive 98/2003 still needs several
upgrades to contribute to the goal; its revision is one more of the focal points
of the *Digital Agenda*.[30]

If we combine the three "action plans", we can see that, while certainly
they do not amount—and do not intend to amount—to a roadmap to Berne
2.0, they bring together three components which are vital to reconciling
IP and the new digital environment. CRMOs are called to overcome their
national limitations to operate cross-border along the routes opened up
by digital technology. Orphan works are seen as a possible area for a more
flexible statutory license regime, unless their holders show up and opt out
of it. The enormous wealth of data sets generated by public sector bodies
engaged in their primary function is increasingly made available to the
pioneers of the third innovation paradigm.

Whether these test beds of legislative innovation are to take off in
actual legislative innovation and coalesce into a normative environment
which brings us closer to a reconciliation of copyright law and the digital
environment, we do not know yet. I surely hope so.

---

28 Robert P. Merges, "Contracting Into Liability Rules: Intellectual Property Rights and
Collective Rights Organisations", *California Law Review*, 84 (1996), 1293–393.

29 *A Digital Agenda for Europe*, pp. 7–8.

30 Ibid., pp. 9–10. The specific copyright issue in the PSI Directive is whether the rules
concerning government IP right may help or hinder the process, as illustrated in detail
by Estelle Derclaye, "Does the Directive on the Re-use of Public Sector Information Affect
the State's Database Sui Generis Right?", in *Knowledge Rights: Legal, Societal and Related
Technological Aspects* ed. by J. Gaster, E. Schweighofer and P. Sint (Austrian Computer
Society, 2008), pp. 137–69.

3. Evaluating Directive 2001/29/EC in the Light of the Digital Public Domain

Lucie Guibault

This chapter presents an evaluation of Directive 2001/29/EC on the harmonisation of certain aspects of copyright and related rights in the digital information society.[1] The Directive entered into force on 22 June 2001,[2] and its objectives were twofold: (1) to adapt legislation on copyright and related rights to reflect technological developments; and (2) to transpose into community law the main international obligations arising from the two treaties on copyright and related rights adopted within the framework of the World Intellectual Property Organisation (WIPO) in December 1996.[3] The Directive was one of the centrepieces of the original Lisbon Agenda of 2000. The renewed Lisbon Agenda aims at fostering economic prosperity, jobs and growth, in particular by boosting the knowledge-based economy, and by enhancing the quality of community regulation ("better regulation"). In doing so, the original Lisbon aim of making the European Union "the most dynamic and competitive knowledge-based economy in

---

1 This chapter is partly based on Lucie Guibault et al., "Study on the Implementation and Effect in Member States' Laws of Directive 2001/29/EC on the Harmonisation of Certain Aspects of Copyright and Related Rights in the Information Society", report to the European Commission, ETD/2005/IM/D1/91, DG Internal Market (February 2007), available at http://www.ivir.nl/publications/guibault/Infosoc_report_2007.pdf.

2 OJ 2001 L 167 of 22.6.2001, p. 10 (hereafter "Directive 2001/29/EC" or "Information Society Directive").

3 WIPO Copyright Treaty (WCT) and WIPO Performers and Phonograms Treaty (WPPT) both signed at the WIPO Diplomatic Conference, Geneva, 20 December 1996.

the world" by 2010, remains intact. A legislative framework for copyright and related rights in the information society that fosters the growth of the knowledge-based economy in the European Union was therefore seen as a crucial element in any strategy leading towards that goal.

At the same time, the European Commission is an active promoter of the digitisation and online accessibility of cultural material and digital preservation by libraries, archives and museums. In connection with the "i2010 initiative", the Commission published a recommendation on the digitisation and online accessibility of cultural material and digital preservation.[4] The objective of this initiative is to develop digitised material from libraries, archives and museums, as well as to give citizens throughout Europe access to its cultural heritage, by making it searchable and usable on the Internet. The achievement of these goals inevitably raises copyright issues. As noted in Recital 10 of the Recommendation, only part of the material held by libraries, archives and museums is in the public domain, while the rest is protected by intellectual property rights.

To what extent do the provisions of the Information Society Directive affect the way digital works are being used? Do the provisions of the Directive pertaining to the limitations on copyright and the legal protection of technological protection measures (TPMs) allow libraries, archives and museums to comply with the objectives of the Recommendation on the digitisation and online accessibility of cultural material and digital preservation? In other words, are the goals of the Information Society Directive compatible with those of the Recommendation on digitisation and accessibility of material?

This chapter is divided into a further four sections. Section 2 puts Directive 2001/29/EC in the context of the digital public domain, by describing the public domain from a continental European law perspective and the position of libraries, archives, museums and scientific research. Section 3 analyses the impact that the implementation of the provisions of the Directive dealing with the exceptions and limitations on copyright has on the activities of libraries, archives and museums. The provisions of the Directive on the legal protection of TPMs are put to a comparable test in section 4. Section 5 sums up with a number of concluding remarks.

---

4 Commission of the European Communities, Recommendation 2006/585/EC on the digitisation and online accessibility of cultural material and digital preservation O.J.C.E. L 236/28, 31 August 2006.

1. Directive 2001/29/EC in context

Before turning to the analysis of the impact of the implementation of the provisions of Directive 2001/29/EC on the use of copyright protected works and the activities of libraries, archives and museums, it is important to put the Directive into context. To this end, the first subsection briefly describes the public domain from a continental European law perspective, while the second subsection gives a portrait of the main interests and concerns of libraries, archives and museums.

1.1 Defining the public domain

When trying to map the public domain from a continental European law perspective,[5] it must be emphasised that intellectual property regimes are designed to strike a delicate balance between the interests of authors, inventors or other rights holders in the control and exploitation of the fruit of their intellectual labour on the one hand, and society's competing interest in the free flow of ideas, information and commerce on the other hand. To this end, most intellectual property regimes admit a number of inherent limits that are designed to promote the dissemination of new works or inventions and to ensure the preservation of a vigorous public domain. These limits are the definition of protectable subject matter (the idea/expression dichotomy), the criteria for protection (the requirement of originality or substantial investment), the fixed duration of the intellectual property protection, and the exhaustion doctrine.

Apart from the copyright regime's inherent limits, a balance of interest between encouraging the creation and the dissemination of new creations is further achieved through the recognition of limitations on the rights owners' exclusive rights. Limitations on rights are designed either to resolve potential conflicts of interests between rights owners and users from within the intellectual property system or to implement a particular aspect of public policy. Technically, limitations should reflect the legislator's assessment of the need and desirability for society to use a protected subject matter against the impact of such a measure on the

---

5   See Pamela Samuelson, "The Challenges of Mapping the Public Domain", in *The Future of the Public Domain: Identifying the Commons in Information Law*, ed. by Lucie Guibault and P. Bernt Hugenholtz (The Hague: Kluwer Law International, 2006), pp. 7–25; and Stéphanie Choisy, *Le domaine public en droit d'auteur* (Paris: Litec, 2002), p. 53.

economic interests of the rights holders. This weighing process often leads to varying results from one country to the next. Potential conflicts between the interests of rights owners and those of society take place at different levels and have different grounds. Limitations typically protect freedom of expression and the right to privacy;[6] they safeguard free competition, promote the dissemination of knowledge, or respond to symptoms of market failure. Of course, certain limitations may have been adopted on more than one ground and the justifications underlying a particular limitation may change over time.

National laws are generally silent on the subject of the imperative character of copyright limitations. The legislator's silence could be interpreted either way, i.e., as providing arguments for or against the imperative character of limitations on copyright. Generally speaking, limitations on copyright have been adopted as an express recognition by the legislator of the "legitimate interests" of users. However, whether the limitations embodying such "legitimate interests" are to be considered imperative or not is likely to depend on a number of factors, including the lawmakers' conception of the overall objectives pursued by the copyright regime. The imperative or default character of the limitations must therefore be determined by examining the legislator's intent, as revealed in the legal commentaries and the jurisprudence.[7]

In view of the small volume of literature available in continental Europe on the subject of the public domain, it is difficult to tell whether the notion of public domain would generally be deemed in Europe as extending also to the user privileges recognised under intellectual property law, as it has been suggested in the American literature.[8] However, even if the statutory user privileges are not to be considered as part of the public domain in the strict sense, the widespread use of TPMs in conjunction with contractual restrictions on the exercise of the privileges recognised by copyright law does affect the free flow of information or, as Madison calls it, the "open space".[9]

---

6   P. Bernt Hugenholtz, "Fierce Creatures: Copyright Exemptions Towards Extinction?", keynote speech, IFLA/IMPRIMATUR Conference, *Rights, Limitations and Exceptions: Striking a Proper Balance*, Amsterdam (30–31 October 1997), p. 18; and *Urheberrecht Kommentar*, ed. by G. Schricker (Munich: Verlag C.H. Beck, 1999), p. 735.

7   Lucie Guibault, *Copyright Limitations and Contracts: An Analysis of the Contractual Overridability of Limitations on Copyright* (The Hague: Kluwer Law International, 2002), p. 109.

8   See Samuelson (2006), pp. 7–25.

9   Michael J. Madison, "Legal-ware: Contract and Copyright in the Digital Age", *Fordham Law Review*, 67 (1998), 1025–1143 (p. 1029).

1.2 Libraries, archives and museums

Typical functions of any library are the collection, preservation, archiving and dissemination of information. The preservation and archiving of copyrighted works often involves the making of reproductions from original works, either because they have been damaged, lost or stolen.[10] The dissemination of information takes place in a number of ways, either by lending exemplars of works; by permitting the public consultation of works on the premises of the library or the consultation of electronic material at a distance; by allowing patrons to make their own reproductions of works for personal purposes using freely accessible machines (photocopy, microfiches or printer); or finally by transmitting works at the request of individual patrons in the context of a document delivery service or an interlibrary loan service.[11]

Public and research libraries occupy a central role in the supply of information to the public. They make current social and cultural information available to the public on a non-profit basis through catalogues, (electronic) databases, compilations of press articles and other sources. In this context, one can easily understand the libraries' wish to be able to continue to provide the same services in the digital environment as they are providing in the analogue world. With the digitisation of works, several of the libraries' and archives' main activities have given rise to an intensification of use of works by the public, either offline or online, on the premises or at a distance. A number of these activities, when carried out in the digital environment, raise some uncertainty under copyright law, the most problematic of which are electronic document delivery services and the digitisation of copyright protected material held in the collections of libraries and archives.

Libraries and archives see in digital technology the ideal means to preserve or restore their collections. The question therefore arises of whether public libraries, archives and other similar institutions should be allowed to make digital reproductions of works and under what circumstances such reproductions could be allowed. Also, can a library or archive make a copy of a digital work in its collection? A library or archive could consider making such a digital reproduction in the case where the original of a work

---

10 Instituut voor Informatierecht, *Auteursrechtelijke aspecten van preservering van elektronische publicaties*, Universiteit van Amsterdam, February 1998, IViR Rapporten – 7, p. 1.

11 J. Krikke, *Het bibliotheekprivilege in de digitale omgeving* (Deventer: Kluwer Law, 2000), p. 21; Dirk J. G. Visser, "Naar een multimedia-bestendig auteursrecht", *ITeR* No. 10, Samsom Bedrijfs Informatie, Alphen aan den Rijn, 1998, pp. 1–81 (p. 45).

is currently in an obsolete format, where the technology required in order to consult the original is unavailable or where the institution's copy of a work has been stolen or is deteriorating.[12]

Contrary to the making of reproductions of works for the library patrons' personal use, an activity which is usually limited to the reproduction of only portions of works, the digitisation of works for preservation or restoration purposes involves the reproduction in digital form of entire works. Recognising the library's and archive's capital role in the preservation of a nation's cultural and historical heritage, the copyright systems of a number of industrialised countries expressly allow the digitisation of certain categories of works, albeit under more or less strict conditions. Most laws are silent, however, on the question of whether libraries and archives may convert hardcopies of works into digital copies for purposes of preservation and restoration of their collections. Moreover, even if digitisation is allowed in certain circumstances, the law is not always clear on whether digitisation is permitted only for printed works or also for sound and audiovisual works.

At another level, scientific publishers offer an impressive number of online publications, research tools per discipline, access to the full text of works (pay-site), and "contents alert" services allowing those who register to receive the tables of contents of the journals of their choice by email. Electronic publishing not only makes it possible to consult the articles, whether free of charge of otherwise, but also to track down other sources of knowledge through a document search, links, interactive services, electronic commerce, etc. The Internet and email increasingly offer the research community opportunities that it did not previously have. Access to information has increased as has access to and discussion with those working in similar areas. One other aspect of digital technology, currently in its infancy but which presents enormous possibilities to the research community, is the use of the Internet to reach individuals as research subjects. In particular, there may be significant research benefits to be gleaned where the group being researched is normally difficult to reach and/or the issues being researched are of a particularly sensitive nature.

---

12 See Lucie Guibault, "The Nature and Scope of Limitations and Exceptions to Copyright and Neighbouring Rights with Regard to General Interest Missions for the Transmission of Knowledge: Prospects for their Adaptation to the Digital Environment", *Copyright Bulletin* (December 2003).

2. Exceptions and limitations in Directive 2001/29/EC

With the adoption of the Information Society Directive, the European legislator actually pursued several objectives among which was the creation of a harmonised legal framework that is consistent with international norms that would provide legal certainty to market players, would be sustainable and would preserve a balance between protecting the rights of right holders and the freedoms of users. Whether the legislator has achieved its goal, particularly from the point of view of libraries, archives and museums, is discussed below.

2.1 General remarks

Besides harmonising the rights of reproduction, communication to the public and distribution, the Directive ended up dealing extensively with an issue that was mentioned only incidentally in the Green Paper: copyright limitations.[13] The European Commission was of the opinion that without adequate harmonisation of these exceptions, as well as of the conditions of their application, Member States would continue to apply a large number of rather different limitations and exceptions to these rights and, consequently, apply these rights in different forms. The harmonisation of limitations proved to be a highly controversial issue, which explains in large part the delay experienced not only in the adoption of the Directive itself, but also in its implementation by the Member States. The difficulty of choosing and delimiting the scope of the limitations on copyright and related rights that would be acceptable to all Member States also proved to be a daunting task for the drafters of the Information Society Directive. Between the time when the Proposal for a directive was first introduced in 1997 and the time when the final text was adopted in 2001, the amount of admissible limitations went from seven to twenty.[14]

The regime of limitations established by the Information Society Directive leaves Member States ample discretion to decide if and how they implement the limitations contained in article 5 of the Directive. This latitude not only follows from the fact that all but one of the twenty-three

---

13 European Commission, "Copyright and Related Rights in the Information Society", Green Paper, COM (95) 382 final, Brussels, 19 July 1995, p. 35.

14 Stefan Bechtold, "Comment on Directive 2001/29/EC", in *Concise on European Copyright Law*, ed. by Thomas Dreier and P. Bernt Hugenholtz (Alphen aan den Rijn: Kluwer Law International, 2006), p. 373.

limitations listed in the Directive are optional, but more importantly from the fact that the text of the Directive does not lay down strict rules that Member States are expected to transpose into their legal order. Rather, articles 5(2) to 5(5) of the Directive contain two types of norms: one set of broadly worded limitations, within the boundaries of which Member States may elect to legislate; and one set of general categories of situations for which Member States may adopt limitations.[15] Moreover, instead of simply reproducing the wording of the Directive, most Member States have also chosen to interpret the limitations contained in the Directive according to their own traditions. The outcome is that Member States have implemented the provisions of articles 5(2) to 5(5) of the Directive very differently, selecting only those exceptions that they consider important.

The European legislator's decision to opt for a list of optional limitations is all the more surprising given that the possible consequences of a lack of harmonisation for the functioning of the Internal Market were already known. The result is that Member States have implemented articles 5(2) and 5(3) very differently, selecting such exceptions as they saw fit, and implementing specific categories in diverse ways. With such a mosaic of limitations throughout the European Community, the aim of harmonisation most likely has not been achieved, and legal uncertainty persists. The fact that Member States have implemented the same limitation differently, giving rise to a variety of different rules applicable to a single situation across the European Community, could ultimately constitute a serious impediment to the establishment of cross-border services. Especially for smaller users, the lack of harmonisation of the limitations on copyright is a serious issue. The level of knowledge required for the conclusion of the necessary licensing agreements per territory is too high and costly to make the effort worthwhile. Larger content providers who wish to extend their services across Europe also suffer from the lack of harmonisation, because it raises transaction costs.

2.2 Limitations to the benefit of libraries, archives and museums

Limitations adopted for the benefit of libraries are thus meant to allow these institutions to perform their general tasks and to encourage the dissemination of knowledge and information among members of

---

15 Martin Senftleben, *Copyright, Limitations and the Three-Step-Test* (The Hague: Kluwer Law International, 2004).

society at large, in furtherance of the common good. Article 5(2)c) of the Information Society Directive allows Member States to adopt a limitation on the reproduction right in respect of specific acts of reproduction made by publicly accessible libraries, archives, educational establishments or museums which are not for direct or indirect economic or commercial advantage. As the Explanatory Memorandum to the Directive specifies, the provision does not define those acts of reproduction which may be exempted by Member States. Moreover, this provision must be read in conjunction with Recital 40 of the Directive, which makes it clear that the European lawmaker intended to restrict the application of this limitation to certain special cases covered by the reproduction right, and not to allow uses made in the context of online delivery of protected works or other subject-matter. Regarding acts of electronic delivery, libraries are encouraged to negotiate specific contractual arrangements with rights holders. The making of digital reproductions of works in a library's collection for purposes of preservation, however, falls clearly within the ambit of this provision, since it makes no distinction between reproductions made in analogue or digital format.[16]

Not all Member States have implemented this optional limitation, and those that did have often chosen different ways to do it, subjecting the act of reproduction to different conditions of application and requirements. Some Member States only allow reproductions to be made in analogue format; others restrict the digitisation to certain types of works, while yet other Member States allow all categories of works to be reproduced in both analogue and digital form.[17] In addition, Member States have identified different beneficiaries of this limitation. Some have simply replicated the wording of article 5(2)b), while others have limited its application to public libraries and archives to the exclusion of educational institutions. The prevailing legal uncertainty regarding the manner in which digitised material may be used and reproduced, is likely to constitute a disincentive to digitisation. This militates against cross-border exchange of material, and may discourage cross-border cooperation.[18] However, as already mentioned in the Staff Working Paper of 2004, libraries face another problem

---

16 Krikke, p. 156.
17 Urs Gasser and Silke Ernst, "EUCD Best Practice Guide: Implementing the EU Copyright Directive in the Digital Age", University of St. Gallen Law & Economics Working Paper No. 2007-01 (December 2006), p. 16.
18 See European Commission, "i2010: Digital Libraries", SEC (2005) 1194, Brussels (30 September 2005), p. 9.

by the fact that pursuant to article 1(2) of the Directive, which leaves the provisions of earlier directives unaffected, the limitation of article 5(2)c) of the Information Society Directive does not apply to databases.[19] This may create severe practical obstacles for the daily operations of libraries.

With respect to the making available of the digital archives, article 5(3)n) of the Directive states that Member States may adopt limitations on the reproduction and the communication to the public rights for "use by communication or making available, for the purpose of research or private study, to individual members of the public by dedicated terminals on the premises of establishments referred to in paragraph 2(c) of works and other subject-matter not subject to purchase or licensing terms which are contained in their collections". Not only is the implementation of this provision, just like the previous one, not mandatory, but even where it has been implemented, its scope remains extremely narrow: a work may only be communicated or made available to individual members of the public if each patron establishes that the use is for his exclusive research or private study. The works may only be communicated or made available by means of dedicated terminals on the premises of non-commercial establishments, which excludes any access via an extranet or other protected network connection that users can access at a distance. Moreover, this provision only finds application insofar as no purchase or licensing terms provide otherwise, which is in practice rarely the case. As the following remark illustrates, this provision was met with much scepticism within the library community:

> While this is a laudable regulation, it is incomprehensible that this exception is tied to "dedicated terminals on the premises" of named establishments and to the condition that these works are not subject to purchase or licensing terms. (...) The second condition is another example of the lack of balance in the Infosoc Directive. By allowing rights holders to contractually evade any exception, it grants them unlimited exclusive rights in the online realm. This condition prevents public libraries from fulfilling their public task of making published works available to their users without prejudice to their ability to pay their market price.[20]

In countries that chose to implement it, article 5(3)n) was transposed almost word-for-word in the national legislation. Several Member States have, however, decided not to incorporate this article into their law; the

---

19 Commission Staff Working Paper on the Review of the EC legal Framework in the Field of Copyright and Related Rights, SEC (2004) 995, Brussels, 19 July 2004, p. 13.
20 Privatkopie.net & Aktionsbuendnis Urheberrecht & FIfF, Response to Consultation on Staff Working Paper 2004, p. 8.

extent to which library patrons are allowed, in these Member States, to consult digital material on the library network is therefore unclear. However, considering the default nature of this provision and the fact that its application is most often overridden by contract, libraries advocate for specific contracts or licenses which, without creating an imbalance, would take account of their specific role in the dissemination of knowledge.

3. Technological Protection Measures in Directive 2001/29/EC

The emergence of the digital network environment as a commercially viable platform for the distribution of copyright protected content sparked, in the early 1990s, the need on the part of rights holders to increase legal protection in order to safeguard content from unauthorised access and use. At the international level, the call for the recognition of legal protection for TPMs became particularly vibrant during the last phase of the negotiations leading to the adoption of the WIPO Internet Treaties in December 1996.[21] Indeed, in the preamble to the WIPO Copyright Treaties (WCT), the Contracting Parties said to recognise "the need to introduce new international rules (…) in order to provide adequate solutions to the questions raised by new economic, social, cultural and technological developments". This Treaty, together with the WIPO Performers and Phonograms Treaty (WPPT), introduced a new form of protection to the benefit of rights holders by establishing, for the first time in an international copyright instrument, that technological measures used by authors and related right holders to protect their works or related subject matter enjoy independent protection.[22]

3.1 General remarks

Article 6 on the legal protection of TPMs turned out to be one of the most intricate and controversial provisions of the entire Information Society Directive. Its complexity is also reflected at the national level. In this context, the question arises whether the provision offers sufficient legal certainty to allow users to know what they can and cannot do with

---

21 Sam Ricketson and Jane C. Ginsburg, *International Copyright and Neighbouring Rights* (Oxford: Oxford University Press, 2006), p. 976.

22 Urs Gasser, "Legal Framework and Technological Protection of Digital Content: Moving Forward Towards a Best Practice Model", *Fordham Intellectual Property, Media and Entertainment Law Journal*, 17 (2006), 39–113 (p. 45).

respect to a protected work. Although the legal protection of TPMs does not confer, as such, an exclusive right on the rights holder, article 6 of the Information Society Directive deserves attention for two main reasons: first, because this article constitutes the main adjustment to Europe's copyright framework as a result of the implementation of its international obligation under the WIPO Internet Treaties; and second, because the use of TPMs—and their legal protection—is seen as one of the main components to the establishment of digital rights management systems (DRMs).[23]

According to article 6(1) of the Information Society Directive, Member States must "provide adequate legal protection against the circumvention of any effective technological measures, which the person concerned carries out in the knowledge, or with reasonable grounds to know, that he or she is pursuing that objective". In other words, this provision requires that Member States prohibit acts of circumvention of TPMs by any person who knows or should have reasonable grounds to know that she is committing an act of circumvention. As a complement to the protection afforded under article 6(1) of the Directive, article 6(2) provides for a prohibition on the supply of any product or service which primarily enables or facilitates the circumvention of TPMs or a prohibition on acts preparatory to actual circumvention. According to article 6(2), Member States must provide:

> adequate legal protection against the manufacture, import, distribution, sale, rental, advertisement for sale or rental, or possession for commercial purposes of devices, products or components or the provision of services which:
>
> (a) are promoted, advertised or marketed for the purpose of circumvention of, or
> (b) have only a limited commercially significant purpose or use other than to circumvent, or
> (c) are primarily designed, produced, adapted or performed for the purpose of enabling or facilitating the circumvention of, any effective technological measures.

In addition, the expression "technological measures" as defined under article 6(3) of the Directive means any technology, device or component that, in the normal course of its operation, is designed to prevent or restrict acts, in respect of works or other subject-matter which are not authorised by the right holder of any copyright or any right related to copyright. This formulation differs from article 11 of the WCT, which protects TPMs only

---

23 Jeffrey P. Cunard, Keith Hill and Chris Barlas, *Current Developments in The Field of Digital Rights Management* (Geneva: WIPO, 2004), SCCR/10/2 Rev., p. 39.

to the extent that they restrict acts that are not authorised by the authors *or permitted by law*. Must one infer from this that the European legislator did not intend to allow the circumvention of a TPM solely for the purpose of exercising a limitation on copyright?[24]

Be that as it may, there is broad consensus that the use of TPMs should take account of the users' interest in exercising certain limitations on copyright and related rights. Accordingly, article 6(4) of the Directive prescribes affirmative action by the rights owners, including by means of agreements between them and other parties concerned, or in its absence, by the Member States. This is to ensure that users benefit from certain limitations with respect to works protected by TPMs to the extent necessary to benefit from these limitations and where that beneficiaries have legal access to the protected work concerned. This provision is extremely complex, vague and prone to differing interpretations. As a result, lawmakers in the 27 Member States have once again used their imagination to interpret the provision and come up with their own solutions, which they hope meet the requirements of article 6(4) of the Directive.

Not all limitations appearing in the list of article 5 of the Directive are covered by this measure, but only a selection of the limitations included in articles 5(2) and 5(3) are subjected to the obligation of the rights holder to provide users with the means to exercise them.[25] Among these limitations are acts of reproduction by publicly accessible libraries, educational establishments or museums, or by archives (article 5(2) c)) as well as use for the sole purpose of illustration for teaching or scientific research (article 5(3)a)). Rights holders and Member States alike are obliged to provide the means to exercise these—otherwise optional—limitations on copyright and related rights only insofar as these have indeed been transposed in the national order. The list of limitations that are subject to the obligation therefore risks being even shorter in reality since, for example, the limitation on reproductions of broadcasts made by social institutions pursuing non-commercial purposes has not been implemented in a number of countries.

However, according to the fourth paragraph of article 6(4) of the Directive, "the provisions of the first and second subparagraphs shall not apply to works or other subject-matter made available to the public on agreed contractual terms in such a way that members of the public may

---

24 Bechtold (2006), p. 393.
25 André Lucas and Pierre Sirinelli, "Chroniques: Droit d'auteur et droits voisins", *Propriétés intellectuelles*, 20 (2006), pp. 297–316, 322.

access them from a place and at a time individually chosen by them". The last sentence of Recital 53 specifies that "non-interactive forms of online use should remain subject to those provisions". What constitutes a non-interactive transmission is unclear. According to one commentator, "only live webcasting, web radio and similar transmissions where the user cannot choose the time of the transmission qualify for non-interactive transmissions".[26] This means that the exclusion actually extends to any work offered "on-demand", covering any work transmitted over the Internet, as long as the user is able to choose and initialize that transmission. In view of the fact that most works offered on-demand through DRM systems rely on the conclusion of contracts and the application of TPMs, the scope of this provision is potentially very broad.

In the absence of any clear guideline in the Directive on how to accommodate the exercise of limitations on copyright, it is safe to say that no real harmonisation has been achieved regarding the implementation of article 6(4) of the Directive in the European Union. The implementation of this provision at the national level has led to an array of different solutions and procedures. In some Member States, only individual beneficiaries may claim the application of the limitation, while in other countries, interest groups and other third parties also have the right to do so. In yet other Member States, administrative bodies may be entitled to force rights holders to make the necessary means available to beneficiaries of limitations. Some Member States have adopted the "wait and see" approach, and done nothing to implement the provision.

3.2 TPMs and libraries, archives and museums

When reading the text of article 6(4), it is clear that the negotiation of agreements between rights owners and parties concerned is the European legislature's preferred method to achieve its objective. As Dusollier points out, the way to contractual negotiations is only realistic when users are easily identifiable, like libraries and archives, broadcasting organisations, social institutions, educational institutions, groups of disabled persons and public entities. However, this is not necessarily the case for all users who may invoke the right to benefit from a limitation pursuant to article 6(4).[27]

---

26 Bechtold (2006), p. 394.
27 Séverine Dusollier, *Droit d'auteur et protection des oeuvres dans l'univers numérique: droits et*

This voluntary path is actually being pursued in various Member States, with varying results. For example, the Motion Pictures Association has entered into negotiations with the British Film Institute (BFI) regarding the right to make archival copies of films.[28] In January 2005, the German National Library has reached an agreement with the German Federation of the Phonographic Industry and the German Booksellers and Publishers Association on the circumvention of such TPMs as access and copy controls on CDs, CD-ROMs, and e-books. According to the press release, the German National Library has obtained a "license to copy" technologically protected digital content for its "own archiving, for scientific purposes of users, for collections for schools or educational purposes, for instruction and research as well as of works that are out of print." To avoid abuses, the library "will check user's interest" for a copy of the technologically protected content. Further, the copies, which are subject to a fee, "will as far as possible be personalized by a digital watermark".[29]

Until recently, libraries were able to offer digital articles as unprotected downloads that could be obtained by anyone who registered with the institution. But the deployment of DRM may become more restrictive in the near future, because major scientific publishers may want to increase the control over their products and possibly charge for individual access. The supply of a key to decrypt protected content is not considered a viable option, since for a single library subscribing to 2,000 electronic journals and periodicals, removing DRM from every single article would be too complicated in practice and impossible to manage with the available organisational resources. This would be aggravated by the multitude of different DRM systems on the market, which prevent a single approach to circumvention. Moreover, the lack of clarity with regard to the limitations on copyright leads to a multitude of different individual initiatives from the sides of rights holders, libraries and publishers. This contradicts the value proposition of digital libraries, i.e. to make knowledge broadly and easily available over the Internet. The British Library notes that the great majority of agreements relating to electronic licences also undermined

---

exceptions à la lumière des dispositifs de verrouillage des œuvres (Brussels, Larcier, 2005), p. 175.
28 Motion Pictures Associations, MPA Response to the UK All Party Parliamentary Internet Group (APIG) Inquiry into Digital Rights Management (DRM), Brussels (13 January 2006).
29 See http://blogs.law.harvard.edu/ugasser/2005/01/26/german-national-library-license-to-circumvent-drm.

exceptions provided for in UK and international copyright law.[30]

The deployment of DRM systems as envisaged by the Information Society Directive not only presupposes the application of technological protection measures to protected works, but it also entails the use of contractual agreements spelling out the acts that users are permitted to accomplish with respect to the licensed material. The digital network's interactive nature has created the perfect preconditions for the development of a contractual culture. Through the application of technical access and copy control mechanisms, rights owners are capable of effectively subjecting the use of any work made available in the digital environment to a set of particular conditions of use.[31] While the Directive contains extensive provisions on the protection of TPMs and rights management information, it fails to deal with the use of contracts in the context of DRM systems or otherwise. At most, the Directive contains a few statements encouraging parties to conclude contracts for certain uses of protected material. Since neither the Directive nor the relevant international instruments on copyright and related rights, such as the WCT and the WPPT, prescribe any rules on the subject, the specific regulation of licensing contracts has been left to the Member States. Thus, the contractual framework generally remains voluntary and market-driven, knowing that the principle of freedom of contract constitutes a cornerstone of European contract law.

In effect, the licence terms often act in conjunction with technological measures as a substitute to the system of exclusive rights and limitations established by traditional copyright law.[32] A quick survey of the current licensing practices carried out by European website operators indicates that information providers increasingly tend to restrict or even to prohibit certain uses with respect to the content made available via the Internet, in a manner that goes far beyond the bounds of copyright law.[33] Often, the wording of a click-wrap licence will seem to imply that the restriction on

---

30 *Gowers Review of Intellectual Property*, London, HM Treasury, December 2006, p. 73.

31 P. Bernt Hugenholtz, "Copyright, Contract and Code: What Will Remain of the Public Domain?", *Brooklyn Journal of International Law*, 26 (2000), 77–90 (p. 79); Paul Goldstein, "Copyright and its Substitutes", *Wisconsin Law Review* (1997), 865–71 (p. 867).

32 Jacques de Werra, "Moving Beyond the Conflict Between Freedom of Contract and Copyright Policies: In Search of a New Global Policy for On-Line Information Licensing Transactions: A Comparative Analysis Between U.S. Law and European Law", *Columbia Journal of Law and the Arts*, 25 (2003), 239–375 (p. 251); Haimo Schack, "Anti-Circumvention Measures and Restrictions in Licensing Contracts as Instruments for Preventing Competition and Fair Use", *University of Illinois Journal of Law, Technology and Policy* (2002), 321–32 (p. 329).

33 Lucie Guibault et al. (2007), pp. 141 et seq.

use of the website's content also extends to the elements of such content that are in principle part of the public domain, because they lack originality or because they are no longer protected by any intellectual property right. Other common terms of use that can be found on the Internet prohibit the making of "any reproduction [of the content] for any purpose whatsoever", clause which purports to restrict the use of protected as well as non-protected material posted on the website.[34]

This chapter examined to what extent the provisions of the Information Society Directive affect the way digital works are being used. More particularly, this contribution considered whether the implementation of the provisions of the Directive pertaining to the limitations on copyright and the legal protection of TPMs allows libraries, archives and museums to comply with the objectives of the Recommendation on the digitisation and online accessibility of cultural material and digital preservation.

The analysis of the provisions of Directive 2001/29/EC inevitably leads to the following general observation: these provisions fail to contribute to the establishment of a clear framework for either rights owners or users, particularly as far as limitations on copyright and the legal protection of TPMs are concerned. The non-uniform implementation of the provisions of the Directive in the Member States gives rise to a mosaic of different rules applicable to a single situation across the European Community, which forms the main source of legal uncertainty. As a result, the lack of harmonisation may constitute a serious impediment to the establishment of cross-border online services and fails to offer a consistent approach with respect to the recognition of user interests, among which are those of libraries, archives, museums and scientists.

The transposition of article 5(2)c of the Directive, permitting specific acts of reproduction by publicly accessible libraries and similar institutions, provides a good illustration of the prevailing uncertainty. In some Member States, the limitation applies to libraries and archives who may make reproductions of all types of works for purposes of preservation or restoration of their collection. In other Member States, this very limitation is restricted either to certain categories of works or to specific institutions. Finally, in a number of Member States, this limitation has not been

---

34 Lucie Guibault, "Wrapping Information in Contract: How Does it Affect the Public Domain?", in *The Future of the Public Domain: Identifying the Commons in Information Law*, ed. by Lucie Guibault and P. Bernt Hugenholtz (The Hague: Kluwer Law International, 2006), pp. 87–104.

implemented at all. Legal uncertainty inevitably arises from this mixture of applicable rules.

The provisions concerning the legal protection of TPMs do not fare any better. The Directive's rules on TPMs have had a modest harmonising effect at best. The vague wording of articles 6(1) and 6(2) of the Directive again leave much to be desired in terms of legal certainty. The wording of Article 6(4) is particularly convoluted and obscure. The provision fails to instruct Member States what "appropriate measures" should be taken to protect disenfranchised users, or how long they should wait before taking action. Moreover, Member States are left with complete discretion as to the procedures leading up to such measures. Pursuant to article 6(4) paragraph 4, however, these "appropriate measures" are no longer applicable any time that a work is made available to the public via interactive services on agreed contractual terms. The distinctions in treatment between the different limitations and between works that are made available interactively or not—distinctions for which no convincing justification has been put forward—will inevitably affect the provision's balanced character to the detriment of the users.

The assessment of the boundary between infringing and non-infringing conduct remains, therefore, highly uncertain and unpredictable. One consequence of the prevailing uncertainty regarding the scope of limitations in the digital networked environment has been to force users to negotiate the conditions of use of protected works with every single rights holder, for every territory involved. In an online cross-border setting, this can be a very cumbersome endeavour. Moreover, legal uncertainty is no solid ground for negotiations, for it inevitably leaves the outcome to the strongest party. Even in the absence of any relevant case law examining the legality of mass-market licences that prevent the use of public domain information or that purport to restrict the exercise of user privileges normally conferred under copyright law, there is reason to believe that such licences would be invalidated only in very exceptional circumstances. As a result, the widespread use of online licences may end up posing a threat to the copyright policy objectives and the integrity of the public domain, insofar as they may contribute to displace democratically established public ordering assumptions.

All in all, the regime of limitations and technological protection measures established by the Information Society Directive does not appear to offer the necessary legal certainty to support the deployment of a cross-border European library project as advocated in the Recommendation on the digitisation and online accessibility of cultural material and digital preservation. It is fair to conclude that the goals of the Information Society Directive are not compatible with those of the Recommendation on digitisation and accessibility of material.

4. Building Digital Commons through Open Access Management of Copyright-related Rights

Giuseppe Mazziotti

Without the intermediation of performers and producers of audio and video recordings, a huge stock of creative works which have entered the public domain after the expiration of the copyright protection term will never become available to the public in digital formats as a free resource. This chapter identifies such "free resources" as "commons"; they are a resource which anyone within the relevant community has a right to access without having to obtain anyone else's permission.[1] There are types of creative works (for example, musical works or theatrical plays) whose effective dedication to the public domain for the benefit of the public at large would never reach the full status of commons if digitized performances of these works were not disseminated under open access licences. The term "open access" indicates different initiatives, ranging from "open source" to "commons" that have flourished following the creation of open-source software, and which have spread beyond the world of software.[2] These commons-based initiatives share the objective of guaranteeing the

---

1 Lawrence Lessig, *The Future of Ideas: The Fate of the Commons in a Connected World* (New York: Vintage, 2002), pp. 19–20.
2 Séverine Dusollier, "Sharing Access to Intellectual Property through Private Ordering", *Chicago Kent Law Review*, 82 (2007), 1391–1435 (pp. 1396–97).

openness of certain resources whose access and use would be automatically restricted under copyright law.

From this perspective, digital resources embodying public domain works such as a Bach suite, a Brahms symphony or a Shakespeare play would never become a commons for the public at large if music and theatre performers and/or recording producers did not release their performances and recordings under open access licences. In short, the basic assumption of this chapter is that performers' and producers' open access management of their copyright-related rights in the digital environment enables the public enjoyment of creative works and gives an essential contribution to the building of digital commons.

We will begin by considering how the use of open access licences for recordings and other forms of digital performances protected by rights related to copyright has a legal impact on the notion of digital commons. By giving a few examples of digital platforms which make use of open access licences for the dissemination of music performances we will show that, as European copyright law stands, the most evident and fruitful use of open access licences for the building of digital commons regards the category of old works whose copyright protection is expired and whose copying, dissemination and, possibly, reuse has been preventively authorized on the grounds of an open access licence. Finally this contribution demonstrates that public bodies and other entities that intend to institutionally pursue the policy objective of maximising the dissemination of creative works through the building of freely accessible platforms and repositories of digital commons should promote the implementation of open access licences by holders of copyright-related rights. These rights-holders may be given an incentive (even an economic incentive) to make their creations available to the public for purposes other than those of making an immediate profit from the licensing of digitized items.

1. Legal effects of open access management of rights related to copyright

In legal terms, like author's copyright, rights related to copyright or "neighbouring" rights (according to the traditional lexicon of international conventions in this field) establish exclusive rights which have the effect of restricting any unauthorized use, communication and modification of audio and audiovisual performances and recordings of unprotected works or works whose term of copyright protection has expired. In the digital world, the extension of the copyright scope to the mere use of these works,[3] which stems from the enforcement of a very broad exclusive right of digital reproduction, concerns the rights of the authors as well as the rights of performers, recording producers and broadcasters.[4] The rationale for the legal protection of the type of creativity and economic investment which characterise acts of performance, recording and broadcasting of creative works is very similar to that of copyright, from both an economic and moral point of view. According to the basic economics of intellectual property, performances, recordings and broadcasts are non-excludable and non-rival goods (i.e. "public goods") that are very costly to produce but very cheap to copy and reuse. To avoid underproduction of these goods, a suitable copyright system should seek to foster cultural innovation by providing an incentive (or reward) to performers, recording producers and broadcasters. In addition to that, there is also a moral argument which underlies the protection of performances in all those jurisdictions (mainly civil law jurisdictions) where performers' rights include moral prerogatives which seek to protect the reputation of performers against prejudicial uses which might call into question their paternity or affect the integrity of their performances.[5]

In European copyright systems, the enforcement of neighbouring rights depends on the enforcement of the author's rights, in such a way that each act of performance, recording and broadcasting of a work protected by copyright shall be authorized by the copyright owner in order to be lawful.[6] Before the adoption of Directive 2011/77, the most significant distinction between the exclusive rights of authors and those of performers and record producers was made, at least in the copyright laws of the European Union, by their respective terms of duration: 70 years

---

3   See Séverine Dusollier, "Technology as an Imperative for Regulating Copyright: From the Public Exploitation to the Private Use of the Work", *European Intellectual Property Review*, 27 (2005), 201–04 (p. 201).

4   See articles 1(1), 2, 3(2) of Directive 2001/29 on the harmonisation of certain aspects of copyright and related rights in the information society, OJ L167/10, 22 June 2001.

5   See for instance articles 81 and 83 of the Italian Copyright Act, i.e. Act n. 633/1941 and later amendments.

6   See article 12 of Directive 2006/115 on the rental right and lending right and on certain rights related to copyright in the field of intellectual property (codified version), OJ L 376/28, 27 December 2006 ("Relation between copyright and related rights"): "Protection of copyright-related rights under this Directive shall leave intact and shall in no way affect the protection of copyright".

post mortem autoris for copyright[7] and 50 years lasting from the date of lawful publication or communication to the public of a performance, recording or broadcast for rights related to copyright.[8] As a result of the entry into force of Directive 2011/77, EU law establishes now a further distinction in the field of neighbouring rights. Through an amendment of Directive 2006/116, the term of protection of sound recordings and fixations of performances incorporated into sound recordings was extended from 50 to 70 years from the date of publication or public communication of the recording.[9] The term of protection of broadcasts and fixations of performances otherwise than in sound recordings, instead, remained untouched and is still subject to the previous 50-year term.

In this evolving legislative context, acts of performance, fixation and broadcasting of works which have entered the public domain are automatically protected by neighbouring rights which restrict anyone from lawfully copying, communicating to the public and modifying performances, recordings and broadcasts without the authorisations of the respective rights-holders. This principle entails that creative works in the public domain would never become effectively available to the public at large as "commons" insofar as these legally unprotected pieces of work were embodied by performers, phonogram producers and broadcasters exclusively into tangible and intangible performances released under copyright terms which merely aim to exploit commercially the above-mentioned rights.

If European law- and policy-makers wish to act seriously and effectively for the sake of cultural enrichment of society and for the pursuit of innovation through the enforcement of exclusive rights in sound recordings, they should consider that the economics of digital performance, recording and communication have been evolving very rapidly in the last two decades. Digital technologies and the Internet have changed the way in which performers, recording producers and broadcasters (who have often established themselves even as web-casters) manage their copyright-related rights. Multi-purpose digital technologies which enable acts of recording, editing, storage and dissemination of audio, video and

---

7   See article 1 of Directive 2006/116 of 12 December 2006 on the term of protection of copyright and certain related, OJ L 372/12, 27 December 2006.

8   See article 3 of Directive 2006/116, as amended by article 1(2) of Directive 2011/77 of 27 September 2011 amending Directive 2006/116/EC on the term of protection of copyright and certain related rights, OJ L 265/1, 11 October 2011.

9   See article 1(2), lett. a) and b), of Directive 2011/77.

audiovisual works allow these categories of right-holders to produce and release their creations in a way that is much cheaper than it has been at any other time.[10] Due to the cheap character of digital production and communication techniques, today's holders of copyright-related rights, when releasing their creative works to the public in digital settings, do not seek necessarily to recover the reduced costs of performance, recording and dissemination. These categories of right-holders might increasingly consider a higher exposure on the Internet as more beneficial to their subsequent business opportunities than an immediate monetization of all exclusive rights created automatically by copyright law on their digital items. New open access licensing practices, which have developed considerably in the last years due to the spread of such legal standards as Creative Commons, have mostly attracted emerging performers, virtual recording labels and web-casters. In the case of works where no actual author right exists, these licences have the potential to increase significantly the stock of public domain works (for instance, most of the classical music repertoire) which are performed, recorded and embodied into digital items and made available to the public for free. In this situation, the contractual technique of open access management, while seeking to remove most legal restrictions created by copyright-related rights to the free use and dissemination of digital performances of public domain works, may have a crucial role for the building of digital commons. To enable this function and to achieve the policy objective of the highest dissemination of unprotected works, open access licences such as Creative Commons shall be deemed to be applicable to the management of neighbouring rights in the same way as they apply to the management of copyright.

2. How open access licences complement the notion of digital commons: Creative Commons

At least in civil law (*droit d'auteur*) systems, newly created works are granted copyright protection by default and enter the public domain only after expiration of the protection term of 70 years *post mortem autoris*. Unlike US law, *droit d'auteur* systems which conceive authors' rights as non-waivable *personality* rights do not seem to endorse and confer contractual validity upon

---

10 Giuseppe Mazziotti, *EU Digital Copyright Law and the End-user* (Berlin: Springer, 2008), pp. 3–4.

copyright licences which aim at making new works available in the public domain immediately, through a relinquishment in perpetuity of all present and future rights under copyright law by the author. This means that, in most European copyright systems, the so-called "Public Dedication License" inserted by the US Creative Commons project into its web-based system of licence selection could not be used validly by copyright holders to opt for such a relinquishment in perpetuity.[11] In most European legal systems, the open access management of copyright cannot achieve the result of expanding the legal scope of the public domain through the relinquishment of new works. In those systems where copyright law grants non-waivable author rights, this sort of relinquishment through the adoption of a purely contractual mechanism could never have *erga omnes* effects. At best, the effects of this dedication could be limited to the legal sphere of the sole parties involved in the transaction and would never address the public at large directly.

Considering that in *droit d'auteur* jurisdictions open access initiatives do not have the potential to add new pieces of work to the public domain, it seems evident that the most fruitful use of such licences for the purpose of building digital commons may concern mostly "old" creative works which have already entered the public domain. This can be the case for digital performances and recordings of classical music (up until the works of Debussy and Ravel) whose legal subjection to the enforcement of copyright-related rights has been preventively avoided through the adoption of an open access licence by performers and/or record producers.

As explained in the literature,[12] the fact that the most popular and adopted open access licences, Creative Commons, have been developed in the US in the context of the US copyright system has called into question the same applicability of these licences to the case of management of sole copyright-related rights. This uncertainty has been aroused by the fact that, so far, in the original texts of CC licences and in their translations and adaptations to other jurisdictions, no reference was made to the management of rights related to copyright. After careful examination of these licences, it is easy to understand that this lack of reference should not mean that CC licensing standards are not applicable to the management of these rights.[13]

---

11 See http://creativecommons.org/licenses/publicdomain.

12 Glorioso, Andrea and Giuseppe Mazziotti, "Alcune riflessioni sulle licenze Creative Commons e i diritti connessi degli artisti interpreti ed esecutori, dei produttori di fonogrammi e degli organismi di radiodiffusione televisiva", Il Diritto d'Autore, 79 (2008), 133-63 (pp. 148–50).

13 Ibid., pp. 158–60.

CC licences have been shaped initially on the grounds of a copyright system—the US Copyright Act—which has provided performers with a separate copyright on sound recordings as of 1972.[14] This separate kind of copyright on sound recordings establishes for the benefit of performers the same rights granted to the performer under European copyright laws, except for the rights of public performance and broadcasting.

This gap between US and European copyright laws in the scope of protection of sound recordings was partially filled by the adoption of the Digital Performance Rights in Sound Recording Act of 1995, which granted rights-holders on sound recordings a right to remuneration for the (sole) digital non-interactive communication (i.e. webcasting) of their recordings to be administered under a complex compulsory licence scheme.[15] The necessary inclusion of the management of rights related to copyright such as performer rights in the text of the CC licences was recently upheld by the express extension of the notion of "work" under the "unported" 3.0 version of these licenses to "performances", "broadcasts" and "phonograms".[16] Whereas these items are eligible for copyright protection under US law, European copyright laws protect them through "rights related to copyright". This suggests that, in transposing open access licences which have developed from US law into European jurisdictions (as happened within the CC initiative), the wording of these licences should be preferably adapted by extending explicitly the notion of manageable rights to the realm of what European laws define as copyright-related (or neighbouring) rights.

Two examples show how well the enforcement of open access licences works on the Internet. The first involves Magnatune's digital platform,[17] which stores, transmits for free and sells digital recordings belonging to a great variety of music genres. It includes music downloads embodying works in the public domain (for example, medieval, baroque and symphonic music) performed by artists and recorded by producers who are associated with the platform deviser. All legally protected content made available for free through the Magnatune platform is released under a CC licence which aims to make it clear to the website users that the

---

14 *Intellectual Property in the New Technological Age*, ed. by Robert P. Merges, Mark A. Lemley and Peter S. Menell, 3rd edition (New York: Aspen, 2003), p. 371.
15 See US Copyright Act, Sections 106 and 114, in particular Sect. 114(d).
16 See http://creativecommons.org/licenses/by-nc-nd/3.0.
17 See http://www.magnatune.com.

release for free of certain pieces of content does not necessarily entail a waiver of all exclusive rights covering those pieces of content.[18] The CC licence indicates to users that "some rights" are kept "reserved" by the respective licensors. Magnatune combines this informational purpose with the insertion of a technological protection measure which consists of a (not easily removable) vocal tag providing a reference to the CC licence applicable to the use of each specific item. From a business-related point of view, the main objective of the Magnatune platform is that of making certain uses of its content freely available under CC in order to increase the reputation and appeal of its material. This then encourage Magnatune's users to buy tangible and intangible goods embodying those performances (for example CDs and music downloads); it also enables subsequent uses such as the synchronisation of performances in timed-relation with a moving image (so-called "synching"). A second example is given by Musikethos, which is a digital platform devised and managed by a non-profit association of classical and jazz performers who use mainly recordings of their live performances of public domain works (for example, ancient music and chamber music pieces) in order to foster not only the management of commercial uses not comprised in the CC licence but also the booking of live performances by agents, concert societies and other cultural institutions.[19]

These examples show that the application of flexible open access licences to digital recordings enables the pursuit of objectives which go beyond mere solidarity in order to encompass the creation of new and promising business opportunities for performers and producers. These examples also show that the creation of such business opportunities by performers and producers adopting open access licenses for the release of their digital performances generates what economists call a "positive externality", namely, a self-interested decision by these actors which spills over to parties other than those who explicitly engage in the decision. In these examples, performers and recording producers are not the only ones who capture the benefits of their business decisions to opt for an open access management of their respective rights. The public at large is given the opportunity to freely enjoy performances of creative works that, notwithstanding their legally unprotected status, would not constitute digital commons. In the absence of a "commons-based" release of their performances, musical

---

18 See http://www.magnatune.com/info/licensing.

19 http://www.musikethos.org/wiki/me.php/Main/Copyright.

works by great composers from the past could be enjoyed as commons either "on paper" (by the few people who are capable of reading music sheets) or through the purchase of recordings marketed in a traditional way for merely commercial reasons. For sound recordings to enter the public domain under EU copyright law and become digital commons without the support of commons-based releases, the public should now wait 70 years from their date of lawful publication or communication to the public.

3. Public policy suggestions for maximising the dissemination of creative works in the public domain

The examples given in Section 2 demonstrate that open access initiatives have been carried out with beneficial effects for society by private entities. A company establishing a virtual label and a non-profit association of musicians have both successfully opted for these licensing methods in order to pursue their own business model or their foundational mission. In my view, due to their peculiar characteristics, these licensing models for the dissemination and use of digital recordings should not be developed only by private parties. The most significant beneficial effects for society may come from the adoption of these models by impulse of public bodies that, among their policy objectives, may have that of institutionally pursuing the maximisation of creative works disseminated through the building and operation of freely accessible platforms and repositories of digital commons. Copyright legislators and administrative bodies such as national ministries of culture and the European Commission (EC) have recently endorsed and fostered initiatives which aimed at creating, by expenditure of public funds, digital spaces where right-holders wishing to waive their exclusive rights could make their creations available to the general public under open access conditions.

The objective of building virtual spaces hosting digital commons was expressly embodied into the Third Additional Provision of Spanish Act N. 23/2006 of 8 July 2006 which transposed the EU Copyright Directive of 2001 into the Spanish legal system. This provision, entitled "Promotion of digital works dissemination", encouraged the government to invest in the development of spaces of public utility where freely accessible materials, including works which have entered the public domain and works released under open access licences, may be stored and accessed by everyone through digital media.[20] Another useful example is given by the project undertaken by the Italian Ministry of Culture entitled "Italian Digital Library", which is designed to subsidise the digitisation of wide collections of ancient books, historical reviews and music sheets coming from some of the most prestigious Italian libraries and music academies, and to publish them on a freely accessible digital repository. Moreover, it is to be stressed that the EU recently undertook initiatives such as the Recommendation 2006/585/EC on the digitisation and online accessibility of cultural material and digital preservation.[21] This act of the EU recommends that, in full respect of copyright law, EU Member States encourage, develop and sponsor the digitisation and online accessibility of cultural materials such as books, journals, newspapers, photographs, museum objects, archival documents and audiovisual materials and create overviews of such digitisation in order to prevent duplication of efforts and promote collaboration and synergies at the European level. In addition to that, it is highly significant that the European Research Council—a European funding body, accountable to the EU, which was set up to support investigator-driven frontier research—issued a document which encouraged interested parties to reduce the current six-month gap between the time that research projects subsidised by the Council are published in subscription-only scientific journals and the time of their open access release on free web-based repositories.[22]

All these kinds of publicly-funded initiatives aimed at fostering the implementation of open access licences and building freely accessible archives of digital commons could be usefully developed with regard to freely accessible repositories of audio and audiovisual performances. The adoption of open access management of copyright-related rights on recordings which embody creative works in the public domain enables their immediate and legitimate incorporation into such repositories. If, for instance, educational institutions such as music academies and acting schools subsidised by public bodies were obliged or given an incentive to embrace these licensing models for the release of their most significant performances, this would have highly beneficial effects for the cultural enrichment of society. From an economic point of view, it would make sense

---

20 See Mazziotti (2008), p. 245.
21 See Commission Recommendation 2006/585/EC of 24 August 2006 on the digitisation and online accessibility of cultural material and digital preservation, OJ L 236, 31 August 2006, p. 28.
22 See ERC Scientific Council Guidelines for Open Access, 17 December 2007.

to publicly subsidise these institutions not only for the pursuit of their primary purpose of training the performers of tomorrow, but also for the development of open archives designed to host high quality recordings. The latter activity would add very little costs to those implied by the former and would be abundantly compensated by the benefits for the general public.

This chapter has shown briefly that the open access management of copyright-related rights in the digital environment may have highly beneficial effects for the building of digital commons. Removing legal obstacles to the free dissemination and use of digital recordings enables the enjoyment of creative works which have entered the public domain by the public at large. Private companies and associations that have opted for these licensing methods in order to pursue their own business models or their foundational mission have in turn benefited society. These licensing models should not be developed only by private parties: the most significant beneficial effects for society may come from the adoption of these models by public bodies (for example, national ministries of culture) that may wish to maximise the dissemination of creative works through the building of freely accessible platforms and repositories of digital commons. This objective could be usefully developed by obliging or giving performing arts institutions an incentive to embrace licensing models for the digital release and archiving of high-quality audiovisual and audio recordings of their most significant productions.

III. Developments and Case Studies

5. Contractually-constructed Research Commons: A Critical Economic Appraisal

Enrico Bertacchini

This chapter surveys the main economic issues concerning the emergence of contractually-constructed research commons, with a particular attention to the field of biological/genetic resources and biotechnologies. In the last decade there has been a growing and high-pitched debate about the expansion of exclusionary and proprietary strategies (intellectual property rights and *sui generis* regimes, restrictive licensing, etc) for the appropriation of the value of knowledge and information resources. The main point of contention has centred on the justification for the adoption of these strategies and how actors in this setting manage the production, dissemination and use of knowledge and information.[1] On one hand, the optimists have highlighted the powerful synergies in the coupling of strong rights and contractual freedom, identifying in markets, patent pools and collaborative agreements the mechanisms to efficiently allocate resources to the most productive users. On the other hand, the pessimists contend that the expansion of property rights and exclusionary strategies is likely to delay or deter innovation because of an overall increase in transaction

---

1 See *Expanding the Boundaries of Intellectual Property*, ed. by Rochelle Dreyfuss, Diane L. Zimmerman and Harry First (Oxford: Oxford University Press, 2001).

costs and the emergence of strategic behaviour in the integration of complementary information resources. Further, they see collaborative private arrangements as stifling competition and imposing negative externalities on both consumers and prospective innovators.[2]

With this perspective, the recent developments and initiatives for the implementation of contractually-constructed research commons ask for a reassessment of this debate. These new organisational initiatives seem to provide a balance between the two diverging positions. Crucially, they recognize the benefits that can accrue to innovators from ownership and exclusivity. Nevertheless, these experiences use property rights to go beyond the familiar control of assets that occurs either within organisations, in markets for technologies or among parties of close-knit collaborative agreements. In turn, these experiences elicit a broader cooperative solution in the form of standard contractual regimes that should be adopted and shared by the members of research communities. The final goal is indeed to avoid unnecessary restrictions, to pool resources and to give researches access to the large aggregate that could result from the contributions of all those who adopt such contractual arrangements.

The main research question underlying this chapter is basically the same posed by scholars in the past years when realising the growing trend in the privatisation of scientific and research activities: given the expansion of proprietary and exclusion strategies, are institutions for the transfer of knowledge and information resources emerging or failing?[3] Answering this question is of paramount importance for assessing the viability and sustainability of the research commons initiatives as an alternative institutional framework for coordinating transactions.

If exchanges and transactions are fading, then to what extent are the commons-based forms of knowledge production effective and long-standing solutions to this problem? By contrast, it may be the case that the alleged deadlock in transacting and integrating resources is just a transitory condition, as more actors in the research communities will learn to interact trough market mechanisms or will develop networks of collaborative agreements.

---

2   See Janet Hope, *Biobazaar: The Open Source Revolution and Biotechnology* (Cambridge, MA: Harvard University Press, 2008).

3   See Paul A. David, "Can Open Science Be Protected From the Evolving Regime of IPR Protections?", *Journal of Institutional and Theoretical Economics*, 160 (2004), 9–34; Michael A. Heller, "The Tragedy of the Anticommons: Property in the Transition from Marx to Markets", *Harvard Law Review*, 111 (1998), 621–87; Michael A. Heller and Rebecca S. Eisenberg, "Can Patents Deter Innovation? The Anticommons in Biomedical Research", *Science*, 28 (1998), 698–701.

Arguably, these options put research commons initiatives in a more evolutionary perspective and suggest that different institutional settings may compete and coexist depending on the technological and economic changes as well as on the evolution of agents' beliefs. Further, this option implies that the sustainability of research commons may be affected by agents' adaptive behaviours, collective action and path-dependent dynamics.

In summary, this chapter presents the main economic issues that represent fields of contention among legal and economic scholars when analysing the impact of the expansion of property rights on the access and production of knowledge and information resources. Crucially, the same issues represent the most challenging research paths to deepen our understanding of the prospective viability and success of research commons.

Here we will look at the emergence and rationale of contractually-constructed research commons; we will present the most relevant economic arguments concerning the emergence and sustainability of these organisational forms; finally we will propose an evolutionary perspective that should inspire the design of emerging research commons.

1. Emergence and rationale of contractually-constructed research commons

Contractually-constructed research commons represent emerging institutional forms for the management of knowledge and scientific material. Against the alleged privatisation pressures that have adversely affected research and innovation activities, these initiatives aim to introduce standard contractual forms, which contemplate non-exclusive use and access to information resources and research inputs that are covered by some forms of exclusive rights.

Contractually-constructed research commons have come out in the last decade in many different fields of scientific production and innovation. For instance, Reichman and Uhlir have been engaged in proposing a contractually-reconstructed commons for scientific data, as a response to enhanced copyright protection and new *sui generis* protection for databases.[4] As for genetic resources for food and agriculture, in 2001 states signed the FAO International Treaty on Plant Genetic Resources

---

4   Jerome H. Reichman and Paul F. Uhlir, "A Contractually Reconstructed Research Commons for Scientific Data in a Highly Protectionist Intellectual Property Environment", *Law and Contemporary Problems*, 66 (2003), 315-462.

for Food and Agriculture (ITPGRFA), which devises a multilateral system of facilitated exchange for germplasm. Within this framework, the contracting parties mutually recognize sovereignty rights over their respective genetic resources, as established by the Convention on Biological Diversity (CBD), but use those sovereignty rights to pool the crop genetic resources held in their national collections for agricultural innovation and crop development.[5] A similar movement is also occurring in the microbial research community, where an integrated research commons has been proposed in order to guarantee access to microbial materials, data and knowledge, in the form of scientific publications.[6] Finally, another initiative that is worth mentioning in biotechnology is that undertaken by CAMBIA, a non profit research institute that has since pioneered the use of open-source-like licensing of research tools and enabling technologies.[7]

All these experiences, although different in their nature and scope, unveil a common narrative account that is useful to summarize for understanding the emergence and rationale behind contractually-constructed research commons. Almost all the proposals and initiatives start recognising the great economic and technological changes that have significantly transformed the scientific research landscape. These changes have improved the ways to produce and distribute knowledge and information resources, but at same time have drawn the agents' expectations in capturing and controlling the value of their research assets. The recent evolution of digital technology and knowledge base has created greater opportunities for the integration of different types of knowledge in networked environments and complementarity between increased computational power and greater scientific understanding.

However, the boundaries between basic and applied research have increasingly blurred, especially in those fields of science that refer to the "Pasteur's Quadrant".[8] Being characterized by the achievement of practical objectives, research outputs in these sectors are the most susceptible to

---

5   Lawrence R. Helfer, "Using Intellectual Property Rights to Preserve the Global Genetic Commons: The International Treaty on Plant Genetic Resources for Food and Agriculture", in *International Public Goods and Transfer of Technology Under a Globalized Intellectual Property Regime*, ed. by Jerome H. Reichman and Keith E. Maskus (Cambridge: Cambridge University Press, 2005), pp. 217–24.

6   Tom Dedeurwaerdere and Peter Dawyndt, "Exploring and Exploiting Microbiological Commons: Contributions of Bioinformatics and Intellectual Property Rights in Sharing Biological Information", workshop paper (Brussels, 2005), available at http://biogov. cpdr.ucl.ac.be/bioinf/document.pdf.

7   See Hope (2008).

8   Donald E. Stokes, *Pasteur's Quadrant: Basic Science and Technological Innovation* (Washington, DC: Brookings, 1996).

commercial exploitation and economic return. Further, as technical routines that represent valuable know-how have been increasingly incorporated on or near the face of research tools and materials, subsequent innovators could duplicate without incurring the time and costs of reverse-engineering.[9]

As a result, although there are greater opportunities for the exchange and integration of knowledge, there has been a growing trend towards building up barriers to the access and use of information resources with the objective to appropriate the value of research outputs. The expansion of intellectual property rights, the creation of *sui generis* regimes and the adoption of restrictive licensing strategies are common institutional responses that have proliferated in almost all the fields of knowledge production.[10] In addition, because of the highly diversified environment of R&D, characterized by great heterogeneity of players in the public and private sector, the enclosure movement has followed a "domino effect". The privatisation pressure that has been initially supported by some players internal to the system has created a shifting balance in favour of proprietary interests. This has eventually led to defensive reactions by other players, who conform to the changes in the legal framework by adopting exclusionary strategies against the erosion of open access models.

While the adoption of exclusionary and proprietary strategies is usually justified with the objective to appropriate the value of research and to enhance a market-based allocation of research inputs,[11] this move has been perceived to generate unintended consequences and to engender negative effects to the flow of resources in R&D activities. Many commentators have highlighted the risk that the new institutional settings may stifle scientific production and innovation because of the increase in transaction costs, the erosion of norms of science in the dissemination of knowledge or the emergence of strategic behaviour in the integration of complementary information resources. These concerns have found a powerful metaphor in the tragedy of anti-commons.[12] Further, the new scenario tends to have a

---

9   Jerome H. Reichman, "Of Green Tulips and Legal Kudzu: Repackaging Rights in Subpatentable Innovation", *Vanderbilt Law Review*, 53 (2000), 1743–98.

10 See Heller and Eisenberg (1998).

11 Robert P. Merges, "Intellectual Property and the Costs of Commercial Exchange: A Review Essay", *Michigan Law Review*, 93 (1995), 1570–1615; Ashish Arora, Andrea Fosfuri and Alfonso Gambardella, *Markets for Technology: The Economics of Innovation and Corporate Technology* (Cambridge, MA: MIT Press, 2004); and Henry E. Smith, "Intellectual Property as Property: Delineating Entitlements in Information", *Yale Law Journal*, 116 (2007), 1742-1822.

12 See Heller (1998); and Heller and Eisenberg (1998).

dual equilibrium.[13] On one hand, there exists a formal system of exchange of information resources where, albeit with increasingly restrictive conditions, the highest value transactions take place. On the other hand, there is growing evidence of an informal system where lower value and routine transactions take place without entering into any formal legal undertakings. This system, based on the ties of a close-knit research community, is less restrictive but nevertheless creates club goods closed to distrusted parties and generates potential negative externalities on the quality control of the resources exchanged in cumulative research.[14]

With this perspective, it is because of the concerns for unintended consequences and drawbacks that contractually reconstructed research commons have been proposed. Crucially, the rationale behind such new approaches is twofold. First, coping with the new proprietary framework, research commons envisage new institutional arrangements such as compensatory liability regimes or standardized agreements that contractually regulate the relations between all the participating research communities and their members. Secondly, research commons aim to reconstruct a pre-competitive environment, which has been eroded by the defensive attitude and strategic behaviour adopted by different players in the research community.

2. Economic arguments for and against emerging research commons

Although the narrative account used to justify contractually based research commons seems to provide meaningful arguments, the attitude for their adoption is hardly shared in the policy and academic debate. For this reason, understanding whether contractually based research commons are viable solutions for the management of knowledge production is an empirical and theoretical question of considerable complexity. In this context, it is possible to identify three main economic issues that should be analysed in order to understand the strengths and weaknesses of proposed research commons.

---

13   See Reichman and Uhlir (2003).
14   Jeffrey L. Furman and Scott Stern, "Climbing Atop the Shoulders of Giants: The Impact of Institutions on Cumulative Research", NBER working paper 12523 (National Bureau of Economic Research, 2006).

2.1 Transaction costs and the quest for the anti-commons tragedy

The issue of increasing transaction costs and the reality or absence of an anti-commons tragedy may be deemed as the primary economic field of contention among detractors and supporters for contractually-constructed research commons. An anti-commons tragedy is caused when multiple owners each have the right to exclude others from a scarce resource, leading to under-utilisation due to the lack of coordination among the various rights holders.[15] The metaphor of the anti-commons tragedy has been promptly ported in the intellectual property debate by Heller and Eisenberg.[16] In their much-cited paper, the authors use the anti-commons image to highlight the concern for the emerging proliferation of concurrent fragments of intellectual property rights or the restricted access to upstream discoveries due to stacking licenses strategies. Likewise, David identifies three analytically distinct layers of the anti-commons tragedy, namely, search costs, negotiation costs and multiple-marginalization costs.[17] While the first two types of costs are clearly incurred before any deal can be concluded, costs derived from multiple marginalization result in inefficiency by raising the price of complementary research assets.

Increased transaction costs are therefore one of the key ingredients for explaining the troubles arising from the proliferation and strengthening of exclusive rights, but this is not enough by itself to bring about an anti-commons tragedy. Even in the presence of proliferating exclusive rights, the anti-commons tragedy may be avoided, provided transaction costs can be kept low by intermediaries, infrastructures and institutional mechanisms other than the proposed research commons.[18] In addition, even royalty stacking by multiple owners highlighted in the multiple-marginalization problem may be less severe than expected.

As a result, evidence of an anti-commons tragedy in all its forms may be a hint in favour of the proposal of a contractually based research commons. Unfortunately, the scarce empirical evidence addressing this subject does

---

15 See Heller (1998).
16 See Heller and Eisenberg (1998).
17 Paul A. David, "New Moves in 'Legal Jujitsu' to Combat the Anticommons: Mitigating IPR Constraints on Innovation by a 'Bottom-up' Approach to Systemic Institutional Reform", paper presented at the first Communia conference, Louvain-la-Neuve, Belgium (30 June 2008).
18 See Hope (2008).

not bear a clear conclusion on whether a tragedy of anti-commons has occurred in any given field of research and innovation activity. For instance, looking at interaction between patent grants and diffusion of knowledge through scientific publications on 169 discoveries, Murray and Stern show that the granting of intellectual property rights is associated with a significant but modest decline in knowledge accumulation as measured by forward citations.[19] More interestingly, two recent works have collected several findings about agents' perceptions and practices in the biomedical research community for exchanging research tools and materials.[20] While almost all the respondents to the surveys reported that the institutional landscape has become more complex due to privatisation pressures, the results provide little empirical basis for claims that restricted access to intellectual property is currently impeding biomedical research. In turn, only for access to tangible research materials and data, the authors find an increasing non-compliance with transfer requests. Crucially, it is important to notice that the actors in private firms, universities and non-profit institutions reported to have adopted different strategies and "working solutions" to cope with the frictions generated by property rights proliferation. These include inventing around blocking patents, going offshore, infringement under an informal research exemption, mutual non-enforcement and cross-licensing agreements.

The perception that emerges from this preliminary evidence is that the quest for anti-commons tragedies is hard for many reasons. First, in technology and innovation systems it is inherently difficult to conduct rigorous studies either of bargaining breakdown or of research projects abandonment and delays. Secondly, from a social welfare perspective, Walsh et al. point out that it is equally hard to assess whether the redirection of a scientist's research effort or reallocation across investigators significantly reduces the chance of scientific progress or does favour a greater variety of projects.[21] Thirdly, while the theoretical models explaining the anti-commons tragedy often rely on static efficiency, it is difficult to

---

19   Fiona Murray and Scott Stern, "Do Formal Intellectual Property Rights Hinder the Free Flow of Scientific Knowledge?: An Empirical Test of the Anticommons Hypothesis", NBER working paper 1146 (National Bureau of Economic Research, 2005).

20   John P. Walsh, Ashish Arora and Wesley M. Cohen, "Effects of Research Tool Patents and Licensing on Biomedical Innovation", in *Patents in the Knowledge-Based Economy*, ed. by Wesley M. Cohen and Stephen A. Merrill (Washington, DC: National Academies Press, 2003), pp. 285–340; and John P. Walsh, Charlene Cho and Wesley M. Cohen, "View from the Bench: Patents and Material Transfers", *Science*, 309 (2005), 2002–03.

21   See Walsh et al. (2005).

capture the social cost implied by this tragedy in a dynamic and evolving world where agents adapt their strategies.[22]

Notwithstanding these obstacles to the inquiry, the absence of clear evidence does not necessarily lead to evidence of the absence of potential anti-commons tragedies. Indeed, the arguments carried out by the critics of the anti-commons tragedy in the field of research and innovation are equally hard to be proven.[23] For instance, the up-growing trend experienced in knowledge intensive industries for many key variables of research activities and outputs (i.e. R&D spending, capital investments and number of research projects) is used as refuting evidence for anti-commons tragedy. However, these variables may increase because the marginal benefits from investing (the discounted values of future returns) can still be higher than the actual marginal costs incurred by the new frictions of anti-commons dynamics. Likewise, increase in R&D spending may be caused by greater research efforts in order to overcome the increasing difficulty in doing research.

2.2 Network governance structure: exclusion and strong ties vs. sharing and weak ties

The second layer of economic issues addresses governance structures for the management of information resources and technological innovation: how emerging research commons could perform in integrating knowledge and information resources as compared to other alternative structures. Knowledge is a very complex economic resource, whose nature poses several problems for its management. Both the natural uncertainty associated with innovation and the extent to which knowledge can be tacit, articulated or codified can substantially affect the division of innovative labour as well as the efficiency in exchanging the resource or appropriating its value.[24]

---

22 Armen A. Alchian, "Uncertainty, Evolution and Economic Theory", *Journal of Political Economy*, 58 (1950), 211–21.

23 See Ted Buckley, "The Myth of the Anticommons" (Biotechnology Industry Organization, 2007); and Richard A. Epstein and Bruce N. Kuhlik, "Is there a Biomedical Anticommons?", *Regulation*, 27 (2004), 54–58.

24 See Kenneth J. Arrow, "Economic Welfare and the Allocation of Resources for Inventions", in *The Rate and Direction of Inventive Activity: Economic and Social Factors*, ed. by Richard R. Nelson (Princeton: Princeton University Press, 1962), pp. 609–26; David J. Teece, "Technological Change and the Nature of the Firm", in *Technical Change and Economic Theory*, ed. by G. Dosi, C. Freeman, R. Nelson, G. Solverberg and L. Soete (London: Printer Publishers, 1998), pp. 242–61; and Sidney G. Winter, "Knowledge and Competence as Strategic Assets", in *The Competitive Challenge: Strategies for Industrial Innovation and Renewal*, ed. by David J. Teece (Cambridge, MA: Ballinger, 1987), pp. 159–84.

With this perspective, in the last two decades the literature has increasingly acknowledged networks and similar forms of collaborative ties as a governance structure distinct from market and firms. Dense networks of relational contracting occur in sectors where the organisation of the innovation process is complex, resources are variable and the environment uncertain.[25] According to Powell, networks are the highest performing systems, as compared to markets and hierarchical organisations, because they create incentives for learning and the dissemination of information, especially when dealing with intangible assets such as tacit knowledge and technological innovation.[26] Networks perfectly fit the transaction dynamics occurring in research communities, mainly because participants share a common background and possess fungible knowledge that is not limited to a specific task but applicable to a wide range of activities. Further, the advances in digital technology have enhanced the opportunity for interacting and exchanging information resources in a network-like form.

However, the dual equilibrium dynamics caused by privatization pressures seem to have generated two different forms of networks. On one hand, networks among firms and universities are observable in the formal zone of regulated access, where research and technological collaborations are a well-documented phenomenon. This form of collaborative ties depends on exclusive rights and business models that use exclusion to appropriate the value of research outputs. In this case, the players in the formal zone often use knowledge protected by intellectual property rights as a bargaining chip for long-term research cooperation. On the other hand, the dark zone of informal exchange of data, materials and research tools aims to circumvent the limitations of restrictive access imposed by privatization pressures. This system generates an informal networked commons, particularly suited for routine low-value transactions. However, this system tends to be closed as it is based on direct reciprocity, strong ties and long-term collaborative relationships among the members of the research community. While this may be an effective system in exchanging resources for the parties involved, it may increase search costs and costs of mistakes in cumulative research.

---

25   Walter W. Powell, "Neither Market Nor Hierarchy: Network Forms of Organization", *Research in Organizational Behavior*, 12 (1990), 295–336; Mark Granovetter, "Coase Revisited: Business Groups in the Modern Economy", *Industrial and Corporate Change*, 4 (1995), 93–130; Merges (1995); and *Technological Collaboration: The Dynamics of Cooperation in Industrial Innovation*, ed. by Rob Coombs, Albert Richards, Pier Paolo Saviotti and Vivien Walsh (Cheltenam: Edward Elgar, 1996).

26   See Powell (1990).

The analysis of the formal and informal system of exchange highlights how knowledge dissemination and integration in networked environments is still based on exclusionary strategies and strong ties. In the long term, this may create high entry barriers to prospective innovators and researchers or hinder the collective good of shared quality standards that favour cumulative research. In turn, effective and facilitated access to research tools, guaranteed materials and knowledge allows for the comparison of results, validation and replication of scientific findings. Then the question is how the existent governance structure in a networked environment could mitigate these problems?

Recent contributions looking at open source models of information production and exchange have highlighted new emerging conditions for distributing and integrating knowledge in a more open and weakly tied network organisation. Arguably, this line of inquiry is particularly relevant to sustain the design of contractually based research commons. As noted by Benkler, advances in digital technology and knowledge base is favouring a "commons based peer production" model for managing and disseminating knowledge.[27] This organisational model is based on sharing resources and outputs among widely distributed, loosely connected individuals who cooperate with each other within a decentralized, collaborative and non-proprietary framework. The basic conditions which make commons-based production economic viable are similar to those identified for the emergence of relational networks, namely, when the productive process is characterized by high uncertainty, there is the need for exchange information that price signals or hierarchical mechanisms cannot provide, and when capital (i.e. human capital, creativity or fungible knowledge) is highly variable and diffused across the agents.[28] However, the crucial difference between commons-based peer production and relational networks lies in the fact that this new form of governance structure is based on non-exclusionary strategies and weak tied network relationships. For instance, in commons-based peer production models the productive activity is coordinated by open source-like standard contractual regimes that allow for the dissemination of information resources to any would-be user. Further, commons-based peer production does not presuppose any strong ties between

---

27   Yochai Benkler, *The Wealth of Networks: How Social Production Transforms Markets and Freedom* (New Haven: Yale University Press, 2006).

28   See Powell (1990).

agents. Crucially, the information resources—which are continuously shared, modified and improved by the users—are the real channel for communication between agents.[29] Considering that innovation and learning are the two faces of R&D activity,[30] exclusion and strong ties are institutional mechanisms that mainly favour agents' appropriation of innovation and research output. By contrast, sharing resources in a commons-based peer production model enhances positive network externalities in cumulative research and favours learning effects among agents in the network.

Finally, it is also noted that the incentives for participating in commons-based peer production may diverge from the standard economic benefits of producing information in familiar governance structures. In this context, a set of indirect benefits and social rewards have been highlighted as the main factors for motivation. Indirect benefits, like hedonic gains or peer-reputation may improve rather than reduce people performance.[31] With regard to social incentives, psychological and anthropological literature stresses that the weight a community puts on social and economic rewards is a function of the cultural values associated with the actions.[32] Economic factors are not the unique forces to determine benefits and costs of actions. On the contrary, social norms contribute in shaping different costs and benefits for individual transactions. As a result, organisation of activities in different contexts of social norms may not follow the same economic and social set of incentives.

2.3 Institutional change and mechanisms of expectations formation

A rather overlooked economic factor that can be of interest for understanding the effectiveness and future sustainability of emerging research commons is the mechanisms that led to the expansion of property

---

29   See Benoît Demil and Xavier Lecocq, "Neither Market nor Hierarchy nor Network: The Emergence of Bazaar Governance", *Organization Studies*, 27 (2006), 1447–66; and Hope (2008).

30   R. R. Nelson, "Innovation and Learning: The Two Faces of R&D", *The Economic Journal*, 99 (1989), 569–96.

31   Josh Lerner and Jean Tirole, "Some Simple Economics of Open Source", *Journal of Industrial Economics*, 50 (2002), 197–234.

32   For example, *Property Relations: Renewing the Anthropological Tradition*, ed. by C. M. Hann (Cambridge: Cambridge University Press, 1998); and Ernst Fehr and Armin Falk, "Psychological Foundations of Incentives", *European Economic Review*, 46 (2002), 687–724.

rights and exclusionary strategies by the actors involved in the research community. While many scholars, when dealing with the expanding boundaries of intellectual property rights, have recognized a set of changing norms, incentives and behaviours that increasingly led to the actual setting, it would be interesting to understand why and how this institutional setting has been reached through a self-sustaining system of shared beliefs and expectations.

One promising line of inquiry is to study the evidence of a current detachment between the marginal value of research assets scattered among the many actors of the research communities and the expected high payoff (especially from downstream commercial applications) those holders perceive regarding their own resources.[33] On this matter, the economic literature concerned on the measurement of the value of information resources is far less optimistic about the high value the owners expect to extract from their assets, especially for genetic and biologic resources.[34] The basic idea is that the total value of all the data and material collections put together is clearly high as a source of leads for research output and downstream commercial applications. However, individual agents and organisations in the research community will only consider the value of the marginal resource with respect to its potential use for research and commercial exploitation. In this case, the marginal value is likely to be low. If there is a large number of potential sources, with approximately the same prospect of success and the same testing cost, all the resources are expected to be close substitutes. When numerous substitutes exist, the marginal value and the corresponding price of each will be low.

As a result, it seems that privatization pressures have come out from "cognitive biases" by the players in the research and innovation community. Eisenberg has clearly highlighted this stylized fact in the surveys conducted for the NIH Working Group on Research Tools.[35] What emerge from this survey is that universities and biotechnology

---

33 See Heller and Eisenberg (1998).

34 For example, George Frisvold and Kelly Day-Rubenstein, "Bioprospecting and Biodiversity: What Happens When Discoveries are Made?", *Arizona Law Review*, 50 (2008), 545–76; and R. David Simpson and Roger A. Sedjo, "Valuing Biodiversity for Pharmaceutical Research", *Journal of Political Economy*, 104 (1996), 163–85.

35 Rebecca Eisenberg, "Bargaining Over the Transfer of Proprietary Tools: Is This Market Failing or Emerging?", in *Expanding the Boundaries of Intellectual Property*, ed. by Rochelle Dreyfuss, Diane L. Zimmerman and Harry First (Oxford: Oxford University Press, 2001), pp. 223–49.

firms, which specialize in earlier stage discoveries, have often unrealistic expectations of making money from research tools, albeit if these entities do not share in the full costs and risks of the complex process of drug discovery. At the same time, pharmaceutical firms, which have a broader view on the research pipeline, are less concerned in directly appropriating the value through collecting cash payments or garnering a share of future profits for outgoing research tools and materials. However, they put high value on research input used in the product development phase and for this reason set restrictive conditions to academic laboratories and biotechnology firms because of the fear of losing competitive ground.

The implication for the sustainability and viability of emerging research commons is straightforward. These initiatives provide standard contractual mechanisms that are particularly suited for exchanging research assets still having unknown or likely low payoff as commercial applications. However, identifying resources with unknown or likely low payoff could be very difficult and skewed by the cognitive biases described above. For this reason, the risk is that the same expectations for high value that led to the adoption of restrictive licensing strategy and privatisation pressures could eventually undermine the willingness to adopt contractually based research commons.

With this perspective, initiatives for contractually-constructed research commons have to be seen as institutional arrangements that nevertheless have to interact and compete with the current system of agents beliefs and expectations in order to be adopted. In this context, literature about institutions and institutional change may be useful to highlight specific dynamics such as adaptive behaviour, collective action problems, path dependency and agents' complex feedback mechanisms that can lead to the successful adoption of emerging research commons initiatives.[36] However, this line of inquiry, particularly developed in generalized models or applied in other institutional domains, seems to still lack a wide application as for the "rules of the game" that govern research communities.

---

36 See, for example, Masahiko Aoki, *Toward a Comparative Institutional Analysis* (Cambridge, MA: MIT Press, 2001); and Benjamin Coriat and Giovanni Dosi, "The Institutional Embeddedness of Economic Change: An Appraisal of the 'Evolutionary' and 'Regulationist' Research Programmes", in *Institutions and Economic Change: New Perspectives on Markets, Firms and Technology*, ed. by Klaus Nielsen and Björn Johnson (Cheltenham: Edward Elgar, 1998), pp. 3–32.

3. Concluding remarks: research commons in an evolutionary perspective

This chapter has proposed a critical appraisal of the main economic issues concerning the proposal and design of contractually-constructed research commons. These initiatives represent a step ahead in the debate that characterizes the expansion of exclusionary and proprietary strategies in research and innovation activities. However, the main economic questions that address the necessity and viability of contractually-based research commons are basically the same scholars have posed at the outset of the enclosure movement occurring to science and information resource for the last two decades. In the new scenario of proliferating exclusive rights, are agents learning to use their contractual freedom to put forward research projects and innovation activities? Conversely, are there reasons to fear that transaction costs, strategic behaviour and cognitive biases will stifle the opportunities for exchanging and integrating knowledge?

The three economic arguments presented in this chapter try to respond to these questions and consequently address the necessity and future sustainability of contractually-based research commons. The issue concerning the increased transaction costs and the evidence of an anti-commons tragedy is probably a foundational one. In this context, two main facts emerge. First, although there is evidence of frictions caused by proliferating property rights and exclusionary strategies, agents have already started adopting private arrangements to cope with the new restrictive legal rules. Arguably, these strategies represent alternative institutional solutions that will compete with the initiatives for adoption of contractually-based research commons. Secondly, although there is little evidence of an anti-commons tragedy, the works surveyed clearly show the emergence of an informal research commons based on informal research exemption, mutual non-enforcement or simply transactions taking place without entering into any formal legal undertakings.

This latter point is particularly relevant for justifying contractually-based research commons as a new governance structure in research activities based on a weakly tied network organisation of exchanges. Indeed, the theoretical examination of commons-based peer production models described in the second economic argument points out the benefits for formalising the informal commons through standard contractual regimes. Further, it also highlighted how this new form of governance structure could be effective in promoting the dissemination of knowledge under social sharing mechanisms.

However, this optimism has to find a balance with the third economic issue, which concerns institutional change and mechanism of expectation formation. As noted before, contractually based research commons represent new institutional arrangements that lower the frictions for the exchange of research assets. For this reason, they will have to interact and compete with the other institutional mechanisms developed by agents and that are currently at play for favouring transactions. As the dynamic of institutions and institutional change is deeply rooted in the system of agents' beliefs and expectations, path dependence and collective action dynamics will inevitably affect the adoption and long standing viability of research commons initiatives.

One of the main challenges is therefore to understand whether the increasing adoption of exclusive strategies can be reverted by changing the system of agents' beliefs and expectations that have generated the domino effect towards the enclosure movement. Putting contractually-based research commons in a comprehensive evolutionary perspective suggests that these initiatives are endogenous responses occurring in the complex ecology of research and scientific activity. As a result, imitative dynamics may be relevant even if small groups among the research communities start adopting or constructing contractually-based research commons.

6. Social Motivations and Incentives in Ex Situ Conservation of Microbial Genetic Resources

Tom Dedeurwaerdere, Per M. Stromberg and Unai Pascual

Innovation in life science depends on Public Service Microbial Collections (PSMCs) for facilitating acquisition of and access to existing microbial research materials through a worldwide network of centralised deposit and access services.[1] Microorganisms are critical to maintaining the health of other life forms that depend on them for energy recycling, nutrients and minerals, while conversely, causing infectious disease when they overlap with susceptible hosts.[2]

1   Scott Stern, *Biological Resource Centres: Knowledge Hubs for the Life Sciences* (Washington, DC: Brookings, 2004).
2   The authors are grateful for the fruitful collaboration with Philippe Desmeth (BCCM), Dr. David Smith (WFCC), Lucy Hoareau (MIRCEN) and Julia Hasler (MIRCEN). Special thanks to all collection staff that shared their expertise, especially Dr. Dagmar Fritze (DSMZ), Dr. Francois Bimet (Pasteur), Pierre-Alain Fonteyne (formerly at BCCM-IHEM), Dr. Matthew Ryan (CABI), Dr. Camacho (USCNCMCC), Dr. H. Marie-Daniel (BCCM/MUCL), Prof. R. Mutters (MCCM), F. Van-Hove of the Belgian collection BCCM/MUCL as well as Dr. Alexandre Bartsev (OECD), and Dr. George Garrity. Financial support was provided by Belgian Science Policy of the Belgian Government through IUAPVI/06, Department of Land Economy at the University of Cambridge, the Cambridge European Trust, the CT Taylor Fund and St Edmund's College, Cambridge.

The World Federation of Culture Collections (WFCC) is a network of over 500 public culture collections that are publicly available for research.[3] It is the WRCC's historical mission to organise the collection, authentication, maintenance and global distribution of cultures of microorganisms and cultured cells. Through the culture collections network, cultures are distributed and made available for research and development under marginal distribution costs, often with the possibility to further distribute the cultures to qualified third parties (for example, the standard agreement of the European Culture Collection Organisation). This results in major benefits for the development of downstream applications in important sectors such as biofuel production, plant symbionts and biocontrol agents providing environmentally sound alternatives to fertilizers and pesticides in agriculture and probiotic bacteria in the diary industry.[4] The use of certified materials from culture collections diminishes the cost from mistakes in cumulative research[5] and decreases the search costs for finding appropriate materials.[6] Therefore, the socio-economic benefits of the investment in public culture collections are substantial.

At present, the situation of exchange of biological materials within a global commons, which prevailed during the early days of the emergence of the modern life sciences, is facing a set of important challenges. The commoditization even of upstream research resources may hamper some of the most promising new scientific opportunities made possible by current advances in high throughput screening and increasing availability of full genome sequencing of entire microorganisms.[7]

The most important concern regarding culture collections is the quality management of their holdings and the associated costs. This does not only include biosecurity related issues, but also problems of cell contamination and misidentification. The German DSMZ collection (Deutsche Sammlung

3   See http://www.wfcc.info.

4   Jerome H. Reichman, Tom Dedeurwaerdere and Paul A. Uhlir, *Global Intellectual Property Strategies for the Microbial Research Commons* (Cambridge: Cambridge University Press, forthcoming 2012).

5   Jeffrey L. Furman and Scott Stern, "Climbing Atop the Shoulders of Giants: The Impact of Institutions on Cumulative Research", NBER working paper 12523 (National Bureau of Economic Research, 2006).

6   Douglas Gollin, Melinda Smale and Bent Skovmand, "Searching an Ex Situ Collection of Wheat Genetic Resources", *American Journal Agricultral Economics*, 82 (2000), 812–27; and Bert Visser, Derek Eaton, Niels Louwaars and Jan Engels, "Transaction Costs of Germplasm Exchange Under Bilateral Agreements", FAO/Global Forum on Agricultural Research Document, No. GFAR/00/17–04-04, Dresden (2000).

7   See Reichman, Dedeurwaerdere and Uhlir (forthcoming 2012).

fur Microorganisms) estimates that approximately 20% of all cell lines used in tumour research are misidentified, and thousands of studies based on faulty cell lines have been published. This problem is not as acute for all types of microbial materials. There have been efforts to develop systematic tests for cell culture identification and certified standard reference cultures at the collections, meaning that microbiologists have been able to limit their exposure to contamination. As a consequence, quality management standards, such as ISO (International Standards Organisation) certification of collections or certification standards of Biological Resources Centres play an important role in the exchange of ex situ microbial material.[8]

A second important concern is the capacity problem of the collections and the related problem of making the appropriate conservation choices. Because of the high cost of isolation and the extraordinary scope of the microbial diversity, the main efforts have been on the collection and identification of the diversity of the microbial species with known scientific and commercial value. However, only a tiny percentage of microbial diversity has even been identified — probably less than 1% — and only a small fraction of this known diversity can actually be effectively cultured. The rest is in situ and part of it will remain that way for a very long time. Researchers are still going back to collect in situ for local microbes to be studied and bring them in the public culture collection system in ways that we do not hear about — for example, in the plant breeding world. Moreover, the situation of the public culture collections is characterized by a high level of interdependency between the various countries involved. The largest public culture collection, with approximately 25,000 strains, holds less than 2% of the total number of strain holdings of the WFCC members and only an estimated 1.5% of the total biodiversity of unique strains holdings in the WFCC collections. Intense collaboration and exchange amongst culture collections is a necessary consequence of this situation.

Social and industry needs in relation to the culture collections raise important coordination and collective action problems that have been dealt with mainly through public sector involvement in the financing of their operations. The reason for this is the evident public good nature of many of the microbial strains, such as the investment in collecting and conserving general purpose microbial resources used on a non-exclusive basis in scientific research, or the conservation of reference strains used for

---

8 See *OECD Best Practice Guildelines for Biological Resource Centres* (Paris: OECD, 2007), available at http://www.oecd.org/dataoecd/7/13/38777417.pdf.

quality management and biosecurity controls.

With the biotechnology revolution, however, new actors have gained influence over the microbial actors network.[9] Technological advances have increased the value of microbes by creating new commercial applications such as pharmaceutical drugs based on micro-organisms, and by lowering the uncertainty of product success. Market oriented social planners in the USA and elsewhere realized the opportunity to diminish time laps between basic research findings and commercialized products (Bartsev, Pers. Comm.). In the mid 1980s, financial pressure among PSMC mounted under rapidly accumulating stocks of microbes and governments' finances were put under increasing stress.[10] Hence the conditions existed for private cost sharing of public collections as a way for industry to access the microbe flow and to diminish time lags between innovation and consumer products.[11] A new climate of business orientation started to influence some social planners and public collections, adopting more formal exchange practices and quality management through certification, even for upstream research tools such as those held in the network of the public culture collection. The management of these new markets directly developed on the basis of public domain assets further added to the complex set of challenges that the culture collections already have to face in the global context.

To understand how this transformation of the publicly accessible research infrastructure affects the governance choices of the culture collection, we conducted a series of interviews in order to address the following research questions: Who are the actors that shape the governance choices of the public culture collections? What distinguishes the basic research tier of the publicly accessible research infrastructure from the emerging commercial tier within the PSMCs? How are the governance problems of coordination for providing essential research materials on the global scale addressed by these two tiers? A preliminary set of in-depth structured interviews were conducted with the staff of five microbial collections in Europe and Latin America. Based on the insights of these interviews, we conducted shorter structured telephone interviews with members of a large number

9   Alex Weedon, "Implementing the Microbial Commons: Legal and Institutional Perspectives", discussant presentation at the Microbial Commons conference, Ghent, Belgium (11 June 2008).

10 Dwight Baker, "Microbial Diversity and Pharmaceutical Industry Culture Collections" in *Genetic and Functional Diversity of Agricultural Microorganisms*, ed. by Jun-ichi Kurisaki, et al. (Tsukuba, Japan: National Institute of Agrobiological Sciences, 2005), pp. 56–61.

11 Furman and Stern (2006).

of collections worldwide, and a large-scale survey of member collections of the WFCC. The results highlight, firstly, the multifunctionality and public good properties of micro-organisms for users in both basic research and product development of, for example, pharmaceutical drugs. Secondly, they show that a two-tier system is developing of one traditional, more scientifically oriented kind of PSMCs, and another, more commercially oriented tier.

1. Analysing actor networks in the World Federation for Culture Collections

Actor Network Theory will be used to contrast the governance attributes of the research sector and analyse the policy implications of the two-tier regime in the PSMCs: the basic research tier with a set of governance attributes characterized by informal exchanges and reciprocity amongst researchers on the one hand, and the emerging commercial tier which has recourse to the use of formal contracts and certification of management standards.

The inherent interdependence among actors causes a complex system of interests and incentives. Actor Network analysis can be used to disentangle and simplify the different motivations in these networks.[12] In this framework, all actions are viewed as being interrelated, within and between networks. It is by inducing other actors to act in a special way that the influence is achieved, for example, by persuading other actors to enrol in the network, and to gain the right to speak on behalf of other actors. Successful "translation" happens when actors accept their roles; translation fails when it cannot overcome heterogeneous preferences and motivations. For the purpose of this study the term actor is used for non-humans in the sense of Strathern (1999), i.e. anything mobilised in the course of action. Here we consider individuals, organisations, microbes and even policies to be actors in order to acknowledge their influence on the microbe flow.

The data for studying the actor networks was gathered in close collaboration with the WFCC, which is the largest international collaboration organisation of PSMCs and United Nations Educational Scientific and Cultural Organisation's (UNESCO) Microbial Resources

---

12   Michel Callon, "The Sociology of an Actor-Network: The Case of the Electric Vehicle", in *Mapping the Dynamics of Science and Technology*, ed. by Michel Callon, John Law and Arie Rip (London: Macmillan, 1986), pp. 19–34.

Network (MIRCEN) with 22 member collections in industrialised and developing countries.

A survey based on a written questionnaire was organized amongst members of WFCC and MIRCEN and completed by in-depth personal interviews. 119 collections returned the written questionnaire and 12 follow-up personal interviews were organised. The written questionnaire specifically addressed the distribution patterns of the culture collections to other actors in the actor networks and aimed to quantify the relative importance of the commercial tier as expressed through the importance of formal Material Transfer Agreements and the adoption of International Standards Organisation (ISO) certification. The personal interviews with staff and researchers at the culture collections were focused on a selection of six collections in European countries, which are representative of different degrees of use of formal contracting and adherence to ISO certification. They were chosen within a relative homogeneous policy context (Europe), in order to better assess the impact of the adoption of commercial practices on the conservation and distribution choices in the PSMCs. They were completed with two interviews with officials of the umbrella organisations (WFCC and ECCO) and four interviews in developing countries to check the consistency of the results in a wider geographical context.

2. The importance of the basic research tier and the commercial tier

This section presents the analysis of the governance choices for conservation and distribution of microbial genetic resources in the PSMCs. It focuses on the identification of the players in the two major actor networks that play a role in the publicly available science infrastructure: the basic research tier and the commercial tier. The next section will analyse how these major actor networks increased or decreased in importance and assess their role in the governance choices on conservation and distribution of microbial materials.

The first question that needs to be asked concerns the role of the various actors in the organisation of conservation and distribution of strain holdings. This question was addressed in our survey amongst the WFCC members, the results of which are presented in Figure 1. The results show the significant number of new strains coming directly from in situ settings into the culture collections (37% from own collecting activities in the field by the culture collections, and 27% from research laboratories in academia and hospitals who principally do their own collecting), the dominance of public sector transactions (77% to entities that are largely public) and the importance of reciprocity amongst collections (16% of new material comes from other public culture collections and 9% of existing material goes to other public culture collections).

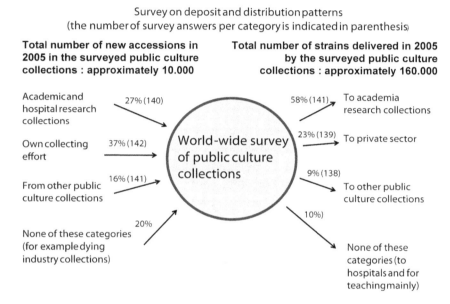

Survey on deposit and distribution patterns
(the number of survey answers per category is indicated in parenthesis)

Total number of new accessions in 2005 in the surveyed public culture collections : approximately 10.000

Total number of strains delivered in 2005 by the surveyed public culture collections : approximately 160.000

Academic and hospital research collections — 27% (140)

Own collecting effort — 37% (142)

From other public culture collections — 16% (141)

None of these categories (for example dying industry collections) — 20%

World-wide survey of public culture collections

58% (141) To academia research collections

23% (139) To private sector

9% (138) To other public culture collections

10%) None of these categories (to hospitals and for teaching mainly)

Figure 1. Providers and users of microorganisms in PSMCs

A socio-technical actor network is built around these transactions, which connect the main actors to the various user groups and ensures their influence. The quantitative survey already shows some of the direct mechanisms of influence of the main actors, mainly by mechanisms of direct reciprocity between collections and researchers. Not only do the collections help each other to complete the gaps in their own reference holdings, but they also allow other collections to further redistribute strains that they provide to them, insofar as the other collection has the capacity and the intent to do so. The influence of the industry appears clearly as an important client of the culture collections' strains.

Even if the industry client is not the most important recipient of the strain holdings, it is a vital one, because it provides a complementary income stream to the collections, which would otherwise be entirely dependent on public funding. Moreover, the selling of strains is often complemented by other services such as identification services for industry and research contracts. The results of the survey show that of all the funding streams other than core funding, the selling of strains (both to public and private institutions) topped the supplementary income streams, followed by contract research, other services and lastly income from patent and safety deposits.

The industry clients exercise their influence not only through bringing an income stream to the collections, but also through the indirect mechanisms which are the standard procedures, technical tools and cognitive approaches imposed in the actors' networks. The original quantitative survey that was conducted for this study showed the importance of the procedures that are imported from commercial practices and adopted by the research sector. 40% of the interviewed collections received some or all of their strains through some formal agreement, either through material transfer agreements, accession forms or other contracts. Therefore, formalization is still not the major practice in the PSMCs but the major international collections obtain the vast majority of their materials through contracts and the trend is clearly in the direction of more formal contracting. A 2009 semi-structured questionnaire on exchange and distribution patterns in PSMCs shows similar results and confirms the increase in formal transactions. Amongst a group of 43 culture collections from Europe (20), America (11), Asia (5), Australia (5) and Africa (1) more than 50% used formal means of transaction in most of the cases (that is, written agreements in their accession and distribution forms); 25% never used formal means and the remaining group used them only occasionally.[13] These results were equally distributed over OECD and non-OECD collections that participated in the survey. Another indicator of the adoption of commercial standards for exchange is the use of ISO certification of management procedures. 13% out of 113 collections that answered this question of the survey had adopted the ISO certificate. The survey shows that the proportion of collections adopting certification is still substantially less than their involvement in

---

13   Tom Dedeurwaerdere, Maria Iglesias, Sabine Weiland and Michael Halewood, "The Use and Exchange of Microbial Genetic Resources for Food and Agriculture", Background Study Paper of the Commission on Genetic Resources for Food and Agriculture, 46 (2009); and Tom Dedeurwaerdere, "Global Microbial Commons: Institutional Challenges for the Global Exchange and Distribution of Microorganisms in the Life Sciences", *Research in Microbiology*, 161 (2010), 414–21.

scientific collaborative networks such as the European Culture Collection Organization (ECCO) or the Global Biodiversity Information Facility (GBIF). However, it is fair to say that the recourse to certification is also increasing in the culture collections' community.

3. Social motivations and incentives in the Actor Networks

Based on these results, further in depth interviews were conducted to analyse two different categories of motivations among PSMCs, in one public sector driven regime of managing and distributing microbes, and in an emerging business-oriented regime. The resulting conflict is studied through the lens of how to organise the exchange of micro-organisms based on reciprocity or based on market-based exclusive license contracts.

3.1 The traditional role of PSMCs within the research infrastructure

An important role of public collections is to distribute its microbial holdings, to make them available for present use in science or applied research or hold them as option value for future uses. For instance, traditionally microbes have been transferred free of charge to all users, including to teachers for educational purposes. This is a way to minimise transaction costs in exchanges among relatively few participants, i.e. taxonomists and researchers within, for example the same university, or in different organisations in one single country. Relatively homogeneous aims within those networks facilitate the creation of trust. The "glue" that motivates such microbe transactions is based on relationships, with high informal excludability, reputation based sanctions, and scarce use of private property rights.

In the traditional actor network, social planners support the network through financial incentives, principally core funding to enable day-to-day operation, and ear-marked support to, for example, major research projects. Financial support to traditional PSMCs is provided by governments through host organisations or through competitive grants from many different types of donor organisations including multilateral organisations such as the European Commission. Of the 423 collections registered in WFCC, the majority are university supported (42%) and government supported (41%), with the remaining collections supported by semi-governmental organisations (8%), being private collections (4%), supported by industry (1%) and inter-governmental organisations (1%). This support is generally complemented by revenues from products and services (Smith, Pers.Comm.). Hence microbial collections are influenced by a broad set of incentives, stemming from the PSMCs' founding principles (e.g. public or for profit), type of users (e.g. researchers but also university lecturers using microbes for teaching, hospitals, academia or private sector), and the intended use of the microbes including agriculture, pharmaceutical products and bioremediation.[14]

3.2 Market creation in the public sphere

In order to secure appropriate governance of PSMCs it is important to have updated information about who funds microbe collections and for what purposes. Notably, funding for PSMCs is provided increasingly by industry and auto financing (WFCC 2005).

The complex activities of PSMCs create the need for investment in expert staff and sophisticated storage equipment. The cost of creating a new collection of about five thousand microbe strains is approximated to US$1 million, excluding the substantial costs of storage, maintenance and use.[15] As a consequence of the high costs of creating and operating collections, closures, mergers and grandfathering of abandoned collections is common.[16]

In fact the largest collections of microbes are held by the industry itself.[17] However, starting in the mid-1990s, the pharmaceutical industry has changed its basic research focus, and closed or outsourced many of its in-house collections (Garrity, Pers.Comm). Small niche public service collections provide specialised services to the industry under conditions of relative secrecy. As a consequence, property rights to microbes are changing and there may be concerns that resulting new profit incentives turn collections away from the objective of conserving sufficiently large stocks of general purpose biological materials available for exploratory and basic research.[18]

Technological advances have increased the value of microbes. This is a result of higher and more predictable value from new commercial

---

14   Furman and Stern (2006).
15   Baker (2005).
16   Ibid.
17   Furman and Stern (2006).
18   David Smith, "Culture Collections Over the World", *International Microbiology*, 6 (2003), 95-100.

applications in, for example, pharmaceutical drugs. With the biotechnology revolution, starting in the 1970s, three new actors gained influence over the microbe actor network: new technology, private industry, and a more business oriented way of organising public sector activities.[19] Market-oriented social planners in the USA and elsewhere realised the opportunity to diminish time laps between basic research findings and commercialised products (Bartsev, Pers.Comm.). Growing stocks of microbes made PSMCs costlier to maintain, and government budgets faced increasing stress in general.[20] A new climate of business orientation started to influence some social planners and public collections. Hence the conditions existed for private cost sharing of public collections, which gave industry access to the microbe flow and diminished time lags between innovation and consumer products.[21] Figure 2 synthesises what is shown to be the emergence of a new network, which created a two-tier system in the governance of microbes.

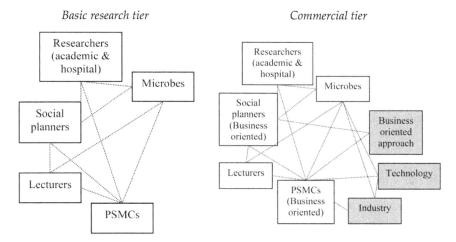

Figure 2. The two-tier actor network that translates the microbe flow in basic and applied research (shaded boxes represent new actors in the second tier)

In Table 1, the two tiers are characterised with respect to their salient attributes. Although in reality the features of the two tiers are often mixed within one collection, the dichotomy is a useful way to understand the incentives and the way PSMCs choose to govern their exchange of micro-organisms. The

19   Weedon (2008).
20   Baker (2005).
21   Furman and Stern (2006).

basic research tier has strong influence from the public sector, is rather homogenous and open, and quality signalling is based on social networks. In contrast, the commercial tier is influenced by industry and adopts a more formal and closed approach to management of the collection's holdings.

Governance attribute	The basic research tier	The commercial tier
Attributes of micro-organism transactions		
Incentives for microbe transactions based on:	Reciprocity	Markets (Fee)
Compliance mechanism for microbe transactions based on:	Social networks (reputation)	Legalistic principle (formal property rights)
Institutional attributes of the public collection		
Strong source of influence from:	Public organisation	Industry
Microbes distributed mainly to:	Public organisations	Industry
Group heterogeneity among PSMCs and demanders:	Low	High
Collaboration with other public collections is:	Open	Closed
Signalling of organisational quality is:	Social network based	Formal (ISO)

Table 1. Attributes of the microbe actor network with respect to management of micro-organisms, of the basic research tier and the commercial tier

Standardisation of management procedures is another business oriented governance mode.[22] Actors outside the traditional networks of PSMCs have difficulty in ascertaining quality of, for example, high quality microbe transfers, since they lack the social networks through which to verify the

---

22   Paul Milgrom and John Roberts, *Economics, Organization and Management* (Englewood Cliffs, NJ: Prentice Hall, 1992).

quality of any given PSMC. Hence standardised procedures to signal the organisational quality (ISO certification) is a way for the industry to inform their choice of PSMC from which to obtain microbes and services. This emerging quality system has been endorsed by some collections, such as DSMZ, while others continue to use informal signalling associated with the traditional actor network.

3.3 Implications for provision of public goods

This section builds on the salient attributes of the two tiers' motivations, roles and resulting ways of organising their interaction, with the view to evaluate briefly their role in microbe conservation as global public goods. In general, regarding the conservation of microbes, the issues of agreeing and building capacity for conservation of option value, monitoring of microbe populations to adapt the conservation choices, and quality control appear to be of particular relevance (e.g. Smith, Pers. Comm.; Baker 2005). PSMCs' individual efforts need to be aligned to global conservation of diversity of microbes, rather than investing in overlapping conservation efforts which generate a small total conserved diversity. In this respect, for those microbes that hold particularly strong public good properties, market signals may provide inappropriate guidance for conservation.

Coordinated action, as in the basic research tier, is well placed to manage such public good properties in contrast to markets.[23] However, heterogeneity and group size can negatively affect the scope for collective action in the coordination among PSMCs internationally. Hence, the entrance of new actors may increase the cost of certain kinds of coordination. Not only has the described entry of industry but also increased international interconnectedness emphasised this vulnerability of the basic research tier. Therefore, while the basic research tier has capability to manage public goods, this capability may become reduced by increased group heterogeneity.

However, the commercial tier has the facility to manage heterogeneous agents by deploying a standardised mode of transactions (in contrast to industry's likely difficulty in accessing trust-based networks). In the light of increased heterogeneity among microbe users it would appear that a formalised mode, based on formalised property rights and fees, is

---

23 Robert Cook-Deegan and Tom Dedeurwaerdere, "The Science Commons in Life Science Research: Structure, Function and Value of Access to Genetic Diversity", *International Social Science Journal*, 188 (2006), 299–318; and Charlotte Hess and Elinor Ostrom, "A Framework for Analyzing Governance and Collective Action in the Microbial Commons", paper presented at workshop on exploring and exploiting microbiological commons, Brussels (7–8 July 2005).

well-aligned to the emerging needs of servicing different users and possibly to decrease lead times between basic research and applied products.

In sum, the basic research tier is well placed to manage information flows needed for the overall coordination of the conservation efforts, while the commercial tier can contribute with formal measures of microbe transfers, and ascertain administrative quality.

In this chapter we have studied the suitability of different institutional designs to manage the conservation of and access to micro-organisms worldwide. Traditionally, microbes have been managed by publicly funded microbial ex situ collections. However, commercial users have come to influence the governance of the flow and diversity of microbes in ex situ collections.[24] By using Actor Network Theory, we argue that the resulting phenomenon can best be described as market creation in the public sphere. Pharmaceutical and other biotechnology firms introduce market incentives, based on formalized property rights. This has important implications: while such commercial co-financing of the microbial flow secures short term input to applied research and product development, the question remains how the collections' long term strategies to meet societal needs are affected. The risk, of course, is that short term market incentives encroach on longer term conservation priorities. Hence, instead of as now having the commercial tier increasing its influence of the basic research tier, the social planner must strengthen the basic research tier in a way that does not impede many of the attributes of market orientation that lead to high effectiveness.

---

24   See, for example, Reichman, Dedeurwaerdere and Uhlir (forthcoming 2012).

7. Open Knowledge: Promises and Challenges

Rufus Pollock and Jo Walsh, Open Knowledge Foundation

"Open knowledge" is material that others are free to access, reuse and redistribute. We are just beginning to witness its great potential. Increasing the visibility and discoverability of open resources is crucial if we are to encourage innovative re-combination and reuse—hence the importance of open metadata for open knowledge. Componentization—or the atomization of a given resource into "packages"—has greatly contributed towards the ease with which software developers are able to reuse and build upon each other's work. In this chapter, we argue that this kind of approach is becoming significantly more important in knowledge development. We will discuss some of the Open Knowledge Foundation's work in these areas, with an emphasis on Public Domain Works and the Comprehensive Knowledge Archive Network (CKAN).[1]

The Open Knowledge Foundation is a not-for-profit organisation founded in 2004 with the aim of protecting and promoting open knowledge in all its forms.[2] By "knowledge" we mean any text, data, image, multimedia and so on. By "open" we mean free for anyone to access, reuse and re-distribute.[3] Our work can broadly be broken down into promoting the idea of open knowledge, doing research and policy

---

1 Substantial parts of this chapter are based on "Componentization and Open Data", a paper delivered by Rufus Pollock and Jo Walsh at XTech (2007).
2 See the Open Knowledge Foundation's website http://okfn.org.
3 For more details see http://www.opendefinition.org.

work, developing various open knowledge projects and tools for open knowledge.

We have created the Open Knowledge Definition to provide a clear set of conditions for openness in relation to knowledge. This provides a common thread to material that is made available under different liberal licenses (such as Creative Commons Attribution and Attribution Sharealike, the GNU Free Documentation License, etc), material in which rights have been waived (CC Zero, the Public Domain Declaration License, etc), material that is in the public domain, and so on. Our "open knowledge" and "open data" web buttons are intended to publicize "openness" regardless of the legal basis of this. We have also drafted an Open Service Definition to fulfil the same function in relation to Software as a Service (SaaS). We aim to act as a hub and partner for the community of users and producers of open knowledge—facilitating discussion through our mailing lists, forums and annual conferences.

We produce material on legal, economic, and domain-specific issues relevant to open knowledge in the UK, EU and internationally.[4] We help to initiate and maintain specific open knowledge projects:

- Open Shakespeare is a complete collection of Shakespeare's works with ancillary information, a concordance and an annotation tool;[5]
- Open Economics is a data store for economic data, plus a visualisation tool;[6]
- Open Text Book is a registry of textbooks that are fully open;[7]
- Public Domain Works is a registry of artistic works that are in the public domain—it merged with the Open Library;[8]

Our KForge project is an open source system for managing software and knowledge projects—integrating tools such as a versioned storage system, a wiki, a tracker and a blog with the system's own facilities for projects, users and permissions.[9] We also run a free service called KnowledgeForge which runs on the Kforge software and currently houses a variety of open knowledge projects, from British parliamentary

---

4   See http://wiki.okfn.org/Research.
5   See http://www.openshakespeare.org.
6   See http://www.openeconomics.net.
7   See http://www.opentextbook.org.
8   See http://www.publicdomainworks.net and http://www.openlibrary.org.
9   See http://www.kforgeproject.com.

data to the works of Ivo of Chartres.[10] The Comprehensive Knowledge Archive Network (CKAN) is a registry of open knowledge packages — we shall return to this later.

1. Databases of metadata and metadata for databases

Openness means cheaper and better access to knowledge; it also encourages richer ecologies of sharing and participation. For example, the Dbpedia project extracts structured information from Wikipedia articles to allow complex querying. The W3C community project, Linking Open Data, is working hard towards inter-linking various open datasets. An increasing number of projects such as Gapminder, Swivel, and Manyeyes seek to socialise the process of visualising and analysing (open) datasets. The "principle of many minds", to which we often allude, states that "the most interesting thing to be done with your material will be thought of by someone else".

In order to encourage this kind of collaboration it is essential that open knowledge resources are as visible and as easily discoverable as possible. Having more and better metadata is one way to facilitate this. Much metadata is of the kind we find in library card catalogues. For our Public Domain Works project we wanted to build up a large registry of metadata for artistic works, and then to use this metadata to determine which of these works are in the public domain, and hence open. Unfortunately we found that a lot of the material we were interested in was closed and prohibitively expensive. We were lucky that several databases from the BBC and from private enthusiasts were donated to us.

In 2007, the project merged into the Open Library project — the brainchild of Brewster Kahle, who also founded the Internet Archive — which aims to provide a very large versioned database of bibliographic data, and has had some donations of data from libraries in the US. We are keen to work with them, and any other interested parties, to create a series of "public domain calculators"[11] which could be used to determine whether a given work is in or out of copyright in a given jurisdiction. While this constitutes a significant development in this area, unfortunately most bibliographic data is proprietary and cannot be reused or built upon by the technical

---

10 See http://www.knowledgeforge.net.
11 http://wiki.okfn.org/PublicDomainCalculators

community. As well as metadata for specific works, we can also have metadata for large collections of knowledge resources. We believe that this is integral to the greater reuse and recombination of knowledge resources.

2. Componentization and Open Knowledge

The collaborative production and distribution of data is gradually progressing towards the level of sophistication displayed in software. Data licensing is important to this progression, but is often over-examined. Instead we believe the crucial development is componentization, which can be defined as the process of atomizing (breaking down) resources into separate reusable packages that can be easily recombined. By focusing on the packaging and distribution of data in a shared context, one can resolve issues of rights, report-back, attribution and competition. Looking across different domains for "spike solutions", we see componentization of data at the core of common concern.

For those familiar with the Debian distribution system for Linux, the initial ideal is of a "debian of data". Through the "apt" package management engine, when one installs a piece of software, all the libraries and other programs which it needs to run are walked through and downloaded with it. The packaging system helps one "divide and conquer" the problems of organising and conceptualising highly complex systems. The effort of a few makes reuse easier for many; sets of related packages are managed in social synchrony between existing software producers.

3. Code got there first

In the early days of software, there was little arms-length reuse of code because there was little packaging. Hardware was so expensive, and so limited, that it made sense for all software to be bespoke and little effort to be put into building libraries or packages. Only gradually did the modern complex, though still crude, system develop. These days, to package is to propagate, and to be discoverable in a package repository is critical to utility.

The size of the data set with which one is dealing changes the terms of the debate. Genome analysis or Earth Observation data stretches to petabytes. Updates to massive banks of vectors or of imagery impact many tiny changes across petabytes. At this volume of data, it helps to establish a sphere of concern—distributing the analysis and processing across many sets of users, in small slices.

Cross-maintenance across different data sets—rebuilding aggregated updates—becomes more important. Having cleanly defined edges, something like a "knowledge API", or many APIs, is envisaged. Each domain has a set of small, concrete common information models. To distribute a data package is to distribute a reusable information model with it—to offer as much automated assistance in reusing and recombining information as possible.

Licensing clarity is important because without it one is not allowed to recombine data sources (though there is still a large gap between being allowed and being able). Code has come a long way with the legal issues, and differently flavoured Free Software Definitions have gained a good consensus. The state of open data is more uncertain, especially looking at the different ways of asserting the right to access and to reuse data in different legislative regions. Open data practice should demonstrate value and utility, and thus it becomes a natural choice, and not an imposition. The Open Knowledge Definition is an effort to describe the properties of truly open data.

4. Knowledge and data APIs

Open knowledge research projects are carried out in an atmosphere of "fierce collaborative competition". The Human Genome Analysis project was a shining example: slices of source data were partitioned out to a network of institutions. Near-to-realtime information about the analysis results led to the redirection of resources and support to centres that were performing better. In the context of open media, people are also "competing to aggregate", to compile not mere volume but more cross-connectedness into indexes and repositories of common knowledge.

Progress on the parts is easier to perceive than on the whole. In the parts, the provenance is clear—who updated data when and why, and how it was improved. The touchstones are to improve reusability, accuracy and currency of data. Working with subsets of datasets, in the absence of significant hardware or bandwidth barriers, anyone can start to carry out and contribute analysis from home. Knowledge is given back into a publically available research space, becoming easier to build on the work of others. The more people who access and analyse data, the more value it has to everybody.

Open source software has shown that openness is complementary to commercial concerns, not counter to them. As the GPL encourages commercial reuse of code, open knowledge is of benefit to commercial activity. Providing a reference system and a common interface, more "added value" applications are built on a base layer. The ability to monitor and report in near-to-realtime on the basis of package development can be useful to more than the "funded community"; it provides real validation of a working (or non-working) business model.

5. What do we mean by componentization?

Componentization is the process of atomizing (breaking down) resources into separate reusable packages that can be easily recombined. It is the most important feature of (open) knowledge development as well as the one which is, at present, least advanced. If you look at the way software has evolved, it is now highly componentized into packages/libraries. Doing this allows one to "divide and conquer" the organisational and conceptual problems of highly complex systems. Even more importantly it allows for greatly increased levels of reuse.

The power and significance of componentisation becomes very apparent when using a package manager (for example, apt-get for Debian) on a modern operating system. A request to install a single given package can result in the automatic discovery and installation of all packages on which that one depends. The result may be a list of tens — or even hundreds — of packages in a graphic demonstration of the way in which computer programs have been broken down into interdependent components.

6. Atomization

Atomization denotes the breaking down of a resource such as a piece of software or collection of data into smaller parts (though the word atomic connotes irreducibility it is never clear what the exact irreducible, or optimal, size for a given part is). For example, a given software application may be divided up into several components or libraries. Atomization can happen on many levels.

At a very low level when writing software we break things down into functions and classes, into different files (modules) and even group together different files. Similarly when creating a dataset in a database we divide things into columns, tables, and groups of inter-related tables.

But such divisions are only visible to the members of that specific project. Anyone else has to get the entire application or entire database to use one particular part of it. Furthermore, anyone working on any given part of an application or database needs to be aware of, and interact with, anyone else working on it—decentralization is impossible or extremely limited. Therefore, atomization at such a low level is not what we are really concerned with; instead it is with atomization into packages.

7. Packaging

By packaging we mean the process by which a resource is made reusable by the addition of an external interface. The package is therefore the logical unit of distribution and reuse and it is only with packaging that the full power of atomization's "divide and conquer" purpose comes into play—without it there is still tight coupling between different parts of a resource.

Developing packages is a non-trivial exercise precisely because developing good stable interfaces (usually in the form of a code or knowledge API) is difficult. One way to provide stability but also to remain flexible in terms of future development is to employ versioning. By versioning the package and providing "releases", those who reuse the packaged resource can stay using a specific (and stable) release while development and changes are made in the "trunk" and become available in later releases. This practice of versioning and releasing is already ubiquitous in software development—so ubiquitous it is practically taken for granted—but is almost unknown in the area of open knowledge.

8. Componentization for knowledge

At present, knowledge development displays very little componentization but, as the underlying pool of raw, "unpackaged" information continues to increase, there will be increasing emphasis on componentization and the reuse it supports. One can conceptualize this as a question of interface versus content. Currently 90% of effort goes into the content and 10% goes into the interface. With components this will change to 90% on the interface 10% on the content. The change to a componentized architecture will be complex but, once achieved, will revolutionise the production and development of open knowledge.

9. The Comprehensive Knowledge Archive Network (CKAN)

Our CKAN project aims to encourage and support the emergence of a culture where knowledge packages can be easily discovered and plugged together as is currently possible with software. Named after software archives such as CPAN for Perl, CTAN for TeX, CRAN for R and so on, it is a registry for knowledge resources.

It is currently in beta and consists of a versioned database of metadata for large datasets and substantial collections of knowledge resources: "from genes to geodata, sonnets to statistics". It gives the "lowest common denominator" of metadata for its packages: author, id, license, user-generated tags and links. We plan to add support for domain specific metadata. We are also planning to make provision for the automated installation of knowledge packages.

8. Science Commons: Building the Research Web

Kaitlin Thaney

Science Commons, a project of Creative Commons (CC), works to encourage the sharing of scientific and academic knowledge. This chapter will look at the technology and infrastructure designed and used at Science Commons to better share knowledge, an approach contextualised here as "building the research Web", in the hope of utilising the power of current Internet technologies to accelerate scientific research.[1] There are three main tenets to consider: open access to the content; access to the physical research materials; and an open source knowledge management system.

This approach requires redesigning information that is already digital into a format that works better for research. This process needs structure, standardised agreements, access to the content and data, metadata that dictates under what terms information is available, common naming systems, and links to repositories, to name just a few. Only then can one start to bring the efficiencies commonly associated with the Internet and a network approach to the world of scientific research.

1. The problem

Printing, delivery and research are rapidly moving into the digital domain. Even with this shift in processes, however, scientific research still largely deals with "paper metaphor" — the idea that knowledge is transmitted by

---

1   This contribution was written following a Communia meeting in September 2007 in Turin, Italy.

an individual, on paper, rather than making the information readable by machines.

Science Commons has identified four key problems. First, there is the issue of cognitive overload, especially as information is translated to a digital form or created that way. We are beginning to know too much for our brain to process and take care of, and in this way face a data deluge. Secondly, most of what we know is poorly fitted for use and reuse—a design problem—making the information impossible to say, text mine. Even the simple act of publishing a document as a PDF adds a barrier to fully utilising the information in the form provided. Documents are poorly linked or annotated, making it increasingly difficult to connect information. Thirdly, there is a licensing problem, where knowledge is licensed in such a way that it is not legally available (this is an issue routinely faced in data integration or text mining). Lastly, the physical materials, the non-digital objects on which this is based (for example, lab mice, DNA, gene snippets and plasmids) is not always freely available in reality.

The first three points—cognitive overload, the design, and licensing problems—all describe problems of the regular Internet, but in order to have "open science" or a "research Web", one must include in this discussion an additional dimension: access to the physical materials.

Current ways of conducting this research are imperfect. Take, for example, the following research question, which could be asked of a "research Web": based on what has been published in journals and databases, what signal transduction genes may be active in pyramidal neurons? This question would serve as a lead to find drug targets in Alzheimer's disease, since signal transduction genes tend to make for good drug targets and pyramidal neurons are implicated. A simple Google search renders approximately 189,000 results. Conducting this search in other information warehouses such as the US National Institutes of Health's PubMed or PubMed Central provides an enormous number of articles, references, and citations. Sorting through all of this knowledge would take far beyond the grant period for any normal researcher—it is an example of the aforementioned data deluge/ cognitive overload problem. What you should be able to access using the power of the Internet is a list of genes that meet the conditions specified in the original research question.

It is currently very difficult to use the network to build on and validate research. There is no technical barrier to doing this, no creative breakthrough nor "eureka moment" needed. It is a matter of reformatting what we already know into a way that works better. Three steps need to be taken to achieve this: first, one has to address the legal issues around accessing the content (be it raw data or scholarly literature); secondly, one has to address the legal, social, and technical issues that surround the physical tools; and thirdly, one has to begin some sort of Open Access knowledge management process. The goal: to go from the old way of collaborating—which was based on the idea of transmitting knowledge through paper, of reading the canon on paper and querying single-access databases—to a new way of collaborating using machines and standardised distribution. Those three areas are critical to building a research Web.

2. Open Access content

Our Scholar's Copyright project began with the promotion of CC licenses to peer-reviewed journals. The most notable adopters are the Public Library of Science, BioMed Central and Hindawi. To date, there are more than 350 peer-reviewed journals using the CC Attribution license for their content. Other adopters include Nature Precedings, the preprint server run by the Nature Publishing Group, in conjunction with the Wellcome Trust, the British Library and Science Commons.

The second part to this project supports the self-archiving route to making scholarly literature freely available. In early 2007, Science Commons released a set of "author addenda" that could be printed, filled in and submitted along with the author's manuscript. This allowed authors to retain certain rights dictated in the text of the addenda and to mark their research for reuse. We took this one step further and created a Web tool that allows authors to fill in the form online, choose an addendum that best suits their needs, and auto-generate the form. The tool can easily be dropped into a university's website and is currently running on the sites of Carnegie-Mellon University, MIT and the Association of Research Libraries. This tool is called the Scholar's Copyright Addendum Engine (SCAE). Since its launch in mid-May 2007, over 900 addenda have been generated.

The SCAE allows a user to plug in very basic publication information and generate a document that can be attached to a copyright transfer agreement in order to reserve a number of rights over their work. All versions reserve the basic right for an author to reuse their work in their own teaching and professional activities as well as in future works. Beyond that basic requirement, each addendum grants the author a variety of rights, whether it be the ability to place a copy of the final PDF version of their work on the Internet upon publication, or whether the work is subject to a six-month delay or otherwise dictated embargo period ("Delayed Access" addendum).

Our most recent work in Scholar's Copyright revolves around the question of licensing data and databases. An extensive amount of research, exploratory conversations and a number of private workshops were convened and conducted to gain a better grasp of the complexity of this issue. On 15 December 2007, Science Commons released the outcome of these conversations — the Protocol for Open Access Data, which, along with the CC Zero Project, do the same things for data as CC licenses do for literature. The idea is to allow databases to be freely integrated with one another, reconstructing the public domain for data through contract, and creating zones of certainty. The protocol incorporated a number of recommendations based on established scientific norms, such as attribution and citation. The CC Zero tool identifies what rights need to be waived (for example, copyright in databases, *sui generis* rights under the European Union database directive, etc) in order to put data back into the public domain.

3. Open Access to physical materials

The Biological Materials Transfer (MTA) Project addresses the accessibility issues surrounding most research materials in biology — the physical research tools upon which the research Web is built. DNA, cell lines, lab mice, and more physical tools are more often than not subject to deliberate withholding, legal slowdowns, difficulties in fulfilling orders and many other kinds of delays that add to the drag on scientific discovery and the research cycle. Our MTA work is built on the idea of building an application that incorporates the principles of an "e-commerce" transaction system but applied to biological materials; we are working towards "one-click" access to these materials wherever possible.

To achieve this, our legal experts worked to create a suite of contracts, known as Materials Transfer Agreements (MTA). There are pre-existing standard MTAs, two of which are included in the suite: the National Institute of Health's Uniform Biological Materials Transfer Agreement (UBMTA) and the Simple Letter Agreement (SLA). These two agreements cover a significant amount of materials already. Each MTA follows the

CC "methodology" and design, consisting of a human-readable deed with iconographic representations of rights and obligations and metadata.

Included in this suite is a set of contracts developed in-house at Science Commons. This follows a two-tiered approach intended to allow for transfer among non-profit institutions as well as for transfers from non-profit institutions to for-profit companies for internal research uses (non-commercial use). For the former, we standardised the existing UBMTA and SLA. For the latter, we developed a suite of standard MTAs with modular options, guided by principles derived from the NIH Principles and Guidelines relating to the sharing of biomedical resources. In particular, we implemented the NIH Guidelines with respect to defining "non-commercial use" in this space.

4. **Open source knowledge management**

The last component needed to achieve a research Web is a way to manage all of this knowledge. Everything that we do at Science Commons takes an open source knowledge management approach. With access to the content, the data, and the physical materials, what remains is a method for fully utilising all of the information available. Science Commons is building its work using the Semantic Web as its platform. We are firm believers that the Semantic Web offers great potential for exploiting the legal access to digital knowledge and research materials through open source data integration and knowledge management.

The work previously discussed in regards to content, data, and physical materials comes together in a single proof-of-concept project: the Neurocommons. The project brings together the tools and techniques from each of these projects, serving as a proving ground for commons-based "e-science" or the research Web as we envision it to be.

The Neurocommons serves as our pilot knowledge management project with a focus specifically on the brain sciences. The goal is to enable scientists to ask very complex questions and receive precise answers, like the aforementioned question looking for potential drug targets for Alzheimer's disease, and receive a list of genes, rather than 250,000 web pages that may be loosely associated with the topic area. This method is not new. Pharmaceutical companies have utilised such systems, in a proprietary and closed manner, for quite some time. However, to our knowledge the Neurocommons is the first iteration of such a system that is open source, making for a data-integration platform for the life sciences that gives researchers easy access to open content.

By reformatting the literature, the data, images, classification systems and ontologies into a common semantic Web frame, it is possible to write a single query asking a question over all of the information. The proof-of-concept we have created to make this tractable technically integrates a series of databases including the content from PubMed Central, gene data, mouse brain images, ontologies about molecular functions and a number of others, all pulled in to make a local system to prove the power of open digital knowledge.

The knowledge base also contains the digital descriptions of the physical research materials through our MTA work, showing the value of using these methods on physical tools. When a scientist gets a precise list of genes they can, with a single click, order those materials directly from a third party, thanks to the metadata. This is one of many opportunities and benefits of building this system on an open, commons-based foundation.

9. The DRIVER Project: The Socio-economic Benefits of a European Scientific Commons

Karen Van Godtsenhoven

The European DRIVER project (the Digital Repository Infrastructure Vision for European Research) builds a repository infrastructure combined with a search portal for open access (OA) European scientific communication. The goal is to aggregate all OA materials into one knowledge infrastructure or scientific commons, with collections, scientific communities and customized portals. For the infrastructure, the DRIVER open source software package D-NET v.1.0 (http://www.driverrepository.eu/index.php/D-NET_release) has been developed. The DRIVER project chose to include only open access full-text materials, which means it does not retrieve reference-only materials, in order to promote the OA movement with readers and authors.

Specific studies about copyright for digital repositories have been issued, and the DRIVER project partners keep advocating an OA mandate for all the publications funded by the European Commission (EC), in parallel with geographically-based or subject-based mandates.[1] The last couple of years have seen a rise in "self-archiving" mandates issued by major research funders and

---

1 See Wilma Mossink, "Intellectual Property Rights", in *A DRIVER's Guide to European Repositories: Five Studies of Important Digital Repository Related Issues and Good Practices*, ed. by Kasja Weenink, Leo Waaijers and Karen van Godtsenhoven (Amsterdam: Amsterdam University Press, 2007), pp. 103–12.

institutions, both in Europe as well as in the US, which is a favourable evolution for authors' rights as well as for the greater public. Since authors are obliged to retain some rights to their work, this allows them to put articles online, which enhances their readership and impact.[2] This, in turn, accelerates science because of the timely and free availability of the publications. The more articles, proceedings, raw data and research results become available, the more DRIVER can build on these data with services for both readers and authors, who will be encouraged by the positive effects (enhanced readership and impact) and deposit more articles. The "V" in the DRIVER acronym embodies this strategic vision: a scientific commons for Europe and the rest of the world.

1. Open Access to scientific communication

1.1 A brief history of Open Access

Although the birth of OA is often rooted in the serials pricing crisis,[3] or the disproportional rise in scientific journal prices during the last decades of the twentieth century, it is not just a libraries' solution to financial issues: OA concerns the whole scientific community, and the movement is rooted within the disciplines themselves. It was the physicists with their arXiv.org who started putting up pre-prints from journal articles online, because they felt the peer review and publishing process took too long and they wanted faster access to research results in order to build upon them.[4] After ten years, the movement became more and more institutionalized and got the famous "BBB" statements as the official declarations of principles for the open access movement.[5] These statements have been signed by over 250 rectors, ministers and research directors worldwide.

Nowadays, OA advocates try to establish institutions' and funders' OA mandates, because researchers need incentives in order to execute the few keystrokes needed to self-archive their articles (the spontaneous

---

2   Heather A. Piwowar, Roger S. Day, Douglas B. Fridsma, "Sharing Detailed Research Data Is Associated with Increased Citation Rate", *PLoS ONE*, 2 (2007), e308.

3   See Jean-Claude Guédon, "In Oldenburg's Long Shadow: Librarians, Research Scientists, Publishers, and the Control of Scientific Publishing", presentation for the Association of Research Libraries, Toronto (May 2001), available at http://www.arl.org/resources/ pubs/mmproceedings/138guedon.shtml; and Judith M. Panitch and Sarah Michalak, "The Serials Crisis: A White Paper for the UNC-Chapel Hill Scholarly Communications Convocation" (January 2005), available at http://www.unc.edu/scholcomdig/ whitepapers/panitch-michalak.html.

4   See http://arxiv.org.

5   "BBB" refers to Budapest (2002) at http://www.soros.org/openaccess; Bethesda (2003); and the Berlin Declaration (2003) at http://www.berlin9.org/about/declaration/index. shtml.

self-archiving rate is a low 15%, according to Swan, 2006). Although the concept of a mandate seems unattractive to researchers (it is a top-down obligation), it is in their own interest (visibility, research impact and storage) and also advantageous for the whole scientific community. The first implementers of OA mandates,[6] such as the University of Minho and the European Oganization for Nuclear Research (CERN) have proven the advantages for their institutions, and were followed by big funding agencies such as the National Institute of Health (US) and the European Research Council, and universities such as Harvard and the University of Liège, Belgium.[7] After last year's recommendations by the ERC and the following mandate, as well as the major EC petition for OA, this will hopefully lead to a generic mandate from the EC. This goal is not easily achieved because of high-level publishers' lobbying with the EC, and the refusal of the EC to take a stand in the discussion, because of the perceived added economic value the publishing industries offer. Thus far, only "strong recommendations" and plans for investments into OA experiments have been published, but none included a very pragmatic approach to the problem of low spontaneous self-archiving rates with European researchers.[8]

1.2 Defining Open Access

Many different "flavours" of OA exist, and there have been a lot of different definitions both from within the community and without, but we will use the definition of the last Berlin Declaration (2003), since that is the most established and widespread document for the OA movement:

Open access contributions must satisfy two conditions:

> 1.   The author(s) and right holder(s) of such contributions grant(s) to all users a free, irrevocable, worldwide, right of access to, and

---

6   Vanessa Proudman, "The Population of Repositories", in *A DRIVER's Guide to European Repositories: Five Studies of Important Digital Repository Related Issues and Good Practices*, ed. by Kasja Weenink, Leo Waaijers and Karen van Godtsenhoven (Amsterdam: Amsterdam University Press, 2007), pp. 49–97; and Alma Swan, "Open Access by Self-archiving: It's an Author Thing", paper presented at the first European conference on scientific publishing in biomedicine and medicine, Lund, Sweden (April 2006), available at http://eprints.ecs.soton.ac.uk/17505/.

7   The Juliet website lists all the funding agencies' open access mandates and conditions: http://www.sherpa.ac.uk/juliet/.

8   For a comprehensive overview of all the official documents by the EC, ERC, EURAB and EUA, as well as the position papers from the publishers, see Peter Suber's Open Access Newsletter, issue 107 (2 March 2007), available at http://www.earlham.edu/~peters/fos/newsletter/03–02-07.htm.

a license to copy, use, distribute, transmit and display the work publicly and to make and distribute derivative works, in any digital medium for any responsible purpose, subject to proper attribution of authorship (community standards, will continue to provide the mechanism for enforcement of proper attribution and responsible use of the published work, as they do now), as well as the right to make small numbers of printed copies for their personal use.

2.   A complete version of the work and all supplemental materials, including a copy of the permission as stated above, in an appropriate standard electronic format is deposited (and thus published) in at least one online repository using suitable technical standards (such as the Open Archive definitions) that is supported and maintained by an academic institution, scholarly society, government agency, or other well-established organisation that seeks to enable open access, unrestricted distribution, interoperability and long-term archiving.

These two conditions ensure that all the materials can be accessed and reused in an appropriate way, thus accelerating research and facilitating a worldwide scientific commons.[9]

1.3 The practical side of OA

The two main roads to OA are either the "green road" (self-archiving of papers in institutional repositories, vehemently defended as the only way by "archivangelist" Stevan Harnad) or the "golden road" (through publishing in OA journals).[10] Both have their positive and negative sides, but the most important factor is that they offer free, immediate and permanent access to scientific communication, the essential principles of OA.

1.4 Copyright issues

One of the biggest concerns of researchers who want to self-archive their articles in a digital repository is the fear of copyright restrictions and possible measures by the publishers. To accommodate these researchers, the UK-based Sherpa/Romeo website lists many scientific journals and publishers with their journal copyright policies.[11] Different categories exist, such as green (allow self-archiving), yellow (only pre-prints can be

---

9   See http://sciencecommons.org.
10   See http://doaj.org.
11   See http://www.sherpa.ac.uk/romeo.

self-archived), blue (only post-prints) and white (no self-archiving allowed). All the different conditions and possible embargoes are listed on the Sherpa website, and it appears that 67% of all the listed publishers are so-called "green publishers", who allow authors to self-archive their final version of a refereed paper. Wilma Mossink thoroughly explains these issues and their solutions, such as the Copyright toolbox by the Dutch SURF foundation, or SPARC's Scholar's Copyright Addendum Engine.[12]

2. The DRIVER project: accomplishments and future goals[13]

2.1 Results from DRIVER I

DRIVER (I) was a project with ten partners from eight countries, funded by the European Commission's Information Society and Multimedia DG, and was included in the i2010 strategy, which promotes the positive contribution that information and communication technologies (ICT) can make to the economy, society and personal quality of life.[14] The i2010 strategy has three aims: to create a Single European Information Space, which promotes an open and competitive internal market for information society and media services; to strengthen investment and innovation in ICT research; and to support inclusion, better public services and quality of life through the use of ICT.

To achieve those aims there are various actions such as regulation, funding for research and pilot projects, promotion activities and partnerships with stakeholders. DRIVER I established a European network of digital scientific repositories, accompanied by a test-bed that aggregated a first list of 51 repositories from Germany, France, the Netherlands, the UK and Belgium.[15] This can be interpreted as the accomplishment of the first goal: creating a single European Information Space for scientific communication. Through the DRIVER search portal, researchers were able to get a first glimpse of the benefits of open access to research materials, through the aggregation of multiple European resources. This way, investments in ICT and innovation (repositories) strengthened the accessibility and

---

12 See Mossink (2007). The Copyright toolbox is at http://copyrighttoolbox.surf.nl and the Scholar's Copyright Addendum Engine is at http://scholars.sciencecommons.org/.
13 Read more on the website: http://driver-community.eu.
14 See http://ec.europa.eu/information_society/eeurope/i2010/strategy/index_en.htm.
15 An example from France is HAL: http://hal.archives-ouvertes.fr/.

visibility of European Research (goal number two). They could, as readers of scientific communication, access all the full-text materials from these 51 repositories through a few mouse clicks: this way, DRIVER tried to make the researchers-as-authors enthusiastic to contribute to the collections of OA materials. Because this was only a test-bed phase, usability studies were carried out in order to optimize the services and benefits for researchers in DRIVER II.[16] The long-term goal of extending the network and building more services on top of the first content base fits neatly into the third goal of i2010: improving quality of life (by facilitating scientific progress) and better public services (by opening up the outputs of publicly-funded research results).

On the political side, the strategy of DRIVER was to advocate the establishment of more OA repositories throughout Europe, and to inform the scientific and greater community of the benefits of OA. An informative and interactive website has been created for that goal, and support services for repository managers and scientific authors were built on this website.[17] On a higher level, a few DRIVER partners co-initiated the "Petition for guaranteed public access to publicly-funded research results", which was handed over to Janosz Potoçnik, the European Commissioner for Research.[18] The petition received over 12,000 signatures from institutions, research funders, individuals and even publishers in no more than two weeks. The counter now stands at 27,280 signatories. This proved that the academic community is ready and willing to conform to an OA mandate by the EC. Indeed, the EC has now implemented an OA mandate for all resulting publications of research projects under FP7. Nevertheless, this mandate is quite limited and leaves a lot of room for non-compliance.[19] The European Research Council, another major European research fund, has set the example and released a mandate in December 2007.[20] DRIVER keeps lobbying on a high level in order to convince the EC of the importance of a mandate for Europe, whilst extending the network of European repositories into a Confederation with international bonds (see 2.2.1). DRIVER also issued technical guidelines for repository managers

---

16   Karen Van Godtsenhoven and Maurits Van der Graaf, "Digital Repository Infrastructure Vision for European Research", DRIVER Usability Assessment Report (2007), available at http://www.driver-support.eu/documents/DRIVER_usability_study_Gent.pdf.

17   See www.driver-support.eu.

18   http://www.ec-petition.eu.

19   See the section "Immediate policy revisions for greater openness" at http://www.openaire.eu/en/component/content/article/223-seizing-the-opportunity-for-open-access-to-european-research-ghent-declaration-published.

20   See http://erc.europa.eu/pdf/ScC_Guidelines_Open_Access_revised_Dec07_FINAL.pdf.

and three OA books concerning practical and political issues for repository managers, university administrators and scientific researchers.

The Belgian DRIVER partner, the University Library of Ghent, established a national network of institutional and subject-based repository managers, supported by a national community website with intranet and mailing lists.[21] This group of content providers met every two or three months, but very soon it appeared that, although the repository managers (often librarians) were very enthusiastic about the OA cause, their management did not allocate enough resources to the establishment and maintenance of the repository (the most pressing problem was man-hours, not so much the servers or technologies). In order to make the repositories more of a priority for university administrations, DRIVER lobbied with the university librarians and rectors by means of fact sheets and information sessions, until all-but-one (14 out of 15) university rectors agreed to officially sign the Berlin Declaration on Open Access to Research in the Sciences and Humanities during a national conference.[22] The two Ministers of Research and Education from Flanders and the French Community also agreed to sign the Declaration, and the two main research funders (FWO and FNRS) had already signed it before. This was a major turning point for the Belgian Open Access landscape: mainly in a strategic sense, since it led to two OA mandates: one by the FWO and one by the University of Liège.[23] The rector of Liège, Bernard Rentier, gave an inspiring speech at the national conference and became a very vehement OA advocate. He founded the European Open Access initiative for university rectors: Europenscholarship.[24] Over the course of one year, Belgium turned from a blind spot in terms of OA and repositories, into a country bustling with activity and enthusiasm. Through the distributed responsibilities and difficulties in the Belgian political landscape, there is not one administration responsible for research which could provide a national network like HAL in France and DAREnet in the Netherlands, but through the goodwill of many involved parties, the national repository community is still extending and getting closer to becoming a real network of content providers.

---

21   More information about the University Library of Ghent can be found at http://lib.ugent.be, and the community website is at www.driver-repository.be.
22   See http://www.driver-repository.be/content1.aspx?PageId=162.
23   See for example http://www.fwo.be.
24   See Bernard Rentier's blog: http://recteur.blogs.ulg.ac.be.

2.2 Plans for DRIVER II

The follow-up project of DRIVER, DRIVER II, financed under DG Research of the EC, sets out to take the accomplishments of DRIVER I a few steps further. The project goals are being extended in many key ways.

- Geographically, the DRIVER consortium is extended with three extra partners: Denmark for Scandinavia, Portugal for South-Western Europe, and Slovenia for Eastern Europe.
- Strategically, the DRIVER Summit meeting in January 2008 launched the European Confederation of Scientific Repositories, a broad European network which liaises with many other OA projects and sets an example for similar projects in other continents.[25]
- Semantically, apart from textual resources, DRIVER II will integrate enhanced publications, which means articles extended with raw data files, images, web resources, extra chapters, etc.
- Technically, in DRIVER II, the search and services portal moves from a test-bed to a state-of-the-art, production mode system using GRID structures such as Géant. The system consists of tools and services for end-users (search portal) as well as for repository managers (validator tools), accompanied by new releases of the open source D-NET software, which enables a larger community of service providers to "plug and play" with the DRIVER tools.[26]

This four-fold extension of the DRIVER vision and ambitions fits into the EC's vision of the "European Research Area":[27] a unified, strong European research community, which can compete with greater powers such as the US or China. This way, DRIVER II creates an economic advantage for Europe: because it is the only infrastructure in its kind, Europe is one step ahead in bringing together its scientific resources in a unified way.

The Belgian activities with repository managers and OA advocacy continue in DRIVER II, and Ghent University Library will also be more involved in the technical work-packages of DRIVER II, with technical tests throughout the country. A distributed project like DRIVER in a divided country like Belgium is no sinecure, but the latest developments have been favourable: many subject-based repository managers have

---

25 See http://www.driver-repository.eu/Summit1/DRIVER_Summit_report_Jan08.pdf.
26 See http://www.driver-repository.eu/D-NET_release.
27 See http://cordis.europa.eu/fp7/ict/e-infrastructure/home_en.html.

joined the Belgian DRIVER community, and with the new release of the D-NET software package it will be possible to build a national network of repositories. The only things lacking are political and therefore financial support for the infrastructure (servers and staff), without which a long-term vision cannot be accomplished.

Both DRIVER I and II fit into the EC's vision of an open, inclusive and integrated knowledge society for Europe, with the socio-economic benefits being the establishment of a unified, robust, state-of-the-art scientific e-infrastructure (with economical advantage for Europe as a continent because of increased research impact), and the opening up of a qualitative science commons to all researchers and readers worldwide (social benefit: developing countries are no longer cut off from vital information, and the greater professional public — for example a specialized doctor or lawyer — can now also freely access the latest evolutions in their field).

The benefits of an open knowledge society are multiple and both benefits (social and economic) have a positive effect on each other: the more a country invests in R&D and innovation, the more it reaps financial rewards, which can in turn provide a better education system resulting in a stronger economy. The DRIVER projects also contribute to the vision of a worldwide open knowledge society by establishing contacts with other repository networks and exchanging best practices with developing nations and continents. The DRIVER and DRIVER II projects have now evolved into OpenAIRE,[28] a project that takes OA a step further and focuses on the distribution and openness of research data. The aim is for the implemented research infrastructures from DRIVER to become fully-grown Open Access scientific information networks.

---

28 See http://www.openaire.eu.

10. CC REL: The Creative Commons Rights Expression Language

Hal Abelson, Ben Adida, Mike Linksvayer and Nathan Yergler

This chapter introduces the Creative Commons Rights Expression Language (CC REL), the standard recommended by Creative Commons (CC) for machine-readable expression of copyright licensing terms and related information.[1] CC REL and its description in this contribution supersede all previous CC recommendations for expressing licensing metadata. Like CC's previous recommendation, CC REL is based on the World Wide Web Consortium's Resource Description Framework (RDF).[2] Compared to the previous recommendation, CC REL is intended to be both

---

1 This chapter contains stylistic, formatting, and minor updates of "ccREL: The Creative Commons Rights Expression Language", a W3C Member Submission of 1 May 2008 by the authors, available at http://www.w3.org/Submission/ccREL. The authors wish to credit Neeru Paharia, past Executive Director of Creative Commons, for the "free-floating" content accountability architecture, Manu Sporny, CEO of Bitmunk, for the Creative Commons Operator code, and Aaron Swartz for the original Creative Commons RDF data model and metadata strategy. More broadly, the authors wish to acknowledge the work of a number of W3C groups, in particular all members of the RDF-in-HTML task force (Mark Birbeck, Jeremy Carroll, Michael Hausenblas, Shane McCarron, Steven Pemberton and Elias Torres), the Semantic Web Deployment Working Group chaired by Guus Schreiber and David Wood, and the tireless W3C staff without whom there would be no RDFa, GRDDL, or RDF, and thus no CC REL: Eric Miller, Ralph Swick, Ivan Herman and Dan Connolly.

2 RDF is a language for representing information about resources in the World Wide Web. We provide a short primer in this paper. Also, see the Web Consortium's RDF website at http://www.w3.org/RDF.

easier for content creators and publishers to provide, and more convenient for user communities and tool builders to consume, extend and redistribute.[3]

Formally, CC REL is specified in an abstract syntax-free way, as an extensible set of properties to be associated with a licensed document. Publishers have wide discretion in their choice of syntax, so long as the process for extracting the properties is discoverable and tool builders can retrieve the properties of CC REL-compliant webpages or embedded documents. We also recommend specific concrete "default" syntaxes and embedding schemes for content creators and publishers who want to use CC licenses without needing to be concerned about extraction mechanisms. The default schemes are RDFa for HTML webpages and resources referenced therein, and XMP for stand-alone media.[4]

For example, using this new recommendation, an author can express CC-structured data in an HTML page using the following simple markup:

```
<div about="http://lessig.org/blog/" xmlns:cc="http://
creativecommons.org/ns#">
    This page, by
    <a property="cc:attributionName" rel="cc:attributionURL"
        href="http://lessig.org/">
     Lawrence Lessig
    </a>,
    is licensed under a
    <a rel="license" href="http://creativecommons.org/licenses
    /by/3.0/">
     Creative Commons Attribution License
    </a>.
</div>
```

From this markup, tools can easily and reliably determine that http://lessig.org/blog is licensed under a CC Attribution License, v3.0, where attribution should be given to "Lawrence Lessig" at the URL http://lessig.org.

---

3   By "publisher" we mean anyone who places CC-licensed material on the Internet. By "tool builders" we mean people who write applications that are aware of the license information. Example tools might be search programs that filter their results based on specific types of licenses, or user interfaces that display license information in particular ways.

4   RDFa is an emerging collection of attributes and processing rules for extending XHTML to support RDF. See the W3C Working Draft "RDFa in XHTML: Syntax and Processing" at http://www.w3.org/TR/rdfa-syntax. The "RDFa Primer: Embedding Structured Data in Web Pages", may be found at http://www.w3.org/TR/xhtml-rdfa-primer. RDF/XML, described briefly below, is a method for expressing RDF in XML syntax. See "RDF/XML Syntax Specification (Revised)," W3C Recommendation 10 February 2004 at http://www.w3.org/TR/rdf-syntax-grammar. XMP (Extended Metadata Platform) is a labeling technology developed by Adobe, for embedding constrained RDF/XML within documents. See http://www.adobe.com/products/xmp.

This chapter explains the design rationale for these recommendations and illustrates some specific applications we expect CC REL to support. We begin with a review of the original 2002 recommendation for CC metadata and we explain why, as CC has grown, we have come to regard this as inadequate. We then introduce CC REL in the syntax-free model: as a vocabulary of properties. Next, we describe the recommended concrete syntaxes. We also explain how other frameworks, such as microformats, can be made CC REL compliant. Finally, we discuss specific use cases and the types of tools we hope to see built to take advantage of CC REL.

1. Background on Creative Commons recommendations

Creative Commons was publicly launched in December 2002, but its genesis traces to the summer of 2000 and discussions about how to promote a reasonable and flexible copyright regime for the Internet in an environment where copyright had become unreasonable and inflexible. There was no standard legal means for creators to grant limited rights to the public for online material, and obtaining rights often required difficult searches to identify rights-holders and burdensome transaction costs to negotiate permissions. As digital networks dramatically lowered other costs and engendered new opportunities for producing, consuming, and reusing content, the inflexibility and costs of licensing became comparatively more onerous.

Over the following year, CC's founders came to adopt a two-pronged response to this challenge. One prong was legal and social: create widely applicable licenses that permit sharing and reuse with conditions, clearly communicated in human-readable form. The other prong called for leveraging digital networks themselves to make licensed works more reusable and easy to find; that is, to lower search and transaction costs for works whose copyright holders have granted some rights to the public in advance. Core to this technical component is the ability for machines to detect and interpret the licensing terms as automatically as possible. Simple programs should thus be able to answer questions like:

- Under what license has a copyright holder released her work, and what are the associated permissions and restrictions?
- Can I redistribute this work for commercial purposes?
- Can I distribute a modified version of this work?
- How should I assign credit to the original author?

Equally important is constructing a robust user-machine bridge for publishing and detecting structured licensing information on the Web, and stimulating the emergence of tools that lower the barriers to collaboration and remixing. For example, if a webpage contains multiple images, not all licensed identically, can users easily determine which rights are granted on a particular image? Can they easily extract this image, create derivative works, and distribute them while assigning proper credit to the original author? In other words, is there a clear and usable connection between what the user sees and what the machine parses? CC REL aims to be a standard that implementors can follow in creating tools that make these operations simple.

1.1 Creative Commons and RDF

As early as fall 2001, CC had settled on the approach of creating machine-readable licenses based on the World Wide Web Consortium's then-emerging Resource Description Framework (RDF), part of the W3C Semantic Web Activity.[5]

The motivation for choosing RDF in 2001, and for continuing to use it now, is strongly connected to the CC vision: promoting scholarly and cultural progress by making it easy for people to share their creations and to collaborate by building on each other's work. In order to lower barriers to collaboration, it is important that the machine expression of licensing information and other metadata be *interoperable*. Interoperability here means not only that different programs can read particular metadata properties, but also that vocabularies — sets of related properties — can evolve and be extended. This should be possible in such a way that innovation can proceed in a distributed fashion in different communities — authors, musicians, photographers, cinematographers, biologists, geologists, and so on — so that licensing terms can be devised by local communities for types of works not yet envisioned. It is also important that potential extensions be backward compatible: existing tools should not be disrupted when new properties are added. If possible, existing tools should even be able to handle basic aspects of new properties. This is precisely the kind of "interoperability of meaning" that RDF is designed to support.

---

5 The Semantic Web Activity is a large collaborative effort led by the W3C aimed at extending the Web to become a universal medium for data exchange, for programs as well as people. See http://www.w3.org/2001/sw.

1.1.1 RDF triples

RDF is a framework for describing entities on the Web. It provides exceptionally strong support for interoperability and extensibility. All entities in RDF are named using a simple, distributed, globally addressable scheme already well known to Web users: the URL, and its generalisation the URI.[6]

For example, Lawrence Lessig's blog, a document identified by its URL http://lessig.org/blog, is licensed under the CC Attribution license. That license is also a document, identified by its own URL http://creativecommons.org/licenses/by/3.0. The property of "being licensed under", which we will call "license" can *itself* be considered a Web object and identified by a URL. This URL is http://www.w3.org/1999/xhtml/vocab#license, which refers to a webpage that contains information describing the "license" property. This particular webpage, maintained by the Web Consortium, is the reference document that describes the vocabulary.[7]

Instantiating properties as URLs enables anyone to use those properties to formulate descriptions, or to discover detailed information about an existing property by consulting the page at the URL, or to make new properties available simply by publishing the URLs that describe those properties.

As a case in point, CC originally defined its own "license" property, which it published at http://creativecommons.org/ns#license since no other group had defined in RDF the concept of a copyright license. When the XHTML Working Group introduced its own license property in 2005, we opted to start using their version, rather than maintain our own CC-dependent notion of license. We were then able to declare that http://creativecommons.org/ns#license is equivalent to the new property http://www.w3.org/1999/xhtml/vocab#license, simply by updating the description at http://creativecommons.org/ns#license. Importantly, RDF makes this equivalence interpretable by programs, not just humans, so that "old" RDF license declarations can be automatically interpreted using the new vocabulary.

In general, atomic RDF descriptions are called *triples*. Each triple consists of a *subject*, a *property*, and a *value* for that property of the subject. The triple

---

6 The term URI (universal resource identifier) is a generalisation of URL (universal resource locator). While a URL refers in principle to a resource on the Web, a URI can designate anything named with this universal hierarchical naming scheme. This generality is used in CC REL for items such as downloaded media files.

7 The vocabulary is also referenced in http://www.w3.org/2011/rdfa-context/rdfa-1.1.html, which sets default vocabulary prefixes and terms for RDFa.

that describes the license for Lessig's blog could be represented graphically as shown in Figure 1: a point (the subject) labelled with the blog URL; a second point (the value) labelled with the license URL; and an arrow (the property) labelled with the URL that describes the meaning of the term "license", running from the blog to the license. In general, an RDF model, as a collection of triples, can be visualized as a graph of relations among elements, where the edges and vertices are all labelled using URLs.

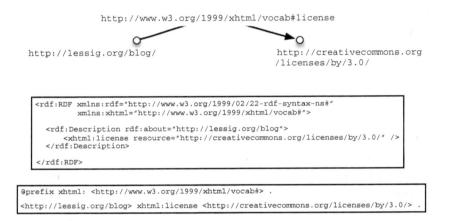

Figure 1: An RDF Triple represented as an edge between two nodes of a graph

1.1.2 Expressing RDF as text

Abstract RDF graphs can be expressed textually in various ways. One commonly used notation, RDF/XML, uses XML syntax. In RDF/XML the triple describing the licensing of Lessig's blog is denoted:

```
<rdf:RDF xmlns:rdf="http://www.w3.org/1999/02/22-rdf-syntax-ns#"
         xmlns:xhtml="http://www.w3.org/1999/xhtml/vocab#">
  <rdf:Description rdf:about="http://www.lessig.org/blog/">
    <xhtml:license rdf:resource="http://creativecommons.org/
        licenses/by/3.0/" />
  </rdf:Description>
</rdf:RDF>
```

One desirable feature of RDF/XML notation is that it is completely self-contained: all identifiers are fully qualified URLs. On the other hand, RDF/XML notation is extremely verbose, making it cumbersome for people to read and write, especially if no shorthand conventions are used. Even this simple example (verbose as it is) uses a shorthand mechanism: the second line of the description beginning xmlns:xhtml defines "xhtml:" to be an abbreviation for http://www.w3.org/1999/xhtml/vocab#, thus expressing the license property in its shorter form, xhtml:license, on the fourth line.

Since the introduction of RDF, the Web Consortium has developed more compact alternative syntaxes for RDF graphs. For example the N3 syntax would denote the above triple more concisely:[8] <http://lessig.org/blog>

```
<http://www.w3.org/1999/xhtml#license>
<http://creativecommons.org/licenses/by/3.0/> .
```

We could also rewrite this using a shorthand as in the RDF/XHTML example above, defining: xhtml: as an abbreviation for http://www.w3.org/1999/xhtml/vocab#:

```
@prefix xhtml: <http://www.w3.org/1999/xhtml/vocab#> .
<http://lessig.org/blog/> xhtml:license
<http://creativecommons.org/licenses/by/3.0/> .
```

The shorthand does not provide improved compactness or readability if a prefix is only used once as above. In N3, prefixes are typically defined only when they are used more than once, for example to express multiple properties taken from the same vocabulary. In RDF/XML, because of the stricter parsing rules of XML, there is a bit less flexibility: predicates can only be expressed using the shorthand, while subjects can only be expressed using the full URI.

1.2 CC's previous recommendation: RDF/XML in HTML comments

With its first unveiling of machine-readable licenses in 2002, CC recommended that publishers use the RDF/XML syntax to express license properties. The CC website included a Web-based license generator, where publishers could answer a questionnaire to indicate what kind of license they wanted, and the generator then provided RDF/XML text for them to include on their webpages, inside HTML comments:

```
<!-- [RDF/XML HERE] --> XXX
```

---

8   N3 (Notation 3) was designed to be a compact and more readable alternative to RDF/ XML. See http://www.w3.org/DesignIssues/Notation3.html.

We knew at the time that this was a cumbersome design, but there was little alternative. RDF/XML, despite its verbosity, was the only standard syntax for expressing RDF. Worse, the Web Consortium's Semantic Web Activity was focused on providing organisations with ways to annotate databases for integration into the Web, and it paid scant attention to the issues of intermixing semantic information with visible Web elements. A task force had been formed to address these issues, but there was no W3C standard for including RDF in HTML pages.

One consequence of CC's limited initial design is that, although millions of webpages now include CC licenses and metadata, there is no uniform, extensible way for tool developers to access this metadata, and the tools that do exist rely on ad-hoc techniques for extracting metadata.

Since 2004, CC has been working with the Web Consortium to create more straightforward and less limited methods of embedding RDF in HTML documents. These new methods are now making their way through the W3C standards process. Accordingly, CC no longer recommends using RDF/XML in HTML comments for specifying licensing information. This chapter supersedes that recommendation. We hope that the new CC REL standard presented in here will result in a more consistent and stable platform for publishers and tool builders to build upon Creative Commons licenses.

2. The CC REL abstract model

This section describes CC REL, CC's new recommendation for machine-readable licensing information, in its abstract form, i.e., independent of any concrete syntax. As an abstract specification, CC REL consists of a small but extensible set of RDF properties that should be provided with each licensed object. This abstract specification has evolved since the original introduction of CC properties in 2002, but it is worth noting that all first-generation licenses are still correctly interpretable against the new specification, thanks in large part to the extensibility properties of RDF itself.

The abstract model for CC REL distinguishes two classes of properties: *work properties* describe aspects of specific works, including under which license a work is distributed; and *license properties* describe aspects of licenses.

Publishers will normally be concerned only with work properties: this is the only information publishers provide to describe a work's licensing terms. License properties are used by CC itself to define the authoritative specifications of the licenses we offer. Other organisations are free to use these components for describing their own licenses. Such licenses, although related to CC licenses, would not themselves be CC licenses nor would they be endorsed necessarily by CC.

2.1 Work Properties

A publisher who wishes to license a work under a CC license must, at a minimum, provide one RDF triple that specifies the value of the work's license property (i.e. the license that governs the work), for example: <http://lessig.org/blog/> xhtml:license <http://creativecommons.org/licenses/by/3.0/>.

Although this is the minimum amount of information, CC also encourages publishers to include additional triples giving information about licensed works: the title, the name and URL for assigning attribution, and the document type. An example might be: <http://lessig.org/blog/> dc:title "The Lessig Blog".

```
<http://lessig.org/blog/> cc:attributionName "Larry Lessig" .
<http://lessig.org/blog/> cc:attributionURL <http://lessig.org/> .
<http://lessig.org/blog/> dc:type dcmitype:Text .
```

The specific work properties illustrated here are:

- dc:title—the document's title. Here dc: is shorthand for the Dublin Core vocabulary defined at http://purl.org/dc/terms and maintained by the Dublin Core Metadata Initiative.[9]

- cc:attributionName—the name to cite when giving attribution when the work is modified or redistributed under the terms of the associated CC license.[10] The prefix cc:, as mentioned above, is an abbreviation for http://creativecommons.org/ns#.

- cc:attributionURL—the URL to link to when providing attribution.

- dc:type—the type of the licensed document. In this example, the associated value is dcmitype:Text, which indicates text. Lessig's blog sometimes includes video, in which case the type would be dcmitype:MovingImage. Recommended use of dc:type is explained at http://dublincore.org/documents/dces. Individual types like

---

9   DCMI promotes the widespread adoption of interoperable metadata standards, and maintains a vocabulary of DCMI Metadata Terms. See http://dublincore.org.

10   All current CC licenses require attribution, and give the publisher the option of specifying a URL with attribution information. The cc:attributionURL property is the preferred way to provide this URL in machine-readable form.

> dcmitype:Text and dcmitype:MovingImage are part of the
> DCMI Vocabulary.

Incidentally, the above list of four triples could be alternately expressed
using the N3 semicolon convention, which indicates a list of triples that all
have the same subject:

```
@prefix dc: < http://purl.org/dc/terms/> .
@prefix cc: <http://creativecommons.org/ns#> .
@prefix dcmitype: <http://purl.org/dc/dcmitype/> .

<http://lessig.org/blog/>
    dc:title "The Lessig Blog" ;
    cc:attributionName "Larry Lessig" ;
    cc:attributionURL <http://lessig.org/> ;
    dc:type dcmitype:Text .
```

There are two more Work properties available to publishers of CC material:

- dc:source—indicates the original source of modified work, specified
  as a URI, for example:

```
<http://randomblog.example.org/modified_lessig_presentation>
dc:source <http://lessig.org/> .
```

- cc:morePermissions—indicates a URL that gives information on
  additional permissions beyond those specified in the CC license.
  For example, a document with a CC license that requires attribution,
  might, under certain circumstances, be usable without attribution.
  Or a document restricted to non-commercial use could be available
  for commercial use under certain conditions.
  A typical use would then be:

```
<http://randomblog.example.org/insightful_posting>
    cc:morePermissions <http://randomblog.example.org/
attribution_free_licensing> .
```

The information at the designated URL is completely up to the publisher,
as are the terms of the associated additional permissions, with one proviso:
the additional permissions must be *additional* permissions, i.e., they cannot
restrict the rights granted by the CC license. Said another way, any use of
the work that is valid without taking the morePermissions property into
account, must remain valid after taking morePermissions into account.

This is the current set of CC REL work properties. New properties may
be added over time, defined by CC or by others. Observe that CC REL
inherits the underlying extensibility of RDF—all that is required to create
new properties is to include additional triples that use these. For example,

a community of photography publishers could agree to use an additional photoResolution property, and this would not disrupt the operation of pre-existing tools, so long as the old properties remain available. We will see below that the concrete syntax (RDFa) recommended by CC for CC REL enjoys this same extensibility property.

Distributed creation of new properties notwithstanding, only CC can include new elements in the cc: namespace, because it controls the defining document at http://creativecommons.org/ns#. The ability to retain this kind of control, without loss of extensibility, is a direct consequence of using RDF.

2.2 License Properties

We now consider properties used for describing licenses. With CC REL, CC does not expect publishers to use these license properties directly, or even to deal with them at all.

In contrast, CC's original metadata recommendation encouraged publishers to provide the license properties with every licensed work. This design was awkward, because once a publisher has already indicated which license governs the work, specifying the license properties in addition is redundant and thus error prone. The CC REL recommendation does away with this duplication and leaves it to CC to provide the license properties.

Tool builders, on the other hand, should take these license properties into account so that they can interpret the particulars of each CC license. The license properties governing a work will typically be found by URL-based discovery. A tool examining a work notices the xhtml:license property and follows the indicated link to a page for the designated license. Those license description pages—the "Creative Commons Deeds"—are maintained by CC, and include the license properties in the CC-recommended concrete syntax (RDFa), as described in section 7.2:

Here are the license properties defined as part of CC REL:

- cc:permits—permits a particular use of the work above and beyond what default copyright law allows.
- cc:prohibits—prohibits a particular use of the work, specifically affecting the scope of the permissions provided by cc:permits (but not reducing rights granted under copyright).
- cc:requires—requires certain actions of the user when enjoying the permissions given by cc:permits.

- cc:jurisdiction—associates the license with a particular legal jurisdiction.
- cc:deprecatedOn—indicates that the license has been deprecated on the given date.
- cc:legalCode—references the corresponding legal text of the license.

Importantly, CC does not allow third parties to modify these properties for existing CC licenses. That say that publishers may certainly use these properties to create new licenses of their own, which they should host on their own servers, and not represent as being CC licenses.

The possible values for cc:permits, i.e. the possible permissions granted by a CC license, are:

- cc:Reproduction—copying the work in various forms.
- cc:Distribution—redistributing the work.
- cc:DerivativeWorks—preparing derivatives of the work.

The possible values for cc:prohibits, i.e. possible prohibitions that modulate permissions (but do not affect permissions granted by copyright law, such as fair use), are:

- cc:CommercialUse—using the work for commercial purposes.

The possible values for cc:requires are:

- cc:Notice—providing an indication of the license that governs the work.
- cc:Attribution—giving credit to the appropriate creator.
- cc:ShareAlike—when redistributing derivative works of this work, using the same license.
- cc:SourceCode—when redistributing this work (which is expected to be software when this requirement is used), source code must be provided.

For example, the Attribution Share-Alike v3.0 Creative Commons license is described as:[11] @prefix cc: http://creativecommons.org/ns#.

```
<http://creativecommons.org/licenses/by-sa/3.0/>
  cc:permits cc:Reproduction ;
cc:permits cc:Distribution ;
```

---

11 *Caveat:* The text descriptions of these property values are indicative only. The precise legal interpretations of the properties can be subtle and even jurisdiction dependent. Consult the full CC licenses ("legal code") for the actual legal definitions.

```
cc:permits cc:DerivativeWorks ;
cc:requires cc:Attribution ;
cc:requires cc:ShareAlike ;
cc:requires cc:Notice .
```

As new copyright licenses are introduced, CC expects to add new permissions, requirements, and prohibitions. However, it is unlikely that CC will introduce new license property types beyond permits, requires and prohibits. As a result, tools built to understand these three property types will be able to interpret future licenses, at least by listing the license's permissions, requirements, and prohibitions: thanks to the underlying RDF framework of designating properties by URLs, these tools can easily discover human-readable descriptions of these as-yet-undefined property values.

3. Desiderata for concrete CC REL syntaxes

While the previous examples illustrate CC REL using the RDF/XML and N3 notations, CC REL is meant to be independent of any particular syntax for expressing RDF triples. To create compliant CC REL implementations, publishers need only to arrange that tool builders can extract RDF triples for the relevant CC REL properties—typically only the work properties, since CC provides the license properties—through a discoverable process. We expect that different publishers will do this in different ways, using syntaxes of their choice that take into account the kinds of environments they would like to provide for their users. In each case, however, it is the publisher's responsibility to associate their pages with appropriate extraction mechanisms and to arrange for these mechanisms to be discoverable by tool builders.

   CC also recommends concrete CC REL syntaxes that tool builders should recognise by default, so that publishers who do not want to be explicitly concerned with extraction mechanisms have a clear implementation path. These recommended syntaxes—RDFa for HTML webpages, and XMP for free-floating content—are described in the following sections. This section presents the principles underlying our recommendations.

3.1 Principles for HTML

Licensing information for a Web document will be expressed in some form of HTML. What properties would an ideal HTML syntax for expressing CC terms exhibit? Given the use cases we have observed over the past several years, we can call out the following four desiderata.

Independence and Extensibility: We cannot know in advance what new kinds of data we will want to integrate with CC licensing data. Currently, we already need to combine CC properties with simple media files (sound, images, videos) and there is a growing interest in providing markup for complex scientific data (biomedical records, experimental results). Therefore, the means of expressing the licensing information in HTML should be extensible: it should enable the reuse of existing data models and the addition of new properties, both by CC and by others. Adding new properties should not require extensive coordination across communities or approval from a central authority. Tools should not suddenly become obsolete when new properties are added, nor when existing properties are applied to new kinds of data sets.

DRY (Don't Repeat Yourself): An HTML document often already displays the name of the author and a clickable link to a CC license. Providing machine-readable structure should not require duplicating this data in a separate format. Notably, if the human-clickable link to the license is changed, for example, from v2.5 to v3.0, a machine processing the page should automatically note this change without the publisher having to update another part of the HTML file to keep it "in sync" with the human-readable portion.

Visual Locality: An HTML page may contain multiple items, for example a dozen photographs, each with its own structured data and a different license. It should be easy for tools to associate the appropriate structured data with their corresponding visual display.

Remix Friendliness: It should be easy to copy an item from one document and paste it into a new document with all appropriate structured data included. In a world where we constantly remix old content to create new content, copy-and-paste, widgets, and sidebars are crucial elements of the remixable Web. As much as possible, CC REL should allow for easy copy-and-paste of data to carry along the appropriate licensing information.

3.2 Desiderata for Free-Floating Content

Some important works are not typically conveyed via HTML. Examples are MP3s, MPEGs, and other media files. The technique for embedding licensing data into these files should achieve the following design principles.

Consistency: There are many different possible file types. The mechanism for embedding licensing information should be reasonably generic, so that a single tool can read and write the licensing information without requiring awareness of all file types.

Publisher Accountability: It can be difficult to provide for accountability of licensing metadata when files are shared in peer-to-peer systems, rather than distributed from a central location. The method for expressing metadata should facilitate providing publisher accountability at least as strong as the accountability of a webpage with a well-defined host and owner.

Simplicity: The process of embedding licensing information should require little more than a simple and free program. In particular, though complex publisher accountability approaches involving digital signatures and certificates can be used, they should not be required for the basic use case.

4. Including CC REL information in webpages

Consider the abstract model for CC REL. Here, again, are the triples from the example of Lessig's blog, expressed in N3:[12] @prefix xhtml: <http://www.w3.org/1999/xhtml#>.

```
@prefix cc: <http://creativecommons.org/ns#> .
<http://lessig.org/blog/> xhtml:license <http://creativecommons.
org/licenses/by/3.0/> .
<http://lessig.org/blog/> cc:attributionName "Lawrence Lessig" .
<http://lessig.org/blog/> cc:attributionURL <http://lessig.org/> .
```

The webpage to which this information refers typically already contains some HTML that describes this same information (redundantly), in human-readable form, for example:

```
<div>
  This page, by
  <a href="http://lessig.org/">
    Lawrence Lessig
  </a>,
  is licensed under a
  <a href="http://creativecommons.org/licenses/by/3.0/">
    Creative Commons Attribution License
  </a>.
</div>
```

---

12 It is worth noting that, while the xhtml:license property has long been a part of the CC specification, the cc:attributionName and cc:attributionURL properties are new with CC REL. Under the independence and extensibility principle, the solution we select for embedding CC REL in HTML should allow for such extensions without breaking tools that already know about xhtml:license.

What we would like is a way to quickly augment this HTML with just enough structure to enable the extraction of the RDF triples, using the DRY principle articulated above: the existing markup and links should be used both for human and machine readability.

4.1 RDFa and concrete syntax for Work properties

RDFa was designed by the W3C with CC's input. The design was motivated in part by the principles noted above. Using existing HTML properties and a handful of new ones, RDFa enables a chunk of HTML to express RDF triples, reusing the content wherever possible. For example, the HTML above would be extended by including additional attributes within the HTML anchor tags, as follows:

```
<div about="" xmlns:cc="http://creativecommons.org/ns#">
  This page, by
   <a property="cc:attributionName"
    rel="cc:attributionURL" href="http://lessig.org/">
       Lawrence Lessig
   </a>,
   is licensed under a
   <a rel="license" href="http://creativecommons.org/licenses/by/3.0/">
    Creative Commons Attribution License
   </a>.
</div>
```

The rules for understanding the meaning of the above markup are:

- about defines the subject of all triples within the <div>. Here we have about="", which defines the subject to be the URL of the current document.
- xmlns:cc associates, throughout the <div>, the prefix cc with the URL http://creativecommons.org/ns#, much as N3 does with @prefix.
- property generates a new triple with predicate cc:attributionName, and the text content of the element, in this case "Lawrence Lessig", as the object.
- rel="cc:attributionURL" generates a new triple with predicate cc:attributionURL, and the URL in the href as the object.
- rel="license" generates a new triple with predicate xhtml:license, as xhtml is the default prefix for reserved XHTML values like license. The object is given by the href.

The fragment of HTML (within the div) is entirely self-contained (and thus remix-friendly). Its meaning would be preserved if it were copied and pasted into another webpage. The data's structure is local to the data itself: a human looking at the page could easily identify the structured data by pointing to the rendered page and finding the enclosing chunk of HTML. In addition, the clickable links and rendered author names gain semantic meaning without repeating the core data. Finally, as this is embedded RDF, the extensibility and independence properties of RDF vocabularies are automatically inherited: anyone can create a new vocabulary or reuse portions of existing vocabularies.

```
<div about="" typeof="cc:Work"
    xmlns:cc="http://creativecommons.org/ns#"
    xmlns:dc=" http://purl.org/dc/terms/"
    align="center">

  <img alt="Creative Commons License"
   src="http://i.creativecommons.org/l/by/3.0/us/88x31.png" />
  <br />

  <span property="dc:title">The Lessig Blog</span>,
  a
  <span rel="dc:type" href="http://purl.org/dc/dcmitype/Text">
    collection of texts
  </span>
  by
  <a property="cc:attributionName"
   rel="cc:attributionURL" href="http://lessig.org/">
      Lawrence Lessig
  </a>,<br />
  is licensed under a
  <a rel="license" href="http://creativecommons.org/licenses/by/3.0/">
      Creative Commons Attribution License
  </a>.<br />

  There are
  <a rel="cc:morePermissions"
    href="http://lessig.org/blog/other-license">
      alternative licensing options
  </a>.
</div>
```

Figure 2: RDFa markup of a Creative Commons license notice, illustrating all the current CC Work properties, including the rendering of this markup in a Web browser

Of course, one can continue to add additional data, both visible and structured. Figure 2 shows a more complex example that includes all work properties currently supported by CC, including how this HTML+RDFa would be rendered on a webpage. Notice how properties can be associated with HTML spans as well as anchors, or in fact with any HTML elements—see the RDFa specification for details.

The examples in this section illustrate how publishers can specify work properties. One can also use RDFa to express license properties. This is what CC does with the license description pages on its own site, as described below in section 7.2.

4.2 Microformats

Microformats are a set of simple, open data formats "designed for humans first and machines second" (http://microformats.org/about). They provide domain-specific syntaxes for annotating data in HTML. At the moment, the two widely deployed "compound" microformats annotate contact information (hCard) and calendar events (hCal). Of the "elemental" microformats, those meant to annotate a single data point, the most popular is rel-tag, used to denote a "tag" on an item such as a blog post. Another elemental microformat is rel-license, which is meant to indicate the current page's license and which, conveniently, uses a syntax which overlaps with RDFa: rel="license". Other microformats may, over time, integrate CC properties, for example, when licensing images, videos and other multimedia content.[13]

---

13   See http://microformats.org.

Microformat designers have focused on simplicity and readability, and CC encourages publishers who use microformats to make it easy for tool builders to extract the relevant CC REL triples. Nonetheless, microformats' syntactic simplicity comes at the cost of independence and extensibility, which makes them limited from the CC perspective.

For example, every time a CC license needs to be expressed in a new context—for example, as videos instead of still images—a new microformat and syntax must be designed, and all parsers must then, somehow, become aware of the change. It is also not obvious how one might combine different microformats on a single webpage, given that the syntax rules may differ and even conflict from one microformat to the next.[14] Finally, when it comes time to express complex data sets with ever expanding sets of properties (for example, scientific data), microformats do not appear to scale appropriately, given their lack of vocabulary scoping and general inability to mix vocabularies from independently developed sources—the kind of mixing that is enabled by RDF's use of namespaces.

Thus, CC does not recommend any particular microformat syntax for CC REL, but we do recommend a method for ensuring that, when publishers use microformats, tool builders can extract the corresponding CC REL properties: use an appropriate profile URL in the header of the HTML document.[15] This profile URL significantly improves the independence and extensibility of microformats by ensuring that the tools can find the appropriate parser code for extracting the CC REL abstract model from the microformat, without having to know about all microformats in advance. One downside is that the microformat syntax then becomes less remix-friendly, with two disparate fragments: one in the head to declare the profile, and one in the body to express the data. Even so, the profile approach is likely good enough for simple data. It is worth noting that this use of a profile URL is already recommended as part of microformats' best practices, though it is unfortunately rarely implemented today in deployed applications.

---

14 See http://microformats.org/wiki/grouping-brainstorming for one discussion.

15 Profile URLs indicate that the HTML file can be interpreted according to the rules of that profile. This property has been used by some microformat specifications to indicate, for example, "this page contains the hCard microformat". The property is also used by GRDDL for generic HTML transformations to RDF/XML, although this approach to RDF extraction from HTML is not fully compliant with the principles laid out in this paper: it is difficult to tell which image on a page is CC-licensed when the RDF extraction is achieved via GRDDL.

4.3 GRDDL for XML Documents

Not all documents on the web are HTML: one popular syntax for representing structured data in XML. Given that XML is a machine-readable syntax, often with a strict schema depending on the type of data expressed, not all of the principles we outlined are useful here. In particular, *visual locality* is not relevant when the reader is a machine rather than a human, and *remix-friendliness* does not apply when XML fragments are rarely remixable in the first place, given schema validation. Thus, we focus on *independence and extensibility*, as well as *DRY*.

When publishing CC licensing information inside an XML document, CC recommends exposing a mechanism to extract the CC REL abstract model from the XML, so that CC tools need not know about every possible XML schema ahead of time. The W3C's GRDDL recommendation performs exactly this task by letting publishers specify, either in each XML document or once in an XML schema, an XSL Transformation that extracts RDF/XML from XML.[16] Consider, for example, a small extension of the Atom XML publishing schema for news feeds:[17] <entry>

```
    <title>Lessig 2.0 - the site</title>
    <link rel="alternate" type="text/html"
      href="http://lessig.org/blog/2007/06/lessig_20_the_site.html" />
    <id>tag:lessig.org,2007:/blog//1.3401</id>
    <published>2007-06-25T19:44:48Z</published>
    <link rel="license" type="text/html"
          href="http://creativecommons.org/licenses/by/3.0/us/" />
    </entry>
```

An appropriate XSL transform can easily process this data to extract the CC REL property that specifies the license:

```
<rdf:RDF about="http://lessig.org/blog/2007/06/lessig_20_the_site.html"
    xmlns:cc="http://creativecommons.org/ns#">
    <cc:license resource="http://creativecommons.org/licenses/by/3.0/us/" />
</rdf:RDF>
```

Similarly, the Open Archives Initiative (OAI) defines a complex XML schema for library resources.[18] These resources may include megabytes

---

16 Gleaning Resource Descriptions from Dialects of Languages (GRDDL) (http://www.w3.org/TR/grddl) is a W3C recommendation for linking Web documents to algorithms that extract RDF data from the document.

17 Atom License Extension. See http://tools.ietf.org/html/rfc4946.

18 See http://www.openarchives.org.

of data, sometimes including the entire resource in full text. Using XSLT, one can extract the relevant CC REL information, exactly as above. Using GRDDL, the OAI can specify the XSLT in its XML schema file, so that all OAI documents are automatically transformable to RDF/XML, which immediately conveys CC REL.

4.4 Direct RDF/XML embedding in XML

Because RDF can be expressed using the RDF/XML syntax, one might be tempted to use RDF/XML directly inside an XML document with an appropriate schema definition that enables such direct embedding. This very approach is taken by Scalable Vector Graphics, and there are cases of SVG graphics that include licensing information using directly embedded RDF/XML.[19]

This approach can be made CC REL-compliant with very little work—a simple GRDDL transform, declared in the XML schema definition, that extracts the RDF/XML and expresses it on its own. Note that, for CC REL compliance, this transform, although simple, is necessary. The reason for its necessity goes to the crux of the CC REL principles: without such a transform provided by each XML schema designer, tools would have to be aware of all the various XML schemas that include RDF/XML in this way. For extensibility and future-proofing, CC REL asks that publishers of the schema make the effort to provide the extraction mechanism. With explicit extraction mechanisms, publishers have a little bit more work to do, while tool builders are immediately empowered to create generic programs that can process data they have never seen before.

5. Embedding CC REL in free-floating files

We turn to the precise CC recommendation for embedding CC REL metadata inside MP3s, Word documents, and other "free-floating" content that is often passed around in a peer-to-peer fashion, via email or P2P networks. We note that there are two distinct issues to resolve: expressing the abstract model using a specific syntax and embedding; and providing minimal accountability for the expressed CC REL data.

We handle accountability for free-floating content by connecting any free-floating document to a webpage, and placing the CC REL information on that webpage. Thus, publishers of free-floating content are just as

---

19 Scalable Vector Graphics, http://www.w3.org/Graphics/SVG, a W3C Recommendation for vector graphics expressed using XML.

accountable as publishers of web-based content: rights are always expressed on a webpage. The connection between the webpage and the binary file it describes is achieved using a cryptographic hash (fingerprint) of the file. For example, the PDF file of Lessig's "Code v2" will contain a reference to http://codev2.cc/download+remix, which itself will contain a reference to the SHA1 hash of the PDF file. The owner of the URL http://codev2.cc/download+remix is thus taking responsibility for the CC REL statements it makes about the file.

For expression, we recommend XMP. XMP has the broadest support of any embedded metadata format (perhaps it is the only such format with anything approaching broad support) across many different media formats. With the exception of media formats where a workable embedded metadata format is already ubiquitous (e.g. MP3), CC recommends adopting XMP as an embedded metadata standard and using the following two fields in particular:

- Web reference: value of xapRights:WebStatement
- License: value of cc:license

Consider our example of Lessig's "Code v2", a CC-licensed, community-edited second version of his original "Code and Other Laws of Cyberspace". The PDF of this book, available at http://pdf.codev2.cc/Lessig-Codev2.pdf, contains XMP metadata as follows:

```
<?xpacket begin="" id=""?>
<x:xmpmeta xmlns:x="adobe:ns:meta/">
  <rdf:RDF xmlns:rdf="http://www.w3.org/1999/02/22-rdf-syntax-ns#">


    <rdf:Description rdf:about="" xmlns:xapRights="http://ns.adobe.com/
xap/1.0/rights/">
       <xapRights:Marked>True</xapRights:Marked>
       <xapRights:WebStatement rdf:resource="http://codev2.cc/
download+remix/" />
    </rdf:Description>

    ...

    <rdf:Description rdf:about="" xmlns:cc="http://creativecommons.org/ns#">
       <cc:license rdf:resource="http://creativecommons.org/licenses/
       by-sa/2.5/" />
    </rdf:Description>

  </rdf:RDF>
</x:xmpmeta>
<?xpacket end="r"?>
```

Notice how this is RDF/XML, including a xapRights: WebStatement pointer to the webpage http://codev2.cc/download+remix, which itself contains RDFa:

```
Any derivative must be licensed under a
<a about="urn:sha1:W4XGZGCD4D6TVXJSCIG3BJFLJNWFATTE"
   rel="license"
   href="http://creativecommons.org/licenses/by-sa/2.5/">
       Creative Commons Attribution-ShareAlike 2.5 License
</a>
```

This RDFa references the PDF using its SHA1 hash—a secure fingerprint of the file that matches only the given PDF file—and declares its CC license. Thus, anyone that finds the "Code v2" PDF can find its WebStatement pointer, look up that URL, verify that it properly references the file via its SHA1 hash, and confirm the file's CC license on the web-based deed.

6. Examples and use cases

This section describes several examples, first by publishers of CC-licensed works, then by tool builders who wish to consume the licensing information. Some of these examples include existing, real implementations of CC REL, while others are potential implementations and applications we believe would significantly benefit from CC REL.

6.1 How publishers can use CC REL

Publishers can mix CC REL with other markup with great flexibility. As a result of CC REL's "independence and extensibility" principle, publishers can use CC REL descriptions in combination with additional attributes taken from other publishers, or with entirely new attributes they define for their own purposes. And CC REL's "DRY" principle means that even small publishers get the benefit of updating data in one location and automatically keeping the human- and machine-readable in sync.

```
<div class="mediaDetails haudio"
     xmlns:xsd="http://www.w3.org/2001/XMLSchema"
     xmlns:dc="http://purl.org/dc/terms/"
     xmlns:commerce="http://example.org/rdf/commerce/elements/1.0/"
     xmlns:hmedia="http://www.microformats.org/2007/12/hmedia/"
     about="#album-6579151">
...
    <a id="mediaImageLink" rel="hmedia:depiction"
       href="http://www.bitmunk.com/view/image/6579151">
...
    <h1 property="dc:title" class="mediaTitle album fn">Lifeseeker</h1>
...
```

```
    <span property="dc:creator" class="fn">Lifeseeker</span>
...
    <span property="dc:contributor" class="fn">(P) 2005 One In A Million
Records</span>
...
    <span property="dc:date" class="published" title="2007-11-18T11
        :23:07-05:00"
            content="2007-11-18T11:23:07-05:00" datatype="xsd:date">
        2002-07-23
    </span>
...
    <a href="/browse/genre/audio_album/59"
        property="dc:type" class="category">Hip Hop and Rap</a>

    <span class="detailLabel">Tracks:</span>
    16 (<abbr property="hmedia:duration" class="duration"
    title="PT1H13M37S" content="PT1H13M37S"
    datatype="xsd:duration">1:13:37</span>)
...
    <span class="detailLabel">Licenses:</span>
    <img property="dc:license" class="licenseIcon"
        src="/themes/bm2/images/licenses/sc-sm.png"
        alt="Standard Copyright" title="Standard Copyright"
        content="Standard Copyright"/>
...
</div>
```

Figure 3: Markup for a Bitmunk Song: this is a real excerpt of the actual
HTML markup used on bitmunk.com, slightly simplified and
indented for readability.

6.1.1 Mixing content with different licenses

A common use case for web publishers working in a mashup-friendly world
is the issue of mixing content with different licenses. Consider, for example,
what happens if Lessig's blog reuses an image published by another author
and licensed for non-commercial use. Recall that the blog is licensed to
permit commercial use.

The HTML markup in this case is straightforward:

```
<div about="" xmlns:cc="http://creativecommons.org/ns#">
    This page, by
    <a property="cc:attributionName" rel="cc:attributionURL"
        href="http://lessig.org/">
            Lawrence Lessig
    </a>,
    is licensed under a
    <a rel="license"
```

```
        href="http://creativecommons.org/licenses/by/3.0/">
           Creative Commons Attribution License
      </a>.

      <div about="/photos/constitution.jpg">
         The photo of the constitution used in this post was originally
  published by
           <a rel="dc:source" href="http://example.org/">Joe Example</a>, and
  is licensed under a
           <a rel="license" href="http://creativecommons.org/licenses/
  by-nc/3.0/">
           Creative Commons Attribution-NonCommercial License
         </a>.
      </div>
  </div>
```

The inner <div> uses the about attribute to indicate that its statements concern the photo in question. A link to the original source is provided using the dc:source property, and a different license pointer is given for this photo using the normal anchor with a rel="license" attribute.

6.1.2 hAudio

Bitmunk is a service that supports artists with a legal, copyright-aware, content distribution service. The service needed a mechanism for embedding structured data about songs and albums directly into their webpages, including licensing information, so that browser add-ons might provide additional functionality around the music, for example, comparing the price of a particular song at various online stores. Bitmunk first created a microformat called hAudio. They soon realized, however, that they would be duplicating fields when it came time to define hVideo, and that these duplicated fields would no longer be compatible with those of hAudio. More immediately problematic, hAudio's basic fields, like the title field, would not be compatible with other "title" fields of other microformats.

Thus, Bitmunk created the hAudio RDFa vocabulary. The design process for this vocabulary immediately revealed separate, logical components: Dublin Core for basic properties (such as title), CC for licensing, a new vocabulary called "hMedia" for media-specific properties (such as duration), and a new vocabulary called "hCommerce" for transaction-specific properties (such as price). Bitmunk was thus able to reuse two existing vocabularies and add features. It was also able to clearly delineate logical components to make it particularly easy for other vocabulary developers to reuse only certain components of the hAudio vocabulary, for example, hCommerce. Meanwhile, all CC licensing information is still expressible without alteration.

Figure 3 shows an excerpt of the markup available from Bitmunk at http://bitmunk.com/view/media/6579151. Note that this particular sample is not CC-licensed: it uses standard copyright. A CC-licensed album would be marked up in the same way, with a different license value: Bitmunk was able to develop its vocabulary independent of CC REL, and can now integrate with CC REL simply by adding the appropriate attributes.

```
<div xmlns:dc="http://purl.org/dc/terms/"
     xmlns:cc="http://creativecommons.org/ns#"
     xmlns:flickr="http://flickr.com/ns#"
     about="http://www.flickr.com/photos/laughingsquid/2034629532/">
...
    <h1 property="dc:title">NewTeeVee Live Game Show</h1>
...
    <img rel="flickr:defaultPhoto"
         src="http://farm3.static.flickr.com/2320/2034629532_02085434dd.
jpg?v=0" />


...

    <div property="dc:description">
        See the blog post for more info:
        <a href="http://laughingsquid.com/a-few-random-newteevee
        -live-photos/">
            A Few Random NewTeeVee Live Photos
        </a>
    </div>
...

    This photo is licensed under a
    <a rel="license" href="http://creativecommons.org/licenses/
by-nc-nd/2.0/">
        Creative Commons license
    </a>.

    If you use this photo within the terms of the license or make
    special arrangements to use the photo, please list the photo credit as

    <span property="cc:attributionName">Scott Beale / Laughing Squid
    </span>

    and link the credit to

    <a rel="cc:attributionURL" href="http://laughingsquid.com">
        laughingsquid.com
    </a>.
```

```
...
    Uploaded on
    <span property="flickr:uploaded" content="2007-11-15">
        November 15, 2007
    </span>
...
    <h4>Tags</h4>
    <a rel="flickr:tag" href="/photos/laughingsquid/tags/
newteevee/">NewTeeVee</a>
    <a rel="flickr:tag" href="/photos/laughingsquid/tags/
gigaom/">GigaOm</a>
...
    <a rel="upcoming:event" href="http://upcoming.org/event/286436">
upcoming:event=286436</a>
...
</div>
```

Figure 4: A Flickr Photo Page with RDFa: this is an excerpt from a Flickr photo page with small amounts of additional markup to show how one would integrate RDFa. The rendering of the HTML is identical with the added RDFa properties. Note the Flickr machine tag upcoming:event, which references an event at upcoming.org. This machine tag is, in fact, an RDF triple, easily expressed in RDFa alongside existing Flickr information and CC licensing.

6.1.3 Flickr

Flickr hosts over 200 million CC-licensed images (as of December 2011). Currently Flickr denotes a license on each image's page with a link to the relevant license qualified by rel="license". This ad-hoc convention, encouraged by the microformats effort, was "grandfathered" into RDFa thanks to the reserved HTML keyword license. Unfortunately, it works only for simple use cases, with a single image on a single page. This approach breaks down when multiple images are viewed on a single page, or when further information, such as the photographer's name, is required.

Flickr could significantly benefit from the CC REL recommendations, by providing, in addition to simple license linking:

- License assertions scoped to the image being licensed.
- Attribution details.
- A cc:additionalPermissions reference to commercial licensing brokers and a dc:source reference to parent works.
- XMP embedding in images themselves.

In addition, Flickr supports "machine tags", where photographers can add metadata about their images using custom properties. Flickr's machine tags are, in fact, a subset of RDF, which can be represented easily using RDFa. Thus, CC licensing can be easily expressed alongside Flickr's machine tags using the same technology, without interfering.

Figure 4 shows how the CC-licensed photo at http://www.flickr.com/ photos/laughingsquid/2034629532 would be marked up using CC REL, including the machine tag upcoming:event that associates the photo with an event at http://upcoming.org.

```
<div xmlns:dc="http://purl.org/dc/terms/"
xmlns:cc="http://creativecommons.org/ns#"
     xmlns:prism="http://prismstandard.org/namespaces/1.2/basic/"
     xmlns:foaf="http://xmlns.com/foaf/0.1/"about="/documents/1290/
version/1">

  <h2 property="dc:title">An Olfactory Receptor Pseudogene whose
Function emerged in Humans</h2>
  ...
  <span rel="dc:creator"><span property="foaf:name">Peter Lai</span>
</span><sup>1</sup>,

  <a rel="dc:creator" href="http://precedings.nature.com/users/
bdaff59be022e709d8b7beab298ccfb8">
     <span property="foaf:name">Gautam Bahl</span>
  </a><sup>2</sup>,
  ...
  <dt class="doctype">Document Type:</dt>
  <dd property="dc:type">Manuscript</dd>

  Received <span property="dc:date">02 November 2007 21:20 UTC</span>;
  Posted <span property="prism:publicationDate">05 November 2007</span>
  ...
  <a rel="prism:category" href="http://precedings.nature.com/subjects/
biotechnology">
     Biotechnology
  </a>,
  ...
```

```
    <ul id="revision-1321-tags" class="taglist">
      <li> <a rel="nature:tag" href="http://precedings.nature.com/tags/
olfactory+receptors">
              olfactory receptors
          </a>
      </li>
      ...
    </ul>
    ...
    This document is licensed to the public under the
    <a rel="license" href="http://creativecommons.org/licenses/by/2.5/">
      Creative Commons Attribution 2.5 License
    </a>
    ...
    <!-- Citation -->
    <dt class="abstract">How to cite this document:</dt>
    <dd>
      <p> <span  property="cc:attributionName">
            Lai, Peter, Bahl, Gautam, Gremigni, Maryse, Matarazzo, Valery,
            Clot-Faybesse, Olivier, Ronin, Catherine, and Crasto, Chiquito.
            An Olfactory Receptor Pseudogene whose Function emerged in
Humans.
          </span>
          Available from Nature Precedings &#060;
          <a rel="cc:attributionURL" href="http://dx.doi.org/10.1038/
npre.2007.1290.1">
            http://dx.doi.org/10.1038/npre.2007.1290.1
          </a>&#062; (2007)
      </p>
    </dd>
...
  </div>
```

Figure 5: Markup for a *Nature Precedings* article, including how RDFa might be integrated seamlessly into the existing markup. The property nature:tag is used to indicate a *Nature*-defined way of tagging content, though another vocabulary could easily be used here.

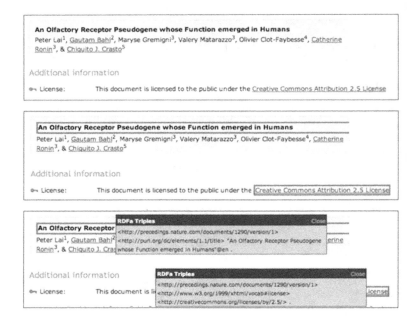

Figure 6: Portions of a *Nature Precedings* paper, marked up with RDFa. An
RDFa-aware browser (in this case any normal browser using the
RDFa Bookmarklets) detects the markup, highlighting the title
and CC license, and revealing the corresponding RDF triples.

6.1.4 Nature precedings

Nature, one of the world's top scientific journals, recently launched a web-only
"precedings" site, where early results can be announced rapidly in advance of
full-blown peer review. Papers on *Nature Precedings* are distributed under a
CC license. Like Flickr, *Nature Precedings* currently uses CC's prior metadata
recommendation: RDF/XML included in an HTML comment. *Nature* could
significantly benefit from the CC REL recommendation, which would let
them publish structured CC licensing information in a more robust, more
extensible, and more human-readable way.

Consider, for example, the *Nature Preceding* paper at http://precedings.
nature.com/documents/1290/version/1. Figure 5 shows how the markup at
that page can be extended with simple RDFa attributes, using the Dublin
Core, CC, FOAF, and PRISM publication vocabularies.[20] Notice how any

---

20 The Publishing Requirements for Industry Standard Metadata (PRISM) provides a
vocabulary for publishing and aggregating content from books, magazines, and journals.
See http://www.prismstandard.org.

HTML element, including the existing H1 used for the title, can be used to carry RDFa attributes. Figure 6 shows how this page could appear in an RDFa-aware browser.

6.1.5 Scientific data

Open publication of scientific data on the Internet has begun, with the Nature Publishing Group recently announcing the release of genomic data sets under a CC license.[21] Beyond simple licensing, thousands of new metadata vocabularies and properties are being developed to express research results. CC is playing an active role to remove barriers to scientific cooperation and sharing.[22] CC is specifically encouraging the creation of RDF-based vocabularies for describing scientific information and is stimulating collaboration among research communities with tools that build on RDF's extensibility and interoperability.

Figure 7: A simple rendering of a bibliographic entry with extra scientific data.

As these vocabularies become more widespread, it's easy to envision uses of CC REL and RDFa that extend the bibliographic and licensing markup to include these new scientific data tags. Tools may then emerge to take advantage of this additional markup, enabling dynamic, distributed scientific collaboration through interoperable referencing of scientific concepts.

Imagine, for example, an excerpt from a (hypothetical) web-based newsletter about genomics research, which references an (actual) article from *BioMed Central Neurosciences*, as it might be rendered by a browser (Figure 7). The words "recent study on rat brains", and "CEBP-beta" are clickable links, leading respectively to a webpage for the paper, and a webpage that describes the protein CEBP-5#5 in the Uniprot protein database.

---

21 See http://www.nature.com/authors/editorial_policies/license.html for details.
22 See http://sciencecommons.org/http://creativecommons.org/science.

The RDFa generating this excerpt could be:

```
<div xmlns:OBO_REL="http://www.obofoundry.org/ro/ro.owl#">

   A <a href="http://www.biomedcentral.com/1471-2202/6/69">
      recent study on rat brains
   </a>
   by von Gertten <em>et. al.</em> reports that

   <div about="http://purl.org/obo/owl/GO#GO_0050729">
      <span property="rdfs:label">inflammatory stimuli</span>

      upregulate expression of

      <a rel="OBO_REL:precedes"
          href="http://purl.uniprot.org/uniprot/P17676">
         <span property="rdfs:label">CEPB-beta</span>
      </a>
   </div>
</div>
```

This RDFa not only links to the paper in the usual way, but it also provides machine-readable information that this is a statement about inflammatory stimuli (as defined by the Open Biomedical Ontologies initiative) activating expression of the CEPB protein (as specified in the UniProt database of proteins). Since the URI of the protein is visually meaningful, it can be marked up with a clickable link that also provides the object of a triple.

6.1.6 Additional permissions

A CC license grants certain permissions to the public; others may be available privately. A coarse-grained "more permissions" link indicates this availability. Creative Commons has branded this scheme CC+. Also, since CC licenses are non-exclusive, other options for a work may be offered in addition to a CC license. Here is an example from http://magnatune.com, showing the use of RDFa to annotate the standard CC license image and also the Magnatune logo:

```
<a href="http://creativecommons.org/licenses/by-nc-sa/1.0/" rel="license">
   <img src="http://he3.magnatune.com/img/somerights2.gif">
</a>

<a href="https://magnatune.com/artists/license/?artist=Anup&album=Embrace&
genre=World"
    xmlns:cc="http://creativecommons.org/ns#" rel="cc:morePermissions">
       <img border=0 src="http://he3.magnatune.com/img/button_license2.gif" />
</a>
```

This snippet contains two statements: the public CC license and the availability of more permissions. Sophisticated users of this protocol will one day publish company, media, or genre-specific descriptions of the permissions available privately at the target URL. Tools built to recognise a CC license will still be able to detect the license after the addition of the morePermissions property, which is exactly the desired behavior. More sophisticated versions of the tools could inform the user that "more permissions" may be granted by following the indicated link.

```
<h3>You are free:</h3>
<ul>
  <li class="license share">
     <strong>to Share</strong> --
     to
     <span rel="cc:permits"
          href="http://creativecommons.org/ns#Distribution">copy</span>,
     <span rel="cc:permits"
          href="http://creativecommons.org/ns#Reproduction">distribute
     </span>,
     display, and
     perform the work
  </li>

  <div id="deed-conditions">
    <h3>Under the following conditions:</h3>
    <ul align="left" dir="">

      <li rel="cc:requires"
          href="http://creativecommons.org/ns#Attribution"
class="license by">
          <p><strong>Attribution</strong>.
          <span id="attribution-container">
          You must attribute the work in the manner specified by
          the author or licensor   (but not in any way that
          suggests that they endorse you or your use of the work).
          </span>
      </li>

      <li class="license nd">
          <p><strong>No Derivative Works</strong>.
            <span>You may not alter, transform, or build upon this work.
            </span>
      </li>
```

```
    <li rel="cc:requires"
        href="http://creativecommons.org/ns#Notice">
        For any reuse or distribution, you must make clear to
        others the license terms of this work. The best way to
        do this is with a link to this web page.
    </li>
  </ul>
 </div>
</ul>
```

Figure 8: Part of the HTML code for the Creative Commons Attribution, No Derivatives Deed (slightly simplified for presentation purposes) showing the use of CC REL License Properties.

6.2 Publishing license properties

CC does not expect content publishers to deal with license properties. However, others may find themselves publishing licenses using CC REL's license properties. Here, too, RDFa is available as a framework for creating license descriptions that are human-readable, from which automated tools can also extract the required properties.

One example of this is CC itself, and the publication of the "Commons Deeds". Figure 8 shows the HTML source of the webpage at http://creativecommons.org/licenses/by-nd/3.0/us/ which describes the US version of the CC Attribution-NoDerivatives license.[23] As this markup shows, any HTML attribute, including LI, can carry RDFa attributes. The href attribute, typically used for clickable links, can be used to indicate a structured relation, even when the element to which it is attached is not an HTML anchor.

In this markup, the "Attribution-NoDerivatives" license permits distribution and reproduction, while requiring attribution and notice. Recall that CC REL is meant to be interpreted *in addition* to the baseline copyright regulation. In other words, the restriction "NoDerivatives" is not expressed in CC REL, since that is already a default in copyright law. The opposite, where derivative works *are* allowed, would be denoted with an additional CC permission.

---

23 The full story is a little more complicated. CC initially used the http://web.resource.org/cc namespace, migrating to http://creativecommons.org/ns# for superior human interaction with the vocabulary when it became apparent RDFa would facilitate this. In 2004, the Dublin Core Metadata Initiative (DCMI) approved a "license" refinement of its "rights" term (see http://dublincore.org/usage/decisions/2004/2004–01.Rights-terms.shtml). Had http://purl.org/dc/terms/license existed in 2002, CC would not have defined http://web.resource.org/cc/license. Thanks to the extensibility properties of RDF, http://creativecommons.org/ns#license describes its relationship to each of these other properties.

Tool builders who then want to extract RDF from this page can do so using, for example, the W3C's RDFa Distiller,[24] which, when given the CC Deed URL http://creativecommons.org/licenses/by-nd/3.0/, produces the RDF/XML serialisation of the same structured data, ready to be imported into any programming language with RDF/XML support:

```
<?xml version="1.0" encoding="utf-8"?>
<rdf:RDF
    xmlns:cc="http://creativecommons.org/ns#"
    xmlns:rdf="http://www.w3.org/1999/02/22-rdf-syntax-ns#">
        <rdf:Description rdf:about="http://creativecommons.org/licenses/
        by-nd/3.0/">
            <cc:requires rdf:resource="http://creativecommons.org/
            ns#Notice"/>
            <cc:requires rdf:resource="http://creativecommons.org/
            ns#Attribution"/>
            <cc:permits rdf:resource="http://creativecommons.org/
            ns#Distribution"/>
            <cc:permits rdf:resource="http://creativecommons.org/
            ns#Reproduction"/>
    </rdf:Description>
</rdf:RDF>
```

6.3 How Tool Builders Can Use CC REL

6.3.1 MozCC

MozCC is an extension to Mozilla-based browsers for extracting and displaying metadata embedded in webpages.[25] MozCC was initially developed in 2004 as a work-around to some of the deficiencies in the prior CC metadata recommendation. That version of MozCC specifically looked for CC RDF in HTML comments, a place most other parsers ignore. Once the metadata is detected, MozCC provided users with a visual notification, via icons in the status bar, of the CC license. In addition, MozCC provided a simple interface to expose the work and license properties.

Since the initial development, MozCC has been rewritten to provide general purpose extraction of all RDFa metadata, as well as a specialised interface for CC REL. The status-bar icons and detailed metadata visualisation features have been preserved and expanded. A MozCC user receives immediate visual cues when he encounters a page with RDFa

---

24   See http://www.w3.org/2007/08/pyRdfa.
25   See http://wiki.creativecommons.org/MozCC.

metadata, including specific CC-branded icons when the metadata indicates the presence of a CC license. The experience is pictured in Figure 9.

Figure 9: The MozCC Mozilla Add-On. The status bar shows a CC icon that indicates to the user that the page is CC-licensed. A click on the icon reveals the detailed metadata in a separate window.

MozCC processes pages by listening for load events and then calling one or more metadata extractors on the content. Metadata extractors are JavaScript classes registered on browser startup; they may be provided by MozCC or other extensions. MozCC ships with extractors for all current and previous CC metadata recommendations, in particular CC REL. Each registered extractor is called for every page. The extractors are passed information about the page to be processed, including the URL and whether the page has changed since it was last processed. This allows individual extractors to determine whether re-processing is needed. The RDFa extractor, for example, can stop processing if it sees the document has not been updated. An extractor which looks for metadata specified in external files via <link> tags, however, would still retrieve them and see if they have been updated.

The results of each extractor are stored in a local metadata store. In the case of Firefox, this is a SQLite database stored as part of the user's profile. The local metadata store serves as an abstraction layer between the extractors and user interface code. The contents are visible through the Page Info interface. The current software only exposes this information as status bar icons; one can imagine other user interfaces (provided by MozCC or other extensions) that expose the metadata in different ways.

6.3.2 Operator

Operator is an add-on to the Firefox browser that detects microformats and RDFa in the webpages a user visits.[26] Operator can be extended with "action scripts" that are triggered by specific data found in the webpage. The regions of the page that contain data are themselves highlighted so that users can visually detect and receive contextual information about the data.

It is relatively straightforward to write a CC action script that finds all CC-licensed content inside a webpage by looking for the RDFa syntax. This allows users to easily identify their rights and responsibilities when reusing content they find on the Web. The simple action script can detect all items, even types of items with properties currently unanticipated, and display the item's name and rights description.

Putting aside for now the definition of some utility functions, an action handler for the license property is declared as follows:[27]

```
RDFa.DEFAULT_NS.cc = "http://creativecommons.org/ns#";
RDFa.ns.cc = function(name) { return RDFa.DEFAULT_NS.cc + name; };

var view_license = {
    description: "View License",
    shortDescription: "View",
    scope: {
        semantic: {
            "RDF": {
                property: RDFa.ns.cc("license"),
                defaultNS: RDFa.ns.cc("")
            }
        }
    },
    doAction: function(semanticObject, semanticObjectType, propertyIndex)
{
        if (semanticObjectType == "RDF") {
            return semanticObject.license;
        }
    }
};

SemanticActions.add("view_license", view_license);
```

Once this action script is enabled, Operator automatically lights up CC-licensed "Resources" it finds on the web. For example, browsing to

---

26 See https://addons.mozilla.org/en-US/firefox/addon/operator.

27 Operator currently does not handle HTML reserved keywords, such as rel="license". Thus, we consider the script for the property cc:license, and provide examples appropriately adjusted.

Lessig's blog, Operator highlights two resources that are CC-licensed: the blog itself, and a CC-licensed photo used in one of its posts. The result is shown in Figure 10.

Figure 10: Operator with a CC action script on Lessig's blog. Notice the two resources, each with its "view license" action.

7. Conclusion

Creative Commons wants to make it easy for artists and scientists to build upon the works of others when they choose to: licensing your work for reuse and finding properly licensed works to reuse should be easy. To achieve this on the technical front, we have defined CC REL, an abstract model for rights expression based on the W3C's RDF, and we recommend two syntaxes for web-based and free-floating content: RDFa and XMP, respectively. The major goal of our technological approach is to make it easy to publish and read rights expression data now and in the future, when the kinds of licensed items and the data expressed about them goes far beyond what we can imagine today. By using RDF, CC REL links CC to the fast-growing RDF data interoperability infrastructure and its extensive developer toolset: other data sets can be integrated with CC REL, and RDF technologies (for example, data provenance with digital signatures) can eventually benefit CC REL.

We believe that the technologies we have selected for CC REL will enable the kind of powerful, distributed technological innovation that is characteristic of the Internet. Anyone can create new vocabularies for their own purposes and combine them with CC REL as they please, without seeking central approval. Just as we did with the legal text of the licenses, we aim to create the minimal infrastructure required to enable collaboration and invention, while letting it flourish as an organic, distributed process. We believe CC REL provides this primordial technical layer that can enable a vibrant application ecosystem, and we look forward to the community's innovative ideas that can now freely build upon CC REL.

11. The Value of Registering Creative Works

Roland Alton-Scheidl, Joe Benso and Martin Springer

In this chapter we present good practices for online registration services. We will be asking the following questions: is reliable and simple registration of works the right way to improve confidentiality and trust? How could rights collecting societies benefit from such registries? What kind of governance is required to run such registries? And do they conflict with public patent laws or authorities? We will conclude with a proposal for either adapting the Digital Media Project (DMP) authority scheme or establishing registration peering and using existing namespaces.[1]

1. Improving confidentiality and trust

Copyright is an automatic right; works are protected by copyright across the world from the moment they are created. As long as a creator of a work does not care about his or her copyright, registration should not be necessary. The purpose of registering works is so that an author can produce a verifiable record of his or her work as it existed before it was published. This record can serve as a proof in case somebody infringes copyright, for instance by publishing the work as their own.

---

1 The authors are affiliated with Registered Commons, a service initiative launched in 2006.

Users in the digital media value-chain frequently have to accept licensing conditions before they can access and use copyrighted content. A certificate that a given piece of content is really the content that has been registered with a trusted agency can improve a user's confidence that he or she may use this content according to the license terms.

Even where license information is available, for example through a web link to a Creative Commons (CC) license, the relation to a given work is not guarded. Companies who may be interested in the commercial distribution and other uses of the material require legal security for their business, notably in the form of reliable authorship information. This reliable link to the author is missing from many websites that offer content for re-use. Even if the work has assigned a license with a weblink, or the work is said to be in the public domain, how can one know that the relation is correct and authorship or the freedom granted is as claimed?

2. Emerging content registries

Registering creative works implies that content must be reliably and unambiguously identified. This task requires specific capabilities, as identification constitutes a key element of trust establishment. The task of content identification needs to be carried out by organisations that are properly accredited with a trusted authority.

Registries are following various goals. First, they provide trust among parties who would like to use or share published works. Secondly, registries are being used to furnish evidence of a work's authorship. A typical use case is to prevent stealing ideas or concepts in the creative sector. People tend to lock their own work in a registry under full copyright and do not necessarily have the intention of publishing it. They register the work in case a similar idea is evolving, for example, after they showed the artwork at a design pitch.

Additionally, many registries offer value added services, such as paper certificates, storage of the work or offering a point of sales for usages beyond a sharing license. CC+ allows people to provide a link, where conditions for commercial use are described.

3. Survey of registries supporting CC

Creative Commons has started to put a focus on providing value added services through registries, funded by the Omidyar Network. Joi Ito, Creative Commons CEO, stated in a press release: "...the grant will allow us to explore providing fee-based, value-added services, which can benefit our community and help support the organization financially. The registry is our first big project in which we plan to explore these possibilities".[2]

Registration of intellectual property has long been a service reserved only for authorities like the US copyright office and the Library of Congress. When authors want to provide proof of ownership of a work, proper registration with a trusted party can be a valuable resource. A traditional registration process can, however, be costly to an artist. One piece of work can cost US$45, and registering may be a time consuming process. Now, in an era of digital distribution, the ability to quickly recognise ownership of content is becoming increasingly important. Licensing models like CC have been adopted by many artists as the preferred licensing solution to their work online. However, with the popular "some rights reserved" CC licensing, there is a growing need to provide users of this content a proof of ownership. This proof is important for all content creators as the copying and distribution of their content becomes increasingly easy.

From the perspective of CC, it would be in their interest to support a trusted authority for registration of CC-licensed material. As the field of CC registries grows, the benefits to the artists are being communicated, and possible relationships between registries and the US copyright office or other design, trademark or patent offices worldwide may emerge. CC started collecting profiles for service providers of registries that support CC licenses. The following table is an early snapshot.

---

2   Eric Steuer, "Creative Commons Announces Major Funding Support from Omidyar Network", Creative Commons Press Release, San Franciso (28 May 2008), available at http://creativecommons.org/press-releases/entry/8322.

Name	Cost	Length of Registration	Types of Works	Online Registration	Serial Numbers	Document Storage	SHA-1 Hashing	Online Verification
DulyNoted	$29 - $37	10 years	Sound MovingImage Image Text	Yes	Yes	Yes	Yes	No
Numly	up to $5 / month	Forever	MovingImage Sound Text InteractiveResource	Yes	Yes	No	Yes	Yes
Registered Commons	Free	Forever	Image Text Sound MovingImage InteractiveResource	Yes	Yes	Yes	Yes	Yes
Safecreative	0		Image Sound Text MovingImage	Yes	Yes	Yes	Yes	Yes
US Copyright Office	US$45		Sound MovingImage Image Text InteractiveResource	No	Yes	Yes	No	No

Table 1: Registries supporting CC licenses (2008)

In the following sections, we will have a closer look at some of the registry services listed above. Still, this list is not exhaustive. There are other ways to register creative works such as national patent offices or the European Office for Harmonization of the Internal Market, which provide services to protect trademarks and design.[3]

3.1 Registered Commons

A creator who registers a work with Registered Commons (RC) benefits from two important advantages. First, a certificate is issued which allows the creator to provide evidence for his or her intellectual ownership of a work. Secondly, and almost as important for evidence of authorship as a certificate, RC digitally records the exact time of a registration with a timestamp, obtained from a trusted third party. Typical users are musicians or photographers who are keen on posting individual works on the Internet, but who wish to retain control over them; or bloggers and even agencies who, prior to giving client presentations, wish to protect their work from plagiarism using the timestamp. These new licensing models render the free distribution of artistic works on the Internet considerably easier, as they free the works from the tight corset of traditional copyright management. However they also exhibit their own significant defects. Firstly, they cannot prevent the unlawful use of works. Secondly, the user's rights of such works for commercial purposes (for example, the use of a piece of music under a non-commercial CC license for the credits of an independent film) are increasingly more difficult to clarify, as many of these works are published without reliable information on the author and the user's rights needed for commercial uses.

As an included service of the current registration and time stamp process, RC provides an automatic backup of the works by default. These works can be directly linked to by way of embedding the generated code for the RC button ⬚RC⬚ ⬚REGISTERED commons⬚ after uploading a work.

RC is a service established and provided by a public-private partnership. The public partner, the Vorarlberg University of Applied Sciences, located in the Austrian Alps close to the Swiss and German border, has been providing infrastructure in the start-up phase. Private partners are organised in the International Media Association, osAlliance.[4] Registered users of the service may also become shareholders. Members of the association keep control over

---

3   See http://oami.europa.eu.
4   See http://osAlliance.com.

the service through their vote in the general assembly. A trademark agreement has been signed with CC in 2007. The transparency of its governance is a core strength of RC which earns the trust of the users.

RC uses Open Source software and runs with a PostGres Database, and the SpunQ database modeller on a BSD platform. Hosting is secured by standardised control and surveillance mechanisms and frequent backups. In 2008, RC could establish agreements with the Austrian Chamber of Commerce, for which the branded version "Creativdepot.at" is being provided. The business model has been slightly adapted in a way that partners may obtain a voucher for their clients or members. The number of free registrations per user has been restricted, unless they use a voucher code. In 2009, RC introduced revenue-generating models for their users. This model aims to incorporate a value-added service that allows a user's work to be licensed for commercial use as a separate contract. Copyright owners can set a price tag—for commercial use of a work, for example—and RC is offering to handle the clearing.

3.2 SafeCreative

SafeCreative is a registration service provided by an investment company called AAR Futuro. They keep a record of work registered for identification purposes. This allows interested parties to consult the registry and obtain information with respect to the rights of use or the distribution. In their service description they want to dissuade third parties from plagiarism or falsely claiming the work as their own. While basic registrations are free, they charge a fee for multi-authorship, extended storage or time-limited custom licenses. Their experience is that only one out of four of those who register chooses options that are not full copyright.

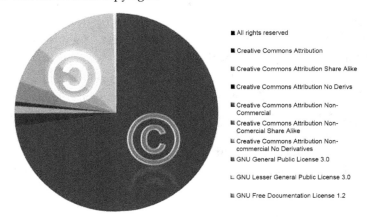

Table 2: Distribution of Licenses used at SafeCreative (http://en.safecreative.net/)

According to SafeCreative's analysis in 2008, the percentages of licenses used in 18,000 registered works are:

72.8% - All rights reserved
12.9% - CC Attribution Non-commercial No Derivatives
6.3%   - CC Attribution Non-commercial Share Alike
3.3%   - CC Attribution Non-commercial
2.1%   - CC Attribution
1.2%   - CC Attribution Share Alike
0.7%   - CC Attribution No Derivs
0.4   - GNU LGPL
0.3%   - GNU GPL
0.1%   - GNU FDL

This seems to be a clear indication that there is a demand for online registries not only for people who are aware of license templates, such as CC, but also for commercial licensing.

3.3 RightsAgent

Registrants should be cautious on the ownership structure of the service provider. RightsAgent promised unified feeds to text, photos or videos, which allowed tracking uses of works. Value could be gained by building a reputation score and by collecting fees for commercial license agreements or when using the CC+ option. However, the service disappeared in 2009.

3.4 Public Domain Registry in Canada

The Canada-based clearing service Access Copyright had announced a partnership with CC and the Wikimedia Foundation on the creation of a Canadian Public Domain Registry.[5] Access Copyright's role in this project was to provide bibliographic information on Canadian published works contained in its Rights Management System (RMS). This list of over 300,000 works, including works that are currently in the public domain and those that will enter the public domain in the future, was provided to CC and the Wikimedia Foundation in September 2007. Since that time, both organisations have used this list to build the registry's database. A Beta

---

5 See Mia Garlick, "Canadian Public Domain Registry Announced" (3 March 2006), available at http://creativecommons.org/weblog/entry/5809.

version of the Public Domain Wiki is still being tested by all three partners.

Once testing is complete, the registry should look similar to the online encyclopaedia Wikipedia. It will allow users to search and edit records in the registry to provide additional information about individual creators, the history of the registry's works and to add additional works to the system. However, their hope according to their public announcement in January 2008—that it will be a model for similar public domain registries around the globe—is still far from becoming realised.[6]

3.5 Open Knowledge Registry (CKAN)

CKAN intended to develop a registry of open knowledge packages and projects, "be that a set of Shakespeare's works, a global population density database, the voting records of MPs, or 30 years of US patents".[7] As of 2011, the project has been merged with their hub of open data sets.[8]

CKAN is looking for people to register "packages", that is, collections with some kind of structure rather than individual items. So a substantial set of photos, datasets of all kinds and the writings of Shakespeare are allowed, but not an individual blog, or your Flickr photo collection (unless it is very big). The material should be free to use, reuse and redistribute without major restrictions, referring to common open definition guidelines.[9] Even if search engines could also be restricted to open content search results, CKAN offers extended metadata on the collections and reuse of the material.

4. What kind of authority is required to run such registries?

In order to guarantee that content identifiers are unique and thus content could be mirrored between registries easily, there needs to be one and only one root authority—called the Registration Authority (RA)—which may have responsibility for many Registration Agencies (RAgs). The RA is responsible for allocating namespaces to RAgs, and it will appoint RAgs on the basis of general rules. The primary role of RAgs is to provide services to

---

6   See http://www.accesscopyright.ca/docs/Public%20Domain%20Registry%20Update%20 Jan%202008.pdf and http://wiki.creativecommons.org/PDWiki.

7   See http://www.ckan.net/.

8   See http://thedatahub.org/.

9   See Open Knowledge Foundation: http://www.okfn.org/.

registrants—allocating identifier name prefixes, registering identifier names and providing the necessary infrastructure to allow registrants to declare and maintain metadata and state data. In general, identifier management policies can be defined on a community-by-community basis. The OASIS committee proposes that a resolution community chooses to create a community root authority.[10] When a community changes the root authority, it should define policies for assigning and managing identifiers under this authority. Furthermore, it should define what resolution protocol(s) may be used for these identifiers. The Digital Media Project has published Approved Document No. 6, which proposes a list of procedural and operational responsibilities for RAs and RAgs.[11] This list can serve as good starting point for the steps that need to be performed for setting up and running content registries.

As an existing example in the music industry, the Global Release Identifier scheme has been established by rights collecting societies.[12] A GRid consists of 18 characters, made up of an Identifier Scheme element followed by an Issuer Code, a Release Number element and a Check Character as follows:

- Identifier Scheme element (2 characters)
- Issuer Code element (5 characters)
- Release Number element (10 characters)
- Check Character element (1 character)

When a GRid is written, printed or otherwise visually presented, the four elements of the GRid shall be separated from each other by a hyphen. The hyphens do not form part of the GRid. It is recommended that when a GRid is visually presented, the font used should clearly distinguish between the number 1 and 0, and the letters I and O.

Example: **A1–2425G-ABC1234002-M**
A1 = Identifier Scheme element
2425G = Issuer Code element
ABC1234002 = Release Number element
M = Check Character element

The Identifier Scheme element distinguishes the GRid Identifier Scheme

---

10   See http://docs.oasis-open.org/xri/xri-resolution/2.0/specs/cs01/xri-resolution-V2.0-cs-01.htm.
11   "Proposal for 'Approved Document No. 5, WD1.1 – Technical Reference: Certification and Registration Authorities, Version 3.0'" (15 July 2007), available at http://www.dmpf.org/open/dmp1015.zip.
12   See http://www.ifpi.org/content/section_resources/grid.html.

from any other standard identification scheme which adopts the same or a similar structure. Registered Commons has adopted this approach by simply issuing codes on the identifier scheme RC; thus their identification scheme should be called RCid. An administrative authority to manage namespaces for the Identifier Scheme Element is missing, and a simple directory service would be sufficient. A peer-to-peer protocol combined with globally unique IDs may also be a good approach to identify any registration process as a singular, retraceable activity.

5. How could rights collecting societies benefit from such registries?

Traditionally, rights collecting societies of Collective Management Societies (CMS) managed the exploitation of any of the rights-holders rights. According to the principle of territorial exploitation, the applicable law is the law of the place of exploitation. For some forms of exploitation (for example, cable retransmission, the making of sound recordings, etc.), collective rights management is compulsory but, in principle, an author can choose between individual and collective management of his or her rights. CMS usually administers, monitors, collects and distributes the payment of royalties for an entire group of right holders, on the basis of the national law of its territory, with respect to that territory.

In order to be compensated by CMS, authors must register works in the country of their residence. Across Europe more than 70 different CMS manage authors' rights. Within the European Union, most CMS are allowed to retain a monopoly status or have conferred on them a monopoly position in relation to their specific fields of activity. The reason is economically persuasive. For users, it is simply more expedient to be directed to one collective body that manages one specific type of right. For decades, CMS have been criticised for lack of transparency (they are not really controlled by their members) and for their unbalanced distribution schemes, favouring blockbusters and top ten-charting music over independent and less commercially successful work.

CMS currently use different schemes to identify works and store the corresponding data in proprietary systems and databases. They wish to protect their assets and defend their monopolies to register and manage works. Many European CMS oblige their members to collectively license all forms of distribution for a certain category of works and thus prevent new forms of individual licensing.

While some years ago legitimate commercial media offers were absent from the Internet, and media content was shared via peer-to-peer (P2P) file-sharing networks, companies today appear to have figured out new business models taking advantage of the "long tail", user-created content and micro-advertising. Apparently this "new deal" is that consumers (users) generate content and the commercial companies use these data for their web services. Consumers can use these services either for free together with advertising content or without ads and with additional features when paying a subscription fee. As the "freemium" model usually compensates neither the user's nor the artist's works, we have clear evidence that an interoperable platform for the management of copyright, the rights-clearing and the micropayment of services is still missing.

Network operators, CMS and providers of Web2.0 services appear to be quite happy with the status quo, which preserves their monopolies. Therefore they maintain technical and legal obstacles, for example, by operating proprietary subscriber management/billing systems or granting access to their services through end-user license agreements (EULAs), which are a mystery to the average consumer. The interesting thing is that in P2P time (Napster and before), there was still some money flowing back to the creators. With Web2.0, there is none. Service providers control the business. Essentially they do not intend to prop up creators by providing them with the means to benefit from their creations, they simply subscribe to the idea that there is "money to make" from those who create. We can ask ourselves why the demand for rights clearing and micropayment has decreased in the past. If the only viable business models on the Internet are flat rates for services and advertising for content, it is clear that users/operators neither require micropayment nor rights compensation.

Meanwhile bis service providers contract artists or labels directly, or creators simply publish content on their own websites. Theoretically, end-users who want to access this content could be charged directly through the publishers' web services. Still, no generic solution for the rights clearing and payment of content is on the horizon, which is cross platform and cross vendor compatible. After all, from the perspective of creators and end-users the best solution would be a decentralised system where individual peers (creators and end-users) can register content and negotiate with each other the usage terms and conditions of content.

With content registration services, converging networks and next-generation P2P environments in place, there will be a new market for micropayment. New concepts of micropayment services, such as Flattr, shortcut the circuit to rights collecting societies, who still could benefit by adapting their terms and allowing CC licensed and voluntary payment schemes on their repertoires.[13]

6. A registration service only for Creative Commons licensed content?

A creator of a work is free to choose the licensing conditions. The decision will usually depend on several factors, for instance if the licensee will use a work for commercial or non-commercial purposes, or if the licensee obtains an exclusive license to use the work. One can also imagine that licensors may want to change conditions after a time, because they find out that another license is more suitable for their business model. The decision about the licensing follows the initial registration of a work. Since content registration precedes the licensing, a registration authority exclusively for commercial content or only for CC content would not make much sense. Therefore, we believe that the setup of a CRA/CRags should be independent of the license.

This raises the question of whether a service like RC, being a service that promotes the publishing of works under a CC license, would be in competition with a service that allows many different licenses. One approach could be that the registration of works which will be released under an open license (such as CC-by) is free of charge, whereas registrants would have to pay a fee for the registration of their works if they intend a commercial deployment or want to reserve the right to decide on the license at a later date. A common technical platform for content registration and licensing of copyrighted content could be developed as an open source project. This would benefit public interests through non-commercial dissemination of content as well as commercial interests. Any co-branding would be neutral in the sense that it would not favour or penalise digital media business models.

A registration service for commercially deployed works would contend with existing service the CMS are offering to their clients. Actually, some CMS, such as the Spanish Sociedad General de Autores y Editores (SGAE), are providing online services for the electronic registration of works.

---

13 See http://flattr.com/.

However, the SGAE Membership Agreement implies that members could not publish their works under a CC license, since SGAE owns the exclusive rights for the reproduction and distribution of their members' works.[14] On the other hand, with fresh ideas and new registration services, the existing CMS monopolies could be stimulated to innovate their activities and business models. The CMS Buma/Stemra in the Netherlands had a one-year test phase that allows musicians to publish their work under a non-commercial CC license, whereas KODA in Denmark was the first to allow CC licensing to all their members.[15]

7. What are the challenges going forward in the digital registry space?

The first challenge is to develop policies for CRA/CRags that are accepted in many countries, by all value-chain players, including the major rights-holders and CMS. Small and independent digital registries could issue different identifiers for copyrighted works. This is not a problem as long as the identification of content is unique and identifiers are accepted everywhere. Large registries operated by major rights-holders or CMS could misuse their monopolies by requiring proprietary technical platforms. As a consequence not every value-chain player could process content identifiers managed by CMS. National societies could decide to refuse content identifiers issued elsewhere.

As mentioned above, RC has prepared the technical means to incorporate other registries that could support the RCid code.[16] GRid provides a system for the unique identification of releases of music over electronic networks. The RC service provides an application programming interface (API) to exchange queries for GRids. Fasttrack, an alliance of major music CMS provides tools to exchange information about their members' works by means of a global decentralised database network.[17] A web interface to their ISWC Network provides a search tool for ISWC identifiers.[18] It is noteworthy that GRid only identifies the electronic release of a work

---

14 The Management Agreement is available at http://www.sgae.es/resources/pdf/5/4/1180694570945.pdf.
15 Florian Philapitsch, "Die Creative Commons Lizenzen", *Medien & Recht*, 2 (2008), 82–97.
16 See http://en.wikipedia.org/wiki/Grid.
17 See http://www.fasttrackdcn.net/.
18 See http://iswcnet.cisac.org/ISWCNET-MWI and http://en.wikipedia.org/wiki/International_Standard_Musical_Work_Code.

whereas ISWC identifies a work independently of its manifestations.

The second challenge is to develop a technical infrastructure based on open standards for the protocols and interfaces to communicate with content registries. In the Digital Media Project we have contributed to the development of technical specifications for content registration and management services. Chillout is a reference implementation of the DMP specifications.[19] Some of the DMP specifications have been standardised in MPEG (for example, ISO/IEC 23000–5 Media Streaming MAF, ISO/IEC FDIS 23000–7 Open Release MAF). We believe that it should be common sense to implement the technical infrastructure for copyright registration and management services using open source software to minimise security risks and gain transparency.

8. Heterogeneous business models

The third challenge is to develop business models to finance registration services. Digital content registries may offer value-added services to users in the digital media value-chain. Primary services may include the secure and reliable storage of digital content for rights-holders. If necessary, the registry must be able to prove that a first fixation (a "digital original") of a work has been deposited at a given time.

We also found that there is an interest of creative sector promoters to offer secondary services. Incremental access restrictions with advanced access for owners of a voucher are attractive to various stakeholders. For example, the Austrian Chamber of Commerce and the City of Linz, both promoting the Creative Industries, have agreed to issue vouchers to their members for the content registry CreativDepot.at.[20] The service includes a personalised feed of registered works from individual artists.

The following use case describes a secondary service of content registries which is being offered to users who intend to re-use existing works for their own creations at OneLoudr.com. In order to produce a remix, sampling artists conduct an exploratory creative process, copying different samples from different musical works, adapting and merging them. All this is legal as long as it is kept private. Samples clearance must only take place when the creator wants to make the resulting creation public, that is, to publish

---

19   See http://chillout.dmpf.org.
20   See http://creativwirtschaft.at.

it online or to produce and distribute copies. The business model is based on a small fee for collecting and redistributing payments of value-added services, such as bonus tracks with remixes produced by fans.

9. Some conclusions on trust and governance

As different registries emerge, the challenge of separating practices and maintaining quality standards and trust with different registries approaches. Registry services should certainly not undermine copyright in the sense that only registered works are protected. As soon as we publish a work it shall be copyrighted, unless we say that we grant specific usages, expressed by licenses like one of CC. However, we want to be able to define usage rules for each work or for sets of works, and those rules need to be described somewhere. For example, automatic enclosure of license-related metadata for pictures would be used by many photographers if it were easy to handle. Still, the photographer needs to sign her works in a trusted way when publishing the pictures.

How can we achieve trust? Registration services need to be able to verify that a person's online identity can be tracked down to his or her real identity. This can be assured by a "web of trust" such as CAcert or by testing the user's postal address and bank account with a pro-forma credit card payment. However, most registration services also offer a simple check of the existence of an email address. This method of identifying a creator may be efficient for the publisher, but not for the commercial user, who needs full trust that the work is by the author that is claimed and nobody else. Fraudulent claims of copyright could not be solved effectively either, and a conflict resolution procedure needs to be offered. Better user identification would result in fewer frauds. Following the guidelines of implementing digital timestamps (RFC 3161), a revocation procedure needs to be provided for objects which have been signed erroneously or by fraud.

Which organisational structures are providing trust? We need to ensure technical operation for decades and we need to show transparency for the processes. According to economic theory, long-term institutions are either public or have incorporated democratic control elements. Purely profit-oriented enterprises may be sold sooner or later, refocus their business or just go out of business. In that case, their limited liability will not be of any use for registrants or users of registered works, unless another registry is taking over the data set, which may be a cumbersome issue for personal data protection. National registries tend to be rather inflexible and non-profit organisations may not take the opportunity to do business.

For RC, a public-private partnership between an academic institution and a for-profit business co-operative of design and IT experts was found to be an ideal structure for running a registry. The co-operative is being steered by the general assembly, a board of directors, a controlling board and an agency for co-operatives. Additionally, an audit on public welfare (*Gemeinwohlökonomie*) has been conducted in 2011. All five levels guarantee high performance, effective conflict resolution and reasonable quality control.

Independently of the organisational structure, any registry must work out a shutdown scenario, which needs to be agreed with the users in the terms of use. An authority to issue global identifier scheme elements would probably be an independent organisation such as International Organization for Standardization (ISO) or the World Intellectual Property Organization (WIPO). That way, registries would efficiently back up confidentiality for all partners involved in the creative sector's value chains, no matter which way copyright regulation evolves.

Select Bibliography of Resources Cited

A. Websites

ARROW: Accessible Registries of Rights Information and Orphan Works
http://www.arrow-net.eu

Berlin Declaration on Open Access
http://www.berlin9.org/about/declaration/index.shtml

Budapest Open Access Initiative
http://www.soros.org/openaccess

CKAN: Open Knowledge Registry
http://www.ckan.net

Communia Project (The European Thematic Network on the Digital Public Domain)
http://www.communia-project.eu

Communia Association
http://www.communia-association.org

Copyright Toolbox
http://copyrighttoolbox.surf.nl

Creative Commons
http://creativecommons.org

DARIAH: Digital Research Infrastructure for the Arts and Humanities
http://www.dariah.eu

Development Agenda for WIPO
http://www.wipo.int/ip-development/en/agenda

Diaspora
https://joindiaspora.com

DOAJ: Directory of Open Access Journals
http://doaj.org

DRIVER: Digital Repository Infrastructure Vision for European Research
http://www.driver-repository.eu

Dublin Core Metadata Initiative
http://dublincore.org

Europeana
http://www.europeana.eu/portal

Europeana Connect
http://outofcopyright.eu

Free Culture Forum
http://fcforum.net

HAL: Hyper Articles en Ligne
http://hal.archives-ouvertes.fr

The Hathi Trust Digital Library
http://www.hathitrust.org

The KForge Project
http://www.kforgeproject.com

Knowledge Exchange
http://www.knowledge-exchange.info

LAPSI: Legal Aspects of Public Sector Information
http://www.lapsi-project.eu

Magnatune
http://www.magnatune.org

Online Books Page
http://onlinebooks.library.upenn.edu

OpenAIRE: Open Access Infrastructure for Research in Europe
http://www.openaire.eu

Open Knowledge Foundation
http://okfn.org

Open Library
http://www.openlibrary.org

osAlliance
http://osAlliance.com

Panton Principles: Principles for Open Data in Science
http://pantonprinciples.org

PRISM: The Publishing Requirements for Industry Standard Metadata
http://www.prismstandard.org

Public Domain Day
http://www.publicdomainday.org

Public Domain Works
http://www.publicdomainworks.net

La Quadrature du Net
http://www.laquadrature.net

Rightscom
http://www.rightscom.com

Scholar's Copyright Addendum Engine
http://scholars.sciencecommons.org

Sherpa/Juliet: Research Funders' Open Access Policies
http://www.sherpa.ac.uk/juliet

Sherpa/Romeo: Publisher Copyright Policies and Self-archiving
   http://www.sherpa.ac.uk/romeo

W3C: The World Wide Web Consortium
   http://www.w3.org

B. Reports, Conference Papers and Working Papers

Abelson, Hal, Ben Adida, Mike Linksvayer, Nathan Yergler "ccREL: The Creative Commons Rights Expression Language", a W3C Member Submission of 1 May 2008, available at http://www.w3.org/Submission/ccREL.

Avocats, Germann et al, "Implementing the UNESCO Convention of 2005 in the European Union" (May 2010), study prepared for the European Parliament Directorate General for Internal Policies, Policy Department B: Structural and Cohesion Policies, Culture and Education, available at http://www.diversitystudy.eu/ms/ep_study_long_version_20_nov_2010_final.pdf.

Bollier, David, "The Commons as New Sector of Value Creation: It's Time to Recognize and Protect the Distinctive Wealth Generated by Online Commons", remarks at the *Economies of the Commons: Strategies for Sustainable Access and Creative Reuse of Images and Sounds Online* Conference, Amsterdam (12 April 2008).

Ted Buckley, "The Myth of the Anticommons" (Biotechnology Industry Organization, 2007), available at http://test.bio.org/ip/domestic/TheMythoftheAnticommons.pdf.

Cousins, Jill, "The Public Domain, the Manifesto, his Charter and her Dilemma", paper delivered at the seventh Communia workshop, Luxembourg (1 February 2010), available at http://www.communia-project.eu/node/361.

Cunard, Jeffrey P., Keith Hill and Chris Barlas, *"Current Developments in The Field of Digital Rights Management"* SCCR/10/2 Rev., prepared for the Word Intellectual Property Organization (2004), available at http://www.wipo.int/edocs/mdocs/copyright/en/sccr_10/sccr_10_2_rev.pdf.

David, Paul A., "New Moves in 'Legal Jujitsu' to Combat the Anticommons: Mitigating IPR Constraints on Innovation by a 'Bottom-up' Approach to Systemic Institutional Reform", paper presented at the first Communia conference, Louvain-la-Neuve, Belgium (30 June 2008), available at http://esnie.org/presentations/124.html.

— and Jared Rubin, "How Many Scanned Books on the Web?" (SIEPER Policy Briefs, December 2008), available at http://siepr.stanford.edu/publicationsprofile/1853.

Dedeurwaerdere, Tom and Peter Dawyndt, "Exploring and Exploiting Microbiological Commons: Contributions of Bioinformatics and Intellectual Property Rights in Sharing Biological Information", workshop paper, Brussels (2005), available at http://biogov.cpdr.ucl.ac.be/bioinf/document.pdf.

—, Maria Iglesias, Sabine Weiland and Michael Halewood, "The Use and Exchange of Microbial Genetic Resources for Food and Agriculture", Background Study Paper of the Commission on Genetic Resources for Food and Agriculture No. 46 (2009), available at ftp://ftp.fao.org/docrep/fao/meeting/017/ak566e.pdf.

Dusollier, Séverine, "Scoping Study On Copyright And Related Rights and the Public Domain", prepared for the Word Intellectual Property Organization (30 April 2010), available at http://www.wipo.int/edocs/mdocs/mdocs/en/cdip_4/cdip_4_3_rev_study_inf_1.pdf.

European Commission, "Copyright and Related Rights in the Information Society", Green Paper, COM (95) 382 final, Brussels (19 July 1995), available at http://ec.europa.eu/internal_market/copyright/docs/docs/com-95-382_en.pdf

European Commission, *A Digital Agenda for Europe*, Communication from the Commission to the European Parliament, the Council, the European Economic and Social Committee and the Committee of the Regions, COM (2010) 245, Brussels (19 June 2010), available at http://ec.europa.eu/information_society/digital-agenda/documents/digital-agenda-communication-en.pdf.

European Commission, "i2010: Digital Libraries", SEC (2005) 1194, Brussels (30 September 2005), available at http://eur-lex.europa.eu/LexUriServ/site/en/com/2005/com2005_0465en01.pdf.

European Commission, Staff Working Paper on the Review of the EC legal Framework in the Field of Copyright and Related Rights, SEC (2004) 995, Brussels (19 July 2004), available at http://ec.europa.eu/internal_market/copyright/docs/review/sec-2004-995_en.pdf.

European Commission, Communication on Copyright in the Knowledge Economy, COM (2009) 532 final, Brussels (19 October 2009), available at http://ec.europa.eu/internal_market/copyright/docs/copyrightinfso/20091019_532_en .pdf.

The European Task Force on Culture and Development, "In From the Margins: A Contribution to the Debate on Culture and Development in Europe", report prepared for the Council of Europe (1997), available at http://www.coe.int/t/dg4/cultureheritage/culture/resources/Publications/InFromTheMargins_EN.pdf.

Expert Group Report, *The Future of Cloud Computing: Opportunities for European Cloud Computing Beyond 2010*, available at http://cordis.europa.eu/fp7/ict/ssai/docs/cloud-report-final.pdf.

Furman, Jeffrey L. and Scott Stern, "Climbing Atop the Shoulders of Giants: The Impact of Institutions on Cumulative Research", NBER working paper 12523, National Bureau of Economic Research (2006), available at http://www.nber.org/papers/w12523.

Garlick, Mia, "Canadian Public Domain Registry Announced" (3 March 2006), available at http://creativecommons.org/weblog/entry/5809.

Gasser, Urs and Silke Ernst, "EUCD Best Practice Guide: Implementing the EU Copyright Directive in the Digital Age", University of St. Gallen Law & Economics Working Paper No. 2007-01 (December 2006).

Ghosh, Rishab Aiyer, "Technology, Law, Policy and the Public Domain", paper delivered at the first Communia workshop, Turin (18 January 2008), available at http://www.communia-project.eu/node/83.

Grassmuck, Volker, "The World is Going Flat(-Rate): A Study Showing Copyright Exception for Legalizing File-Sharing Feasible as a Cease-Fire in the 'War on Copyright' Emerges", *Intellectual Property Watch*, 11 May 2009, available at http://www.ip-watch.org/weblog/2009/05/11/the-world-is-going-flat-rate.

Gray, Jonathan, "Public Domain Calculators", presentation delivered at the third Communia workshop, Amsterdam (20 October 2008), available at http://www.communia-project.eu/communiafiles/ws03s_Public_Domain_Calculators/index.html.

Guédon, Jean-Claude, "In Oldenburg's Long Shadow: Librarians, Research Scientists, Publishers, and the Control of Scientific Publishing", presentation for the Association of Research Libraries, Toronto (May 2001), available at http://www.arl.org/resources/pubs/mmproceedings/138guedon.shtml.

Guibault, Lucie, "The Nature and Scope of Limitations and Exceptions to Copyright and Neighbouring Rights with Regard to General Interest Missions for the Transmission of Knowledge: Prospects for their Adaptation to the Digital Environment", *Copyright Bulletin* (December 2003), available at http://portal.unesco.org/culture/en/files/17316/10874797751l_guibault_en.pdf/l_guibault_en.pdf.

—, "Evaluating Directive 2001/29/EC in the Light of the Digital Public Domain", paper presented at the first Communia conference, Louvain-la-Neuve (1 July 2008), available at http://www.communia-project.eu/communiafiles/conf2008p_Evaluation_of_the_directive_2001-29-EC.pdf; an updated version of Guibault's paper can be found in this volume (Chapter 3).

— et al., "Study on the Implementation and Effect in Member States' Laws of Directive 2001/29/EC on the Harmonisation of Certain Aspects of Copyright and Related Rights in the Information Society" (February 2007), report prepared for the European Commission, DG Internal Market, ETD/2005/IM/D1/91, available at http://www.ivir.nl/publications/guibault/Infosoc_report_2007.pdf.

—, Rufus Pollock and Jo Walsh, "Open Knowledge: Promises and Challenges", paper delivered at the first Communia workshop, Turin (18 January 2008), available at http://www.communia-project.eu/communiafiles/ws01p_Open%20Knowledge%20Promises%20and%20Challenges.pdf. An updated version of this paper can be found in this volume (Chapter 7).

Gurry, Francis, "The Future of Copyright", speech delivered at the Blue Sky Conference, Sydney (25 February 2011), available at http://www.wipo.int/about-wipo/en/dgo/speeches/dg_blueskyconf_11.html

Hess, Charlotte and Elinor Ostrom, "A Framework for Analysing Governance and Collective Action in the Microbial Commons", paper presented at workshop on exploring and exploiting microbiological commons, Brussels (7–8 July 2005).

Horrigan, John, "Home Broadband Adoption 2006", 28 May 2006, available at http://www.pewinternet.org/Reports/2006/Home-Broadband-Adoption-2006.aspx.

Hugenholtz, P. Bernt, "Fierce Creatures: Copyright Exemptions Towards Extinction?", keynote speech, IFLA/IMPRIMATUR Conference, Amsterdam (30–31 October 1997).

—, "Owning Science: Intellectual Property Rights as Impediments to Knowledge Sharing", paper delivered at the second Communia conference, Turin (29 June 2001), available at http://communia-project.eu/node/289.

et al., "The Recasting of Copyright & Related Rights for the Knowledge Economy", report to the European Commission, DG Internal Market (November 2006).

Isherwood, Mark, "European Commission Project: Economic and Social Impact of the Public Domain. Introduction to Methodology", paper presented at the first Communia conference, Louvain-la-Neuve (30 June 2008), available at http://communia-project.eu/communiafiles/conf2008p_The_economic_and_social_impact_of_the_public_domain.pdf.

Jones, Sophia and Alek Tarkowski, "Digital Repository Infrastructure Vision for European Research: DRIVER project", paper delivered at the first Communia workshop, Turin (18 January 2008), available at http://www.communia-project.eu/node/85.

Kroes, Neelie, "A Digital World of Opportunities", speech delivered at the Forum d'Avignon: Les Rencontres Internationales de la Culture, de l'Économie et des Medias, Avignon (5 November 2010), available at http://europa.eu/rapid/pressReleasesAction.do?reference=SPEECH/10/619&format=HTML&aged=0&language=EN&guiLanguage=en.

LeGuel, Fabrice and Fabrice Rochelandet, "P2P Music-Sharing Networks: Why the Legal Fight Against Copiers May Be Inefficient?", Social Science Research Network Working Paper Series (2005), available at http://ssrn.com/abstract=810124.

Liebowitz, Stan J., "How Reliable is the Oberholzer-Gee and Strumpf Paper on File-Sharing?" (University of Texas at Dallas, Working Paper, August 2007), available at http://copyrightalliance.net/files/ssrn-id1014399.pdf.

Motion Pictures Associations, MPA Response to the UK All Party Parliamentary Internet Group (APIG) Inquiry into Digital Rights Management (DRM), Brussels (13 January 2006), available at http://www.apcomms.org.uk/apig/current-activities/apig-inquiry-into-digital-rights-management/apig-drm-written-evidence/MPA_APIG_DRM_Sub_Final_13012006.pdf.

Murray, Fiona and Scott Stern, "Do Formal Intellectual Property Rights Hinder the Free Flow of Scientific Knowledge?: An Empirical Test of the Anticommons Hypothesis", NBER working paper 1146. National Bureau of Economic Research (2005).

Nesson, Charles with Juan Carlos De Martin, "Communia and Universities", welcome address at the third Communia conference, Turin (28 June 2010), available at http://www.communia-project.eu/node/459.

OECD Best Practice Guildelines for Biological Resource Centres, Paris (2007), available at http://www.oecd.org/dataoecd/7/13/38777417.pdf.

Owens, Richard, "WIPO and Access to Content: The Development Agenda and the Public Domain", paper delivered at the fifth Communia workshop, London (27 March 2009), available at http://www.communia-project.eu/node/231.

—, "WIPO Project on Intellectual Property and the Public Domain", paper delivered at the seventh Communia workshop, Luxembourg (1 February 2010), available at http://www.communia-project.eu/node/363.

Panitch, Judith M. and Sarah Michalak, "The Serials Crisis: A White Paper for the UNC-Chapel Hill Scholarly Communications Convocation" (January 2005), available at http://www.unc.edu/scholcomdig/whitepapers/panitch-michalak.html.

Pira International, "Commercial Exploitation of Europe's Public Sector Information", report prepared for the European Commission, Information Society Directorate General (30 October 2000), available at http://ec.europa.eu/information_society/policy/psi/docs/pdfs/pira_study/commercial_final_report.pdf.

Pollock, Rufus and Jo Walsh, "Componentization and Open Data", paper delivered at XTech (2007), available at http://blog.okfn.org/writings/componentization-and-open-data.

Reichman, Jerome H., "Formalizing the Informal Microbial Commons: Using Liability Rules to Promote the Exchange of Materials", paper delivered at the second Communia conference, Turin (30 June 2009), available at http://communia-project.eu/node/339.

Ricolfi, Marco, "Copyright Policies for Digital Libraries in the Context of the i2010 Strategy", paper presented at the first Communia conference, Louvain-la-Neuve (1 July 2008), available at http://www.communia-project.eu/node/110.

Rogers, Thomas, Andrew Szamosszegi and Peter Jaszi, "Fair Use in the U.S. Economy: Economic Contribution of Industries Relying on Fair Use", study prepared for the Computer and Communications Industry Association (September 2007), available at http://www.ccianet.org/CCIA/files/ccLibraryFiles/Filename/000000000354/fair-use-study-final.pdf.

Steuer, Eric, "Creative Commons Announces Major Funding Support from Omidyar Network", Creative Commons press release, San Franciso (28 May 2008), available at http://creativecommons.org/press-releases/entry/8322.

Stiglitz, Joseph E., "Public Policy for a Knowledge Economy", address to the Department for Trade and Industry and Center for Economic Policy Research (1999), available at http://akgul.bilkent.edu.tr/BT-BE/knowledge-economy.pdf.

Swan, Alma, "Open Access by Self-archiving: It's an Author Thing", paper presented at the first European conference on scientific publishing in biomedicine and medicine, Lund, Sweden (April 2006), available at http://eprints.ecs.soton.ac.uk/17505.

Uhlir, Paul, "Measuring the Economic and Social Benefits and Costs of Public Sector Information Online: A Review of the Literature and Future", paper delivered at the first Communia conference, Louvain-la-Neuve, Belgium (30 June 2010), available at http://www.communia-project.eu/node/132.

—, "Revolution and Evolution in Scientific Communication: Moving from Restricted Dissemination of Publicly-Funded Knowledge to Open Knowledge Environments", paper delivered at the second Communia conference, Turin (28 June 2009), available at http://www.communia-project.eu/communiafiles/Conf%202009_P_Uhlir_BS.pdf.

Van Godtsenhoven, Karen, "The DRIVER Project: On the Road to a European Commons for Scientific Communication", paper delivered at the first Communia conference, Louvain-la-Neuve (30 June 2008), available at http://communia-project.eu/node/113. An updated version of Van Godtsenhoven's paper can be found in this volume (Chapter 9).

— and Maurits Van der Graaf, "Digital Repository Infrastructure Vision for European Research", DRIVER Usability Assessment Report (2007), available at http://www.driver-support.eu/documents/DRIVER_usability_study_Gent.pdf.

Van Gompel, Stef, "Extending the Terms of Protection for Related Rights Endangers a Valuable Public Domain", paper presented at the second Communia workshop, Vilnius (31 March 2008), available at http://www.communia-project.eu/communiafiles/Stef_van_Gompel_Position_paper_term_extension_CC.pdf.

Bert Visser, Derek Eaton, Niels Louwaars and Jan Engels, "Transaction Costs of Germplasm Exchange Under Bilateral Agreements", FAO/Global Forum on Agricultural Research Document, No. GFAR/00/17–04-04, Dresden (2000), available at http://www.fao.org/docs/eims/upload/206946/gfar0077.PDF.

Alex Weedon, "Implementing the Microbial Commons: Legal and Institutional Perspectives", discussant presentation at the Microbial Commons conference, Ghent, Belgium (11 June 2008).

Weiss, Peter, "Borders in Cyberspace: Conflicting Government Information Policies and their Economic Impact", summary report, US Department of Commerce, National Oceanic and Atmospheric Administration National Weather Service (February 2002), available at http://www.nws.noaa.gov/sp/Borders_report.pdf.

C. Books, Papers, and Newspaper Articles

Aigrain, Philippe, *Internet and Création: Comment Reconnaître les Échanges sur Internet en Finançant la Création* (Cergy-Pontoise: In Libro Veritas, 2008).

Alchian, Armen A., "Uncertainty, Evolution and Economic Theory", *Journal of Political Economy*, 58 (1950), 211–21.

Andelson, Robert V. (ed.), *Commons Without Tragedy: The Social Ecology of Land Tenure and Democracy* (London: Center for Incentive Taxation, 1991).

Aoki, Masahiko, *Toward a Comparative Institutional Analysis* (Cambridge, MA: MIT Press, 2001).

Arora, Ashish, Andrea Fosfuri and Alfonso Gambardella, *Markets for Technology: The Economics of Innovation and Corporate Technology* (Cambridge, MA: MIT Press, 2004).

Arrow, Kenneth J., "Economic Welfare and the Allocation of Resources for Inventions", in *The Rate and Direction of Inventive Activity: Economic and Social Factors*, ed. by Richard R. Nelson (Princeton: Princeton University Press, 1962), pp. 609–26.

Auteri, Paolo, "Il paradigma tradizionale del diritto d'autore e la nuove tecnologie" in *Proprietà digitale: diritti d'autore, nuove tecnologie e Digital Rights Management*, ed. by M. L. Montagnani and M. Borghi (Milan: Egea, 2006).

Baker, Dwight, "Microbial Diversity and Pharmaceutical Industry Culture Collections" in *Genetic and Functional Diversity of Agricultural Microorganisms*, ed. by Jun-ichi Kurisaki, et al. (Tsukuba, Japan: National Institute of Agrobiological Sciences, 2005), pp. 56–61.

Bechtold, Stefan, "Comment on Directive 2001/29/EC", in *Concise on European Copyright Law*, ed. by Thomas Dreier and P. Bernt Hugenholtz (Alphen aan den Rijn: Kluwer Law Intermational, 2006), pp. 343–404.

Benkler, Yochai, "Free as the Air to Common Use: First Amendment Constraints on the Enclosure of the Public Domain", *New York University Law Review*, 74 (1999), 354–446.

—, "A Political Economy of the Public Domain: Markets in Information Goods Versus the Marketplace of Ideas", in *Expanding the Boundaries of Intellectual Property: Innovation Policy for the Knowledge Society*, ed. by Rochelle Dreyfuss, Diane L. Zimmerman and Harry First (Oxford: Oxford University Press, 2001), pp. 267–94.

—, "Sharing Nicely: On Shareable Goods and the Emergence of Sharing as a Modality of Economic Production", *Yale Law Journal*, 114 (2004), 273–358.

—, *The Wealth of Networks: How Social Production Transforms Markets and Freedom* (New Haven: Yale University Press, 2006).

Birnhack, Michael D., "More or Better? Shaping the Public Domain", in *The Future of the Public Domain: Identifying the Commons in Information Law*, ed. by P. Bernt Hugenholtz and Lucie Guibault (The Hague: Kluwer Law International, 2006), 59-86.

Bollier, David, *Silent Theft: The Private Plunder of Our Common Wealth* (New York: Routledge, 2002).

Bourcier, Danièle, Pompeu Casanovas, Melanie Dulong de Rosnay and Catharina Maracke (eds.), *Intelligent Multimedia: Sharing Creative Works in a Digital World* (Florence: European Press, 2010).

Boyle, James, "Cultural Environmentalism and Beyond", *Law and Contemporary Problems*, 70 (2007), 5–21.

—, "Foreword: The Opposite of Property?", *Law and Contemporary Problems*, 66 (2003), 1–32.

—, *The Public Domain: Enclosing the Commons of the Mind* (New Haven: Yale University Press, 2008).

—, "The Second Enclosure Movement and the Construction of the Public Domain", *Law and Contemporary Problems*, 66 (2003), 33–74.

—, *Shamans, Software, and Spleens: Law and the Construction of the Information Society* (Cambridge, MA: Harvard University Press, 1996).

Braithwaite, John and Peter Drahos (eds.), *Global Business Regulation* (Cambridge: Cambridge University Press, 2000).

Braun, Nora, "The Interface Between The Protection of Technological Measures and the Exercise of Exceptions to Copyright and Related Rights: Comparing the Situation in the United States and the European Community", *European Intellectual Property Review*, 25 (2003), 496–503.

Bromley, Daniel W., David Feeny et al (eds.), *Making the Commons Work: Theory, Practice and Policy* (San Francisco: ICS Press, 1992).

Callon, Michel, "The Sociology of an Actor-Network: The Case of the Electric Vehicle", in *Mapping the Dynamics of Science and Technology*, ed. by Michel Callon, John Law and Arie Rip (London: Macmillan, 1986), pp. 19–34.

Choisy, Stéphanie, *Le domaine public en droit d'auteur* (Paris: Litec, 2002).

Cohen, Patricia, "Digital Keys for Unlocking the Humanities' Riches", *The New York Times*, 16 November 2010.

—, "In 500 Billion Words, New Window on Culture", *The New York Times*, 16 December 2010.

Cook-Deegan, Robert and Tom Dedeurwaerdere, "The Science Commons in Life Science Research: Structure, Function and Value of Access to Genetic Diversity", *International Social Science Journal*, 188 (2006), 299–318.

Coombs, Rob, Albert Richards, Pier Paolo Saviotti and Vivien Walsh (eds.), *Technological Collaboration: The Dynamics of Cooperation in Industrial Innovation* (Cheltenam: Edward Elgar, 1996).

Coriat, Benjamin and Giovanni Dosi, "The Institutional Embeddedness of Economic Change: An Appraisal of the 'Evolutionary' and 'Regulationist' Research Programmes", in *Institutions and Economic Change: New Perspectives on Markets, Firms and Technology*, ed. by Klaus Nielsen and Björn Johnson (Cheltenham: Edward Elgar, 1998), pp. 3–32.

Cornish, W. R., *Intellectual Property: Patents, Copyright, Trade Marks and Allied Rights* (London: Sweet & Maxwell, 1996).

David, Paul A., "Can Open Science Be Protected From the Evolving Regime of IPR Protections?", *Journal of Institutional and Theoretical Economics*, 160 (2004), 9–34.

—, "Intellectual Property Institutions and the Panda's Thumb: Patents, Copyrights, and Trade Secrets in Economic Theory and History" in *Global Dimensions of Intellectual Property Rights in Science and Technology*, ed. by Mitchell B. Wallerstein, Mary Ellen Mogee and Roberta A. Schoen (Washington, DC: National Academy Press, 1993), pp. 19–62.

— and Jared Rubin, "Restricting Access to Books on the Internet: Some Unanticipated Effects of U.S. Copyright Legislation", *Review of Economic Research on Copyright Issues*, 5 (2008), 23–53.

Davison, Mark, "Database Protection: The Commodification of Information", in *The Future of the Public Domain: Identifying the Commons in Information Law*, ed. by Lucie Guibault and P. Bernt Hugenholtz (The Hague: Kluwer Law International, 2006), pp. 167–89.

Dedeurwaerdere, Tom, "Global Microbial Commons: Institutional Challenges for the Global Exchange and Distribution of Microorganisms in the Life Sciences", *Research in Microbiology*, 161 (2010), 414–21.

Demil, Benoît and Xavier Lecocq, "Neither Market nor Hierarchy nor Network: The Emergence of Bazaar Governance", *Organization Studies*, 27 (2006), 1447–66.

Derclaye, Estelle, "Does the Directive on the Re-use of Public Sector Information Affect the State's Database Sui Generis Right?", in *Knowledge Rights: Legal, Societal and Related Technological Aspects*, ed. by J. Gaster, E. Schweighofer and P. Sint (Austrian Computer Society, 2008), pp. 137–69.

Drahos, Peter with John Braithwaite, *Information Feudalism: Who Owns the Knowledge Economy?* (London: Earthscan, 2002).

Dreyfuss, Rochelle, Diane L. Zimmerman and Harry First (eds.), *Expanding the Boundaries of Intellectual Property* (Oxford: Oxford University Press, 2001).

Dusollier, Séverine, *Droit d'auteur et protection des oeuvres dans l'univers numérique: droits et exceptions à la lumière des dispositifs de verrouillage des œuvres* (Brussels, Larcier, 2005).

—, "Sharing Access to Intellectual Property through Private Ordering", *Chicago Kent Law Review*, 82 (2007), 1391–1435.

—, "Technology as an Imperative for Regulating Copyright: From the Public Exploitation to the Private Use of the Work", *European Intellectual Property Review*, 27 (2005), 201–04.

Eisenberg, Rebecca, "Bargaining Over the Transfer of Proprietary Tools: Is This Market Failing or Emerging?", in *Expanding the Boundaries of Intellectual Property*, ed. by Rochelle Dreyfuss, Diane L. Zimmerman and Harry First (Oxford: Oxford University Press, 2001), pp. 223–49.

Elkin-Koren, Niva, "Copyright Policy and the Limits of Freedom of Contract", *Berkeley Technology Law Journal*, 12 (1997), 93–113.

Epstein, Jason, "The Rattle of Pebbles", *The New York Review of Books*, 27 April 2000.

Epstein, Richard A. and Bruce N. Kuhlik, "Is there a Biomedical Anticommons?", *Regulation*, 27 (2004), 54–58.

Feeny, David, Fikret Berkes, Bonnie J. McCay, and James M. Acheson, "The Tragedy of the Commons: Twenty-Two Years Later", *Human Ecology*, 18 (1990), 1–19.

Fehr, Ernst and Armin Falk, "Psychological Foundations of Incentives", *European Economic Review*, 46 (2002), 687–724.

Fennell, Lee A., "Commons, Anticommons, Semicommons", in *Research Handbook on the Economics of Property Law*, ed. by Kenneth Ayotte and Henry E. Smith (Cheltenham: Edward Elgar, 2010), 35–56.

Frisvold, George and Kelly Day-Rubenstein, "Bioprospecting and Biodiversity: What Happens When Discoveries are Made?", *Arizona Law Review*, 50 (2008), 545–76.

Gapper, John, "The Music Labels Can Take a Punch", *The Financial Times*, 3 July 2008.

Gasser, Urs, "Legal Framework and Technological Protection of Digital Content: Moving Forward Towards a Best Practice Model", *Fordham Intellectual Property, Media and Entertainment Law Journal*, 17 (2006), 39–113.

Geiger, Christoph, "Promoting Creativity Through Copyright Limitations: Reflections on the Concept of Exclusivity in Copyright Law", *Vanderbilt Journal of Entertainment and Technology Law*, 12 (2011), 515–48.

Glorioso, Andrea and Giuseppe Mazziotti, "Alcune riflessioni sulle licenze Creative Commons e i diritti connessi degli artisti interpreti ed esecutori, dei produttori di fonogrammi e degli organismi di radiodiffusione televisiva", *Il Diritto d'Autore*, 79 (2008), 133–63.

Goldstein, Paul, "Copyright and its Substitutes", *Wisconsin Law Review* (1997), 865–71.

—, *Copyright's Highway: From Gutenberg to the Celestial Jukebox* (Stanford: Stanford University Press, 1994).

Gollin, Douglas, Melinda Smale and Bent Skovmand, "Searching an Ex Situ Collection of Wheat Genetic Resources", *American Journal Agricultral Economics*, 82 (2000), 812–27.

Gordon, H. Scott, "The Economic Theory of a Common-Property Resource: The Fishery", *Journal of Political Economy*, 62 (1954), 124–42.

Granovetter, Mark, "Coase Revisited: Business Groups in the Modern Economy", *Industrial and Corporate Change*, 4 (1995), 93–130.

Grossman, Sanford J. and Joseph E. Stiglitz, "On the Impossibility of Informationally Efficient Markets", *American Economic Review*, 70/3 (1980), 393–408.

Guibault, Lucie, *Copyright Limitations and Contracts: An Analysis of the Contractual Overridability of Limitations on Copyright* (The Hague: Kluwer Law International, 2002).

—, "Wrapping Information in Contract: How Does it Affect the Public Domain?', in *The Future of the Public Domain: Identifying the Commons in Information Law*, ed. by Lucie Guibault and P. Bernt Hugenholtz (The Hague: Kluwer Law International, 2006), pp. 87–104.

Hann, C. M. (ed.), *Property Relations: Renewing the Anthropological Tradition* (Cambridge: Cambridge University Press, 1998).

Hanna, Susan S., Carl Folke, and Karl-Gören Mäler (eds.), *Rights to Nature: Ecological, Economic, Cultural, and Political Principles of Institutions for the Environment* (Washington, DC: Island Press, 1996).

Hardin, Garrett, "The Tragedy of the Commons", *Science*, 162 (1968), 1243–48.

Heller, Michael A., "The Tragedy of the Anticommons: Property in the Transition from Marx to Markets", *Harvard Law Review*, 111 (1998), 621–88.

— and Rebecca S. Eisenberg, "Can Patents Deter Innovation? The Anticommons in Biomedical Research", *Science*, 28 (1998), 698–701.

Helfer, Lawrence R., "Using Intellectual Property Rights to Preserve the Global Genetic Commons: The International Treaty on Plant Genetic Resources for Food and Agriculture", in *International Public Goods and Transfer of Technology Under a Globalized Intellectual Property Regime*, ed. by Jerome H. Reichman and Keith E. Maskus (Cambridge: Cambridge University Press, 2005), pp. 217–24.

Hess, Charlotte and Elinor Ostrom (eds.), *Understanding Knowledge as a Commons: From Theory to Practice* (Cambridge, MA: MIT Press, 2007).

Hope, Janet, *Biobazaar: The Open Source Revolution and Biotechnology* (Cambridge, MA: Harvard University Press, 2008).

Hugenholtz, P. Bernt, "Copyright, Contract and Code: What Will Remain of the Public Domain?", *Brooklyn Journal of International Law*, 26 (2000), 77–90.

— and Lucie Guibault (eds.), *The Future of the Public Domain: Identifying the Commons in Information Law* (The Hague: Kluwer Law International, 2006).

Hugo, Victor, *Discours d'ouverture du Congrès littéraire international* (Paris: Lévy, 1878).

Koskinen-Olsson, Tarja, "Collective Management in the Nordic Countries", in *Collective Management of Copyright and Related Rights*, ed. by Daniel Gervais (Kluwer Law International, 2006), pp. 257–81.

Krikke, J., *Het bibliotheekprivilege in de digitale omgeving* (Deventer: Kluwer Law International, 2000).

Krugman, Paul, "Bits, Band and Books", *The New York Times*, 6 June 2008.

Landes, William M. and Richard A. Posner, *The Economic Structure of Intellectual Property Law* (Cambridge, MA: Harvard University Press, 2003).

—, "Indefinitely Renewable Copyright", *University of Chicago Law Review*, 70 (2003), 471–518.

Lange, David, "Recognizing the Public Domain", *Law and Contemporary Problems*, 24 (1981), 147–81.

—, "Reimagining the Public Domain", *Law and Contemporary Problems*, 66 (2003), 463–83.

Lerner, Josh and Jean Tirole, "Some Simple Economics of Open Source", *Journal of Industrial Economics*, 50 (2002), 197–234.

Lessig, Lawrence, "The Architecture of Innovation", *Duke Law Journal*, 51 (2002), 1783–1801.

—, *Free Culture: The Nature and Future of Creativity* (London: Penguin, 2005).

—, *The Future of Ideas: The Fate of The Commons in a Connected World* (New York: Vintage, 2002).

—, "Re-crafting a Public Domain", *Yale Journal of Law and the Humanities*, 18 (2006), 56–83.

—, *Remix: Making Art and Commerce Thrive in the Hybrid Economy* (New York: Penguin, 2008).

Liebowitz, Stan J., "File Sharing: Creative Destruction or Just Plain Destruction?", *Journal of Law and Economics*, 49 (2006), 1–28.

Litman, Jessica, *Digital Copyright* (Amherst: Prometheus, 2001).

—, "Real Copyright Reform", *Iowa Law Review*, 96 (2010), 1–55.

Macmillan, Fiona, "Commodification and Cultural Ownership", in *Copyright And Free Speech: Comparative And International* Analyses, ed. by Jonathan Griffiths and Uma Suthersanen (Oxford: Oxford University Press, 2003), pp. 35–65.

—, "Copyright, the World Trade Organization, and Cultural Self-Determination", in *New Directions in Copyright Law*, vol. 6, ed. by Fiona Macmillan (Cheltenham: Edward Elgar, 2007), pp. 307–334.

—, "The Cruel ©: Copyright and Film", *European Intellectual Property Review*, 24 (2002), 483–92.

—, "The Dysfunctional Relationship Between Copyright and Cultural Diversity", *Quaderns Del CAC*, 27 (2007), 101–10.

—, "Public Interest and the Public Domain in an Era Of Corporate Dominance", in *Intellectual Property Rights: Innovation, Governance and The Institutional Environment*, ed. by Brigitte Andersen (Cheltenham: Edward Elgar, 2006), pp. 46–69.

Madison, Michael J., "Legal-ware: Contract and Copyright in the Digital Age", *Fordham Law Review*, 67 (1998), 1025–1143.

—, Brett M. Frischmann and Katherine J. Strandburg, "Constructing Commons in the Cultural Environment", *Cornell Law Review*, 95 (2010), 657–609.

Maskus, Keith and Jerome H. Reichman, "The Globalization of Private Knowledge Goods and The Privatization of Global Public Goods", *Journal of International Economic Law*, 7 (2004), 279–320.

Mazziotti, Giuseppe, *EU Digital Copyright Law and the End-user* (Berlin: Springer, 2008).

Merges, Robert P., "A New Dynamism in the Public Domain", *University of Chicago Law Review*, 71 (2004), 183–203.

—, "Contracting Into Liability Rules: Intellectual Property Rights and Collective Rights Organisations", *California Law Review*, 84 (1996), 1293–393.

—, "Intellectual Property and the Costs of Commercial Exchange: A Review Essay", *Michigan Law Review*, 93 (1995), 1570–1615.

—, Mark A. Lemley and Peter S. Menell (eds.), *Intellectual Property in the New Technological Age*, 3rd edition (New York: Aspen, 2003).

Milgrom, Paul and John Roberts, *Economics, Organization and Management* (Englewood Cliffs, NJ: Prentice Hall, 1992).

Mossink, Wilma, "Intellectual Property Rights", in *A DRIVER's Guide to European Repositories: Five Studies of Important Digital Repository Related Issues and Good Practices*, ed. by Kasja Weenink, Leo Waaijers and Karen van Godtsenhoven (Amsterdam: Amsterdam University Press, 2007), pp. 103–12.

Nelson, R. R., "Innovation and Learning: The Two Faces of R&D", *The Economic Journal*, 99 (1989), 569–96.

Netanel, Neil W., "Copyright and Democratic Civil Society", *Yale Law Journal*, 106 (1996), 283–387.

—, "Market Hierarchy And Copyright In Our System Of Free Expression", *Vanderbilt Law Review*, 53 (2000), 1879–932.

—, "Why Has Copyright Expanded?: Analysis and Critique", in *New Directions in Copyright Law*, vol. 6, ed. by Fiona Macmillan (Cheltenham: Edward Elgar, 2008), pp. 3–34.

Nosetti, Massimo, "Il maestro dell'organo fuori dal copyright", in *Il Giornale della Musica*, November 2008.

Olson, Mançur, *The Logic of Collective Action: Public Goods and the Theory of Groups* (Cambridge, MA: Harvard University Press, 1971).

Ostrom, Elinor, *The Drama of the Commons* (Washington, DC: National Academies Press, 2002).

—, *Governing the Commons: The Evolution of Institutions for Collective Action* (Cambridge: Cambridge University Press, 1990).

—, Roy Gardner and James Walker, *Rules, Games, and Common-Pool Resources* (Ann Arbor: University of Michigan Press, 1994).

Loren, Lydia Pallas, "Slaying the Leather-Winged Demons in the Night: Reforming Copyright Owner Contracting with Clickwrap Misuse", *Ohio Northern University Law Review*, 30 (2004), 495–535.

Pessach, Guy, "Copyright Law as a Silencing Restriction on Noninfringing Materials: Unveiling the Scope of Copyright's Diversity Externalities", *Southern California Law Review*, 76 (2003), 1067–104.

Pettifer, Richard E. W., "Towards a Stronger European Market in Applied Meteorology", *Meteorological Applications*, 15/2 (2008), 305-12.

Peukert, Alexander, "A Bipolar Copyright System for the Digital Networks Environment", *Hastings Communications and Entertainment Law Journal*, 28 (2005), 1–80.

Philapitsch, Florian, "Die Creative Commons Lizenzen", *Medien & Recht*, 2 (2008), 82–97.

Piwowar, Heather A., Roger S. Day, Douglas B. Fridsma, "Sharing Detailed Research Data Is Associated with Increased Citation Rate", *PLoS ONE*, 2 (2007), e308.

Pollock, Rufus, "The Value of the Public Domain" (UK Institute for Public Policy Research, 2006).

Polk, Wagner R., "Information Wants to Be Free: Intellectual Property and the Mythologies of Control", *Columbia Law Review*, 103 (2003), 995–1034.

Pool, Ithielde Sola, *Technologies of Freedom* (Cambridge, MA: Belknap, 1983).

Powell, Walter W., "Neither Market Nor Hierarchy: Network Forms of Organization", *Research in Organizational Behavior*, 12 (1990), 295–336.

Proudman, Vanessa, "The Population of Repositories", in *A DRIVER's Guide to European Repositories: Five Studies of Important Digital Repository Related Issues and Good Practices*, ed. by Kasja Weenink, Leo Waaijers and Karen van Godtsenhoven (Amsterdam: Amsterdam University Press, 2007), pp. 49–97.

Rai, Arti K., Jerome H. Reichman, Paul F. Uhlir and Colin R. Crossman, "Pathways Across the Valley of Death: Novel Intellectual Property Strategies for Accelerated Drug Discovery", *Yale Journal of Health Policy, Law, and Ethics*, 8 (2008), 1–36.

Reichman, Jerome H., "Legal Hybrids between the Patent and Copyright Paradigms", *Columbia Law Review*, 94 (1994), 2432–558.

—, "Of Green Tulips and Legal Kudzu: Repackaging Rights in Subpatentable Innovation", *Vanderbilt Law Review*, 53 (2000), 1743–98.

—, Tom Dedeurwaerdere and Paul A. Uhlir, *Global Intellectual Property Strategies for the Microbial Research Commons* (Cambridge: Cambridge University Press, forthcoming 2012).

— and Jonathan A. Franklin, "Privately Legislated Intellectual Property Rights: Reconciling Freedom of Contract with Public Good Uses of Information", *University of Pennsylvania Law Review*, 147 (1999), 875–970.

— and Paul F. Uhlir, "A Contractually Reconstructed Research Commons for Scientific Data in a Highly Protectionist Intellectual Property", *Law and Contemporary Problems*, 66 (2003), 315–462.

Sam Ricketson, "The Birth of the Berne Union", *Columbia-VLA Journal of Law and the Arts*, 11 (1986), 9–32.

— and Jane C. Ginsburg, *International Copyright and Neighbouring Rights* (Oxford: Oxford University Press, 2006).

Ricolfi, Marco, "Individual and Collective Management of Copyright in a Digital Environment" in *Copyright Law: A Handbook of Contemporary Research*, ed. by Paul Torremans (Cheltenham: Edward Elgar, 2008), pp. 283–314.

—, "Is There an Antitrust Antidote Against IP Overprotection within TRIPs?", *Marquette Intellectual Property Law Review*, 10 (2006), 305–67.

Rodotà, Stefano, "Se il mondo perde il senso del bene comune", *La Repubblica*, 10 August 2010.

Rose, Carol M., "The Comedy of the Commons: Custom, Commerce, and Inherently Public Property", *University of Chicago Law Review*, 53 (1986), 711–81.

Rose, Mark, "Copyright and its Metaphors", *UCLA Law Review*, 50 (2002), 1–15.

Samuelson, Pamela, "The Challenges of Mapping the Public Domain", in *The Future of the Public Domain: Identifying the Commons in Information Law*, ed. by Lucie Guibault and P. Bernt Hugenholtz (The Hague: Kluwer Law International, 2006), pp. 7–25.

—, "Mapping the Digital Public Domain: Threats and Opportunities", *Law and Contemporary Problems*, 66 (2003), 147–61.

Schack, Haimo, "Anti-Circumvention Measures and Restrictions in Licensing Contracts as Instruments for Preventing Competition and Fair Use", *University of Illinois Journal of Law, Technology and Policy* (2002), 321–32.

Schumpeter, Joseph, *Capitalism, Socialism and Democracy* (New York: Harper, 1976).

Senftleben, Martin, *Copyright, Limitations and the Three-Step-Test* (The Hague: Kluwer Law International, 2004).

Simpson, R. David and Roger A. Sedjo, "Valuing Biodiversity for Pharmaceutical Research", *Journal of Political Economy*, 104 (1996), 163–85.

Smith, David, "Culture Collections Over the World", *International Microbiology*, 6 (2003), 95–100.

Smith, Henry E., "Intellectual Property as Property: Delineating Entitlements in Information", *Yale Law Journal*, 116 (2007), 1742–1822.

Sprigman, Christopher, "Reform(aliz)ing Copyright", *Stanford Law Review*, 57 (2004), 485–568.

St Clair, William, "Metaphors of Intellectual Property", in *Privilege and Property: Essays on the History of Copyright*, ed. by Ronan Deazley, Martin Kretschmer and Lionel Bently (Cambridge: Open Book Publishers, 2010), pp. 369–95.

Stern, Scott, *Biological Resource Centres: Knowledge Hubs for the Life Sciences* (Washington, DC: Brookings, 2004).

Stokes, Donald E., *Pasteur's Quadrant: Basic Science and Technological Innovation* (Washington, DC: Brookings, 1996).

Strumpf, Koleman, "File-Sharing and Copyright", *Innovation Policy and the Economy*, 10 (2010), 19–55.

Teece, David J., "Technological Change and the Nature of the Firm", in *Technical Change and Economic Theory*, ed. by G. Dosi, C. Freeman, R. Nelson, G. Solverberg and L. Soete (London: Printer Publishers, 1998), pp. 242–61.

Van Gompel, Stef, "Formalities in the Digital Era: An Obstacle or Opportunity?", in *Global Copyright: Three Hundred Years Since the Statute of Anne, from 1709 to Cyberspace*, ed. by Lionel Bently, Uma Suthersanen and Paul Torremans (Cheltenham: Edward Elgar, 2010), pp. 395–424.

Van Houweling, Molly Shaffer, "Cultural Environmentalism and the Constructed Commons", *Law and Contemporary Problems*, 70 (2007), 23–50.

Varnelis, Kazys (ed.), *Networked Publics* (Cambridge, MA: MIT Press, 2008).

Volokh, Eugene, "Cheap Speech and What It Will Do", *Yale Law Journal*, 104 (1995), 1805–50.

Walsh, John P., Ashish Arora and Wesley M. Cohen, "Effects of Research Tool Patents and Licensing on Biomedical Innovation", in *Patents in the Knowledge-Based Economy*, ed. by Wesley M. Cohen and Stephen A. Merrill (Washington, DC: National Academies Press, 2003), pp. 285–340.

—, Charlene Cho and Wesley M. Cohen, "View from the Bench: Patents and Material Transfers", *Science*, 309 (2005), 2002–03.

Werra, Jacques de, "Moving Beyond the Conflict Between Freedom of Contract and Copyright Policies: In Search of a New Global Policy for On-Line Information Licensing Transactions: A Comparative Analysis Between U.S. Law and European Law", *Columbia Journal of Law and the Arts*, 25 (2003), 239–375.

Winter, Sidney G., "Knowledge and Competence as Strategic Assets", in *The Competitive Challenge: Strategies for Industrial Innovation and Renewal*, ed. by David J. Teece (Cambridge, MA: Ballinger, 1987), pp. 159–84.

Woodmansee, Martha and Peter Jaszi, "The Law of Text: Copyright in the Academy", *College English*, 57 (1995), 769-87.

Yoo, Christopher S., "Copyright and Democracy: A Cautionary Note", *Vanderbilt Law Review*, 53 (2000), 1933–63.

Zittrain, Jonathan, "Lost in the Cloud", *The New York Times*, 20 July 2009.

This book does not end here...

At Open Book Publishers, we are changing the nature of the traditional academic book. The title you have just read will not be left on a library shelf, but will be accessed online by hundreds of readers each month across the globe. We make all our books free to read online so that students, researchers and members of the public who can't afford a printed edition can still have access to the same ideas as you.

Our digital publishing model also allows us to produce online supplementary material, including extra chapters, reviews, links and other digital resources. Find *The Digital Public Domain* on our website to access its online extras. Please check this page regularly for ongoing updates, and join the conversation by leaving your own comments:

http://www.openbookpublishers.com/product/93

If you enjoyed this book, and feel that research like this should be available to all readers, regardless of their income, please think about donating to us. Our company is run entirely by academics, and our publishing decisions are based on intellectual merit and public value rather than on commercial viability. We do not operate for profit and all donations, as with all other revenue we generate, will be used to finance new Open Access publications.

For further information about what we do, how to donate to OBP, additional digital material related to our titles or to order our books, please visit our website.

OpenBook Publishers

Knowledge is for sharing